A Floating Chinaman

A Floating Chinaman

FANTASY AND FAILURE ACROSS THE PACIFIC

Hua Hsu

Harvard University Press

Cambridge, Massachusetts
London, England
2016

First printing

Library of Congress Cataloging-in-Publication Data
   Hsu, Hua, 1977– author.
   A floating Chinaman : fantasy and failure across the Pacific / Hua Hsu.
      pages cm
   Includes bibliographical references and index.
   ISBN 978-0-674-96790-8 (hc : alk. paper)
      1. Tsiang, H. T., 1899–1971.   2. China—Foreign public opinion,
American—History—20th century.   3. Public opinion in literature.
   4. Authors and publishers—United States—History—20th century.
   5. United States—Foreign relations—China.   6. China—Foreign
relations—United States.   I. Title.
   E183.8.C5H74 2016
   951.05—dc23   2015032635

For Carol, and in memory of Ken,
for my parents,
and for Z.

Contents

A Floating Chinaman

Introduction

What Means the World to You?

EDWARD PAYSON VINING was not the first person to believe that the Chinese had discovered America, but he was certainly one of the most dedicated.

In the 1870s, Vining worked as the general freight manager of the Union Pacific Railroad where he was, by all accounts, a meticulous and demanding boss. At least this was what occupied him during business hours. In his free time, Vining poured his energy into a range of eclectic intellectual pursuits, from proving that Shakespeare's Hamlet was "in very deed a woman" to investigating a long-standing suspicion that a Buddhist monk had arrived in the Americas nearly a thousand years before Christopher Columbus. In 1885 he published an imposing volume titled *An Inglorious Columbus.*[1] Eight hundred very dense, very cramped pages long, its sheer mass suggests an author possessed, a researcher who did not know when to stop. Vining's title was not meant as a dis of Columbus; here, "inglorious" meant "obscure" and it referred to Hwui Shan, the unheralded Buddhist monk who, "in the year 499 A.D., reached China, and stated that he had returned from a trip to a country lying an immense distance east."[2] This immense land was America.

The main problem with this account, Vining admitted, was that Hwui Shan did not write it himself. The text under scrutiny was

1

recorded in the seventh-century Liang dynasty annals by a bemused prince who added his own particular flourish to the monk's report. Straying every so often from the task at hand, the prince added his own running commentary to the official body.[3] Over decades, as volumes bulged in the imperial archives, it became necessary to re-evaluate and pare down the passages essential to the maintenance of China's history. Meticulously recorded and carefully preserved stories of travel and war were condensed into shorter ones, the old records were destroyed and the new interpretations—mistakes, mis-understandings, jokes, and all—formed the official archive. In 1321, the eminent Chinese historian Ma Twan-lin published the definitive account of Hwui Shan, drawn from these abridgements.[4] By the time Vining picked up the case five hundred years later, he could only cobble together 746 Chinese characters of information that were reliable or interesting.[5]

This process of archival "natural selection" did not discourage Vining, who generously gave the Chinese the benefit of the doubt. Much of Vining's book inventories the scholarly back-and-forth over this unrecoverable past, the fierce and unambiguous claims rival Sinologists waged over a scant few paragraphs. The level of minu-tiae is what makes *An Inglorious Columbus* so mesmerizing. Nothing is left to chance; nothing can be forgotten. Self-proclaimed experts debate the intricacies of what the Chinese language sounded like a thousand years ago, the climate and botany of lands they have never seen. They argue with stern conviction that Hwui Shan had landed not in the present-day United States but in Mexico or Canada or Siberia; maybe he had lost his way and mistaken nearby Japan for a distant land. It is a string of arguments marshaled on the backs of minuscule bugs; proven, some say, by a specific shade of red dye and the soot-colored feathers of rare chickens; verified by homonyms separated by thousands of miles. In the absence of reliable informa-tion, the Orientalists of yore deferred to suspicion and chauvinism. For example, Vining records one claim that Hwui Shan could not have possibly survived such an extraordinary journey, for everyone knows that the Chinese have always been "mediocre sailors, hardly capable of undertaking long voyages."[6] The evidence is everywhere: in the past as well as the present.

The remoteness of Hwui Shan's account did not deter new voices from entering the fray over the following decades. There is a radiant quality to this shared obsession, this desire to find truth in such an erratic, unstable universe of literature, these quibbles across time and space about the veracity of irretrievable words. The writer and folklorist Charles Leland began researching Hwui Shan in the 1840s, eventually publishing *Fusang, or the Discovery of America by Chinese Buddhist Priests in the Fifth Century* in 1875.[7] So great was his desire to mark his territory that he pressed ahead with his claims despite some inconsistencies and potential inaccuracies—"*let them go,*" he pleaded with his brother, who had been tasked with finding him a publisher, "*don't give it an excuse for not getting it published,* let it rather go, faults and all."[8] The Chinese archeologist Wei Chu-Hsien became so intrigued by these passages that he spent decades chasing their claims through thousands of classical documents, publishing a series of books detailing ancient communication between China and the Americas.[9] In the 1950s, a Chicago patent attorney and independent researcher named Henriette Mertz fell under the spell of Hwui Shan's tale and composed a forceful, concise study titled *Pale Ink*. She remarked that the controversies of the past century had "turned on questions of personalities rather than on facts."[10] Perhaps "personality" was a softer way to suggest prejudice: either you believed that the clever, compassionate Chinese were capable of accomplishing these feats of accidental daring or you believed that the inept, backwards Chinese could not distinguish north from south, let alone navigate their way through choppy waters.

These were debates that raged across continents and civilizations, delivered to the present in obscure books that have been closed for decades. Perhaps Hwui Shan did not precede Columbus by a thousand years. What remains is a different voyage: rumors of things left behind; hypotheses debated and then marooned for seeming madness; a slow, ambling trail of ideas, speculations, and alternate histories. My fascination with *An Inglorious Columbus* is not driven by a vague wish for it to be true—although that would be cool. Rather, I have been drawn to the ways in which previous generations debated the question of whether any of it was even possible. For me, it is a model of how authority accrues, particularly authority on a remote

and fairly obscure subject. Over time, all of it—suspicion and stereotype, careful scholarship and rushed mistranslation—hardens as
fact. All we are left with are the surviving fragments of his account
that, along with the layer upon layer of scholarly scrutiny, assume an
exaggerated importance. A historical debate about a lone monk—
a monk who might actually have come from Afghanistan and not
China—morphed into one about the fitness and ingenuity of the
Chinese civilization.

The construction and refinement of knowledge is a careful, rigorous process. But it is also beholden to whims, passions, prejudices,
and, as Mertz put it, "questions of personalities." Sometimes it embodies its circumstances and sometimes it seems wholly ignorant of
it. Consider Vining's context as he was preparing *An Inglorious Columbus* for publication. One wonders if he ever pondered the irony
of his job as a railroad executive. Chinese laborers had built huge
swaths of America's transcontinental railroad decades earlier but, by
the early 1880s, a grassroots movement of disgruntled, xenophobic
white workers had emerged to drive them out, culminating in the
Chinese Exclusion Act of 1882. Outside his office, the Chinese were
being reimagined as a depraved, heathen threat to American values;
meanwhile, Vining's nose was buried deep in his manuscript, entranced by what the superhuman Chinese had done centuries earlier,
trying to teach himself their wondrous language.

I begin with the story of Vining and Hwui Shan because of these
bewitching juxtapositions: "facts" against "personalities," debates
about China that were purely conceptual, against a backdrop where
the Chinese were anything but. These moments occasion us to wonder about the construction of knowledge and the foundations of
authority, as well as the extent to which both benefit from distant,
often unnamed feelings of prejudice or suspicion. But I also begin
here because it reminds me of the utter precariousness of the arguments and ideas we have left behind, from the whittling down of the
Chinese archives to *An Inglorious Columbus* itself. It is a relatively
obscure book. As I leafed through its pages at the library, it was humbling to imagine how this copy had survived the years. Even the
softest gestures caused the corners and binding to flake free. I swept
the crumbs of these decades-old, browned pages to the floor, hoping

nobody would notice. The handwritten request history suggested that the last person to retrieve this book from the archives had been my friend Ed, who had told me about it years earlier.

There are limitations to what we can know about the past. Only so many books have survived the years to be safe-kept in libraries; a mere fraction of first drafts, diaries, and letters have been salvaged from trash bins to find a place in archives: there is only so much evidence to comb. What possibilities do these old documents foresee? What did their authors desire or fear? Taken together, these scattered remnants of the past seem to trace the circumference of what was once conceivable.

Like many young American journalists coming of age between the two great wars, Harold Isaacs suspected that the next big story was China. He scrapped and saved his way across the Pacific, working as a bellhop on a luxury liner and in the engine room of a freighter, eventually arriving in Shanghai in 1930. Over the next fifteen years, Isaacs was a tireless and prolific writer, filing stories on politics and civil unrest, founding *The China Forum*, an English-language weekly in Shanghai, publishing books about China's revolutionary aspirations, and eventually earning a blacklist from the Chinese government. He was a firsthand witness to how quickly a population's attitudes could be reshaped around new political imperatives. It was an experience that stayed with him.

By the 1950s, Isaacs had settled into a far less exciting life in academia. Now, regarding China at a distance, he wondered: how had Americans come to know this distant place? What role had he played as a journalist and author? "What ideas, notions, and images do Americans have in their heads about these hitherto distant lands and peoples?"[11] Isaacs was baffled by how American perceptions of China could swing so drastically. One hundred years prior, the Chinese had been viewed as subhuman, devious. By the turn of the century, they were admired and revered, a proud civilization in sad decline. Now they were America's hostile, hard-working rivals. How did the typical American come to understand and internalize these larger political contexts? How did they translate these ambient ideas into everyday prejudices?

In 1958, Isaacs published *Scratches on Our Minds*, a fascinating attempt to reckon with the mysterious brew of fact and fiction, experience and innuendo that supplies our imaginations. Isaacs and his assistants spent a little over a year probing 181 Americans for their "associations and impressions," their hazy affections and "unspoken prejudices."[12] Some had spent years in Asia; for others, a nearby Chinatown laundry or "a Chinese restaurant in their home city" was the closest they had come to China.[13] In fact, quite a few of Isaacs's interviewees had grown to admire the Chinese because of "the familiar and pleasurable experience of eating Chinese food."[14] Isaacs pressed his interviewees to think about where they had first learned to view the Chinese as sage or stoic, why the mere mention of China automatically triggered images of "rice fields, temples, pagodas, padded clothing, women with children on their backs."[15] He was not particularly interested in figuring out positions and ideologies; instead he hoped to interrogate questions of mood and feeling, the intuitions that shape our political preferences.

An African American respondent dismissed the Chinese as "international Uncle Toms" and "bootlickers of the whitemen," in part because he had once heard a story about a Chinese politician who had refused to grant an interview to a black reporter.[16] An engineer explained that he had a positive feeling about the Chinese even though he had never met one. He could not explain why. Isaacs encouraged him to think back to where this affection had come from. Eventually, the engineer rattled off a somewhat random list of inputs: carved ivory, best sellers, the journalist Edgar Snow, World War II, a comic strip called *Terry and the Pirates*, a Charlie Chan movie he had just seen on television.[17] The engineer's fondness had not been born out of reason, careful study, or even friendship. What he had described was no less than an entire marketplace of Chinese effects.

Perhaps unsurprisingly, Isaacs found that the primary source for America's impressions of China had been popular culture—and popularity mattered. One figure had been particularly influential to this generation of Americans. Isaacs explained:

No single book about China has had a greater impact than [Pearl Buck's] famous novel, *The Good Earth*. It can almost be said that for a whole generations of Americans, she "created" the Chinese, in the same sense that Dickens "created" for so many of us the people who lived in the slums of Victorian England. The extent of her influence is illustrated in our own panel by the fact that 69 individuals spontaneously mentioned Pearl Buck as a major source of their own impressions of the Chinese and these were almost uniformly impressions of a wonderfully attractive people.[18]

Scratches on Our Minds is absorbing largely because it collects such a random, disparate array of perspectives. Isaacs's 181 interviewees come across as discrete and idiosyncratic voices, even as their viewpoints begin to cohere around a set of commonly shared beliefs. But sometimes, as in the case of Buck, the masses fell under the spell of a single figure. This moment of seeming consensus attested to Buck's unique authority. She "created" China for scores of Americans, teaching them how to envision and love this distant land. Few of Isaacs's respondents, though, could articulate the source of Buck's expertise, beyond her ubiquity. It was the market, then, that had confirmed her authority.

Buck's wild success created a desire for even more books about China. Published in 1931, *The Good Earth* became a prominent reference point for authors and readers interested in this distant land. Within a few years, writers like Buck, Alice Tisdale Hobart, Lin Yutang, and Carl Crow would introduce China to an entire generation of American readers, regaling them with hopeful visions of noble ideas and surplus goods crisscrossing the Pacific. Their works allowed American readers to imagine China in relatable terms: as yeoman and workmanlike; as consumers, customers, and freethinkers. Ultimately, it was not important to Isaacs if the impressions these works left were accurate or not. The responses indexed in *Scratches on Our Minds* accounts were rife with conflations; after all, Chinatown is not China, just as novels are not chronicles of real life. What mattered were the scratches that survived, years into the future, thanks to family legends, worn paperbacks, second-hand stories. For Isaacs, this was America's China. A great distance bridged by popular novels, comic books, movies, newspaper reports, business etiquette manuals.

An exotic land that became a little less abstract after each passing conversation with the local Chinese restaurateur or laundryman. The best-selling author Pearl Buck's "wonderfully attractive" muse.

The same year that *The Good Earth* was published, a Chinese writer named H. T. Tsiang wandered the streets of New York, looking to sell his latest book, *China Red*, to anyone who crossed his path. It was 1931 and America was just beginning to look toward China. Tsiang was a minor Chinese bureaucrat who had originally come to the United States as a graduate student. His exposure to New York's proletarian arts movement had transformed him into a prolific novelist, poet, and playwright. He had published a book of anti-imperialist poetry, *Poems of the Chinese Revolution*, in 1929, though any praise it received owed more to its ethnographic insights into China than his poetic instincts.[19] *China Red*, his first attempt at fiction, was remarkably ambitious. On the surface, it appeared to be an epistolary romance about an aspirational Chinese couple separated by the Pacific Ocean. But it gradually unfolded into something much stranger, as the novel's itinerant Chinese laborer drifts away from his betrothed and toward the embrace of Communism. Portions of *China Red* had appeared in major proletarian publications like the *New Masses* and the *Daily Worker*, as well as the *Daily News* of New York University. Perhaps these successes emboldened him: before self-publishing *China Red*, as he had done for *Poems*, Tsiang had tried to shop the manuscript to various New York publishers. We know this because the back cover reproduces a series of lukewarm and at times negative blurbs from these publishers, politely turning down Tsiang's submission.

A representative from Jonathan Cape and Harrison Smith praised it for being "most unusual" and "well written," but carefully explained that it did not fit with the publisher's list. An agent from Alfred Knopf was more direct: "We doubt very much its popular appeal because of the political discussions we realize are necessary to the book." As if by way of retort, Tsiang included these words at the bottom of the back cover: "Now published by the Author."[20] A note from Theodore Dreiser appears inside the book, though it was hardly glowing. Dreiser offered the faintest of praise, observing:

"'China Red' contains much that is moving and colorful. The idea of presenting both sides of an argument is always interesting."

One imagines that Dreiser's vaguely approving blurb was part of Tsiang's sales pitch, as he dragged his stack of self-published paperbacks through the streets. In actuality, Dreiser never composed these sentences. Tsiang had mailed a copy of *China Red* in December 1930, hoping that the influential author would write an introductory note for him. Dreiser's secretary sent Tsiang a mannered but curt reply, paraphrasing the author's opinions, which Tsiang reprinted as Dreiser's actual words.[21]

If one returns to Tsiang's original letter to Dreiser, there is a fascinating detail that sheds light on the young Chinese writer's ultimate intentions. He describes a manuscript in progress entitled *A Floating "Chinaman"*:

> I have in preparation a novel called "A Floating 'Chinaman'". It is an odyssey of a Chinese proletarian covering the old regime in China and the renascence of the new China. It is in four parts:
>   1. Life in old China's "Lower Depths".
>   2. Unconformity to the American Scene.
>   3. Inspirational regeneration from the Soviet Union.
>   4. Underground revolutionary work and heroic struggle of the Proletariat of the New China.[22]

The scope of *A Floating "Chinaman"* is staggering. It imagines renewal, redemption, and revolution on a global scale, dramatizing the first three-quarters of Tsiang's own life: rising above his meager upbringing, feeling his way through an inhospitable "American scene," and devoting himself to the revolutionary struggle.[23] But *A Floating "Chinaman"* was never published, if it was ever even written. Perhaps it never existed and Tsiang was merely trying to convince Dreiser of his expansive intellect. Or maybe *A Floating "Chinaman"* became *Shanghai Newyork Moscow (An Odyssey of a Chinese Coolie)*, another of Tsiang's never-published, phantom novels, listed as "in preparation" on the inner flap of one of Tsiang's later works.

Perhaps such a novel, one that would narrate the complexities of globalization, from worldwide depression to coming revolution, was simply too ambitious. It could never have existed. Or maybe the market would never allow it. Think of my novels like *The Good Earth*, Tsiang once told a journalist, only much better. But, as Americans in the 1930s devoured Buck's tales of a genteel, far-away China, Tsiang struggled for recognition. After the modest success of *Poems* and *China Red*, the composer Ruth Crawford Seeger adapted two of his poems, "Sacco-Vanzetti" and "Chinaman, Laundryman." In 1935, he self-published *The Hanging on Union Square*, an absurdly dark novel about New York's beleaguered proletarians.[24] He finally convinced a semireputable publishing house to handle one of his novels when, in 1937, Robert Speller issued *And China Has Hands*, a Chinatown satire that bears occasional resemblance to his description of *A Floating 'Chinaman.'*[25] Despite the obstinately leftward trajectory of his career, Tsiang's final published work, *China Marches On*, suggested a softer, spiritual bond uniting the people of China, Japan, and the United States—one that transcended geopolitics or capitalism.[26] Paranoid that his antiestablishment works would result in his deportation, he self-published this play in 1938, as a disavowal of the radical politics that defined his earlier works.[27]

For me, Tsiang's career, defined largely by envy and disappointment, describes a set of possibilities. Collectively, Tsiang's works do not comprise a coherent oeuvre; they suggest a promiscuous attitude toward standards of form and genre. It seemed that no available literary form suited Tsiang's spectacularly expansive visions of solidarity, and this might explain why he experimented with so many, from parody to militantly leftist poetry, sentimental plays to bitterly ironic, experimental novels. He enjoyed very little success, even within the hospitable climate of New York's interwar proletarian arts scene. Yet these frustrations only refined his critical instincts. His works came to express impatience with New York's proletarian dogma, which, despite an inherent hope for global solidarity, privileged the American urban experience.

Tsiang's other natural audience might have been those interested in China—a readership that seemed to grow by the day. But they ignored him as well, opting instead for the more palatable visions of

Buck, Hobart, Lin, and Crow. His frustrations toward this emerging scene of China-watchers pushed him toward increasingly experimental ends. Eventually, he began appearing in his own novels as a downtrodden author wandering the streets of New York, selling his self-published works out of a weathered suitcase, eager to badger his protagonists with his take on the contradictions of the proletarian arts movement or the vacuity of Buck and her clique. For both of these presumed audiences-turned-targets, Tsiang simply did not fit: his perspectives on the global consequences of capitalism could not align neatly with the local struggles of his fellow proletarian artists, while his interest in the local struggles of American laborers and immigrants undermined his credibility as an "authentic" interlocutor of a distant, mysterious China. Tsiang's identity defied categorization, just as his literary works could not be contained within existing notions of form, genre or, in some cases, what constituted a novel.

A Floating Chinaman—my version—is essentially about who gets to speak for China. On one hand, it focuses on a prominent cluster of writers and thinkers in the 1930s and '40s who helped Americans understand China as a land of possibilities—an emerging market, a democratic ally, a mirror for the American future. But *A Floating Chinaman* is also about the conditions that created their authority—about why they were taken seriously in the first place.

Historians have long observed the subtle shift in American attitudes toward China that occurred from the turn of the century to the onset of World War II: after an extended period of condescension and contempt in the late nineteenth century, the early decades of the twentieth century saw public feelings of exotic fascination rise, as China was recast as a rich, unexplored mystery to Western observers.[28] *A Floating Chinaman* fixes on this moment when the United States "rediscovered" China and considers how fantasies of a new, transpacific future animated the period's literary culture: the comfortable, middlebrow literature of Pearl Buck, Alice Tisdale Hobart, and Lin Yutang; the journalism of Carl Crow and Henry Luce; exuberant reports from oil executives and traveling salesmen proclaiming a new era in global trade. On the margins—in Chinatowns, on college campuses, in H. T. Tsiang's failed avant-gardism—a different conversation about what these two nations might learn from one another was taking place. United by a shared investment in China, the figures who comprise *A Floating Chinaman* left behind a dizzying archive of texts: best-sellers to self-published paperbacks, travel literature, corporate newsletters, FBI surveillance files, flowery letters from an Ellis Island detention center.

In order to understand where this paper trail leads, it may be useful to consider where it began. I initially envisioned this as a project looking at representations of Asian American life originating from within this loosely defined community. I had always greeted outside depictions with a degree of skepticism: the history of those representations tracked a sorry history of ever-shifting political expediencies, with Asian immigrants scorned as a subhuman threat one moment and prized as model citizens the next, their relative powerlessness to resist these stereotypes offering the only common thread. But how did these identities travel beyond the borders that had produced them? And what effect did all the overheated stories about the rise and fall of Asia have on domestic attitudes toward Asian Americans? I became interested in how the dramas of American identity sat within global contexts, particularly an American fascination with China that always imagined the Chinese as somewhere else, far across the ocean. I was curious how people like Buck, Luce, or Crow understood the indirect effects their China obsession had on Chinese Americans—whether they recognized the collateral effect their stories about distant China had on nearby Chinatown. And I wanted to learn more about how the Chinese in America—travelers, drifters, students, and settlers alike—understood themselves at a time when they could not access even the most basic language of citizenship.

It seemed to me that the interwar years had a lot to say about our present, especially given America's renewed fascination with China. *A Floating Chinaman* is inspired by critics like Rob Wilson, Yunte Huang, David Palumbo-Liu, Rey Chow, and Aihwa Ong who have envisioned flexible, contingent, and at times playful new models for conceptualizing the space between Asia and America. I use the term "transpacific" because it captures a sense of transience, motion, and flux; it describes a physical space as well as a horizon of possibility. As the anthropologist Janet Hoskins and the literary critic Viet Nguyen have noted, a variety of pasts and futures gather under the capacious sign of the transpacific, from economic trade and political exchange to exploitation and conflict, from networks of new knowledge and beliefs to a purely figurative space where "imaginative constructions, discourses, and fantasies" circulate.[29] In particular, I am drawn to the commingling of fact and fiction at the heart of these exchanges, what the literary critic Yunte Huang evocatively terms the "transpacific imagination." For Huang, "the enactment of poetic imagination" offers a small measure of resistance to the political and economic demands that have long been placed upon this region.[30] On one hand, then, *A Floating Chinaman* revisits a series of optimistic and sometimes opportunistic encounters between writers and audiences, politicians and publishers, corporations and customers, all of which brought the transpacific into focus as a material reality. But *A Floating Chinaman* also attempts to restore the perspectives of those well outside these elite circles, whose experience of the transpacific—as workers, witnesses, students, and provocateurs—left them alienated by the era's general cheeriness.

After all, despite the shift in attitudes, these decades also overlapped with the Chinese Exclusion Act, which was a carryover of a previous era. As a result of Exclusion there was limited contact between the nations' citizens and, as Isaacs's *Scratches on Our Minds* showed, the few accounts that did circulate acquired a greater, at times undue, importance. Specifically, I argue that a re-exploration of the "China question" offers a new way of considering American anxieties toward ideas of progress and "civilization" in the interwar years—China, representative of an older, sager, and no doubt exotic "Oriental" civilization, became a standard of measurement for citizens of a younger, rapidly modernizing United States eager to assess the global status of their nation's ideas and culture. Just as the railroad executive Vining devoted his waking hours to chronicling the centuries-past ingenuity of the Chinese, seemingly deaf to the anti-Chinese sentiment swirling around him, the writers and thinkers who comprise this book were largely entranced with an abstract, possibility-rich China, seldom connecting their interest in this distant land to the fairly dire situation of the Chinese in the United States. I am interested, too, in how this elite fascination with China trickled down to the immigrants in Chinatown. How did this period's interest in China and far-away trade routes shape perceptions about the Chinese Americans across town?

In the broadest sense, *A Floating Chinaman* is about the construction of authority, and here is where Mertz's barb about the undue influence of "personalities" returns. Just as the Sinologists of the past had judged Hwui Shan according to their own, mild prejudices toward the Chinese, the China-watchers of the 1930s and '40s exercised a sense of clubby discretion over which voices were qualified to speak about this prized land. This book is about the circulation of ideas. But it is also a book about writers writing about other writers—about the creation and refinement of those ideas, as well as the spirit of competition that underlies all critical endeavors. These were decades when China represented a new area of inquiry. The stakes for writers like Buck, Crow, Lin, and Tsiang were at once intellectual, personal, and professional. The acquisition of authority is always a contest; there are always other claimants to the status of expert.

A Floating Chinaman begins by considering the context for America's rediscovery of China. Chapter 1 examines the enormous impact of Buck's prize-winning *The Good Earth*, a novel that allowed readers to "go Chinese." Buck's success was, in many ways, the culmination of a longstanding fascination with China that stretched back to America's colonial era. A celebration of the indomitable, thrifty spirit of the Chinese peasant, her novel offered an engaging jumble of old-world idealism and emergent global realities. How did *The Good Earth*—a Pulitzer Prize winner in 1932 and the major achievement of a Nobel Prize-winning career—speak to the anxieties and hopes of its American readers, a decade removed from World War I and deep in the throes of financial depression? What drew these readers to the windswept, pre-modern China of Buck's imagination?

As we admire Buck's rise, we also begin to note the seeds of discontent. She had become perhaps the most famous China expert in the country. Her success helped insure a viable market for sympathetic writings about China. In Chapter 2, we track the career of Tsiang, the idiosyncratic dreamer who, in the wake of this Buck-inspired call to turn our attention to China, began publishing poetry depicting a transpacific future built on revolutionary politics.

Despite his firsthand experience working within the Chinese government, his career stalled. His personal frustrations lurked on the edges of his first novel, *China Red*, an epistolary romance in which a pair of lovers separated by political ideology and the Pacific slowly drift apart. While Tsiang was forced to self-publish *China Red*, readers were devouring other, far less polemical works on China's evolving relationship with America. This was a time when it seemed that any American with half a wit could prosper in China. Chapter 3 returns to this broader stage and the various versions of China that did flourish within the market, most notably Crow's sensational tales of doing business in this new world of "four hundred million customers." Visions of a new economic frontier animated the heroic tales of Standard Oil, one of the first corporations to crack the Chinese market, and their teams of globetrotting American executives and Westernized, English-speaking Chinese sales agents. But not everyone subscribed to these cheery tales of American dreamers abroad. In contrast to the era's triumphalism, we consider Hobart's trilogy of China novels, a series of scathing, interlinked tragedies about the unforeseen effects of American merchants abroad.

These were not the stories Tsiang was capable of telling. Even as Americans craved stories about China, his career continued to stall. Over Chapters 4 and 5, his frustrations mount, as he is unable to find the audience he desires for his next two novels, *The Hanging on Union Square* and *And China Has Hands*. In the mid-1930s he grew desperate, ironic, and vengeful toward the proletarian arts scene, Buck, Lin, and others whose status he coveted. He haunted his own novels, a sad sack badgering his own characters into buying his books. How might we interpret his various experiments with the form of the novel? How did his unique political vantage *compel* him toward flourishes we might today recognize as experimental or postmodern? In Chapter 6, we consider the competing visions of a transpacific future, from the political essays of young Chinatown residents to Buck and Lin's abstract musings on Chinatowns and the theoretical Chinese Americans who populated them. What was at stake as both of these constituencies debated whether the Chinese immigrant community's political destiny was to stay or return to their ancestral home? How did these different versions of the

Chinese American dilemma resonate with broader anxieties about the changing global order, particularly as America was slowly "losing" China?

All of these different figures vied to offer the most authoritative version of America and China's transpacific future. But in all struggles for authority, there is someone who loses. Finally, then, Chapter 7 wonders what we might learn from these various moments of imagined rivalry and professional failure. We return to Buck and Tsiang as their literary careers waned in the late 1940s and 1950s. How did they find creative meaning in rejection, disappointment, and invisibility? What version of Tsiang, now scraping by as an actor in Hollywood, emerges in his personal letters and Federal Bureau of Investigation surveillance files? What did these FBI agents—among his most careful readers and critics—glean from hours spent combing his novels and poems?

Tsiang never got to read his FBI files, which probably would have delighted him. Similarly, it is unlikely that Buck ever read Tsiang's criticisms of her work or the audience she cultivated. For her part, Buck's animosities were directed toward more prominent figures. She, too, lampooned rival visions of the transpacific in print, going so far as to pen an entire novel, 1951's *God's Men*, fictionalizing the life of the only other China-watcher who approached her stature, Henry Luce. Luce, like Buck, grew up in the dying days of the Chinese empire and, in the years leading up to World War II, they were the two most influential interpreters of China for American audiences. But their mutual disdain resulted in a rather bizarre incident of literary character assassination—one of many such acts of revenge I uncover in *A Floating Chinaman*, and a final reminder that the transpacific exists in part as an imagined—and thus passionately, creatively contested—space.

Though Tsiang is the most powerless figure in this book, he is undeniably its heartbeat. My work builds on that of the literary critic Floyd Cheung, whose tireless research helped rescue Tsiang from obscurity. I have often fantasized about what Tsiang's lost work might have contained, what new possibilities of transpacific solidarity it might have imagined. In the conclusion, I imagine Tsiang's representative "Chinaman" floating across continent, across the Pacific, caroming off inhospitable systems and codes, perpetually questing for an identity—Chinese, laborer, transpacific. The image of this "floating" being, contingent and unfixed, captures the critical vantage from which we might reassess this crucial turning point of both American and Asian American cultural formation.

In borrowing Tsiang's evocative title, I embark on my own set of speculations and explorations. *A Floating Chinaman* is not a biography of Tsiang, nor does it hope to overstate his clout. But it is animated at least in part by his stubborn curiosity and relentless whimsy. I have tried to construct a book that drifts between scales and sites, mainstream and margin. I am interested in locating and interpreting Tsiang's "Chinaman" as both a figurative and literal presence floating through interwar American culture—particularly among figures with a greater investment in China than Chinatown or Chinese Americans. Floating toward our present—maybe even beyond it.

The circles at the heart of *A Floating Chinaman*, from Chinese-born Americans and American-born Chinese to traveling scholars, businessmen, students, writers, and the merely curious bore witness to a fascinating moment of internationalism, engaging a series of tropes and ways of describing China that endure to this day. It was a moment, just before the cold war, fraught with possibilities of "transpacific dialogue"—Luce's update of his "American Century"—that remains overlooked in American literary and cultural histories. Contemporary criticism often dismisses figures like Buck and Luce vessels of middlebrow whims, ignoring the nuanced ways in which the consumption of popular writing may have acted as a proxy for deeper global anxieties. What effect might their missionary upbringings have had on American perceptions of China and the "American Century?" How do the stories of Buck's astonishing success and the market for China-related books that resulted enrich our understanding of American publishing history, which has generally overlooked this moment of Orientalist faddishness. Similarly, the Chinese writers of the 1920s and '30s are absent in many major overviews of "Asian American" or "Chinese American" literary history.[31] And, at a time when few Chinese were able to publish, let alone immigrate, the American writings of cosmopolitan writers like Tsiang, Lin, and even

Buck represent seminal interpretations of Chinese American consciousness. How might Lin and Buck's somewhat conservative versions of Chinese American citizenship enrich our understanding of
a population that would, within decades, become known as a "model
minority?" More importantly, what can we learn from Tsiang's frustrations? How do they, too, model a set of wild, desperate responses
to a market uninterested in your stories?

Given how fleeting these moments feel in retrospect—and, bearing in mind that this is a book featuring self-aware authors inserting
themselves and their dramas into their stories—*A Floating Chinaman*
approaches the past with a playful, speculative orientation. This book
is an attempt to explore the concept of the transpacific imagination,
in all the vastness and intangibility that phrase suggests. And it treats
the commingling of fact and fiction that one finds in the trail of writings left behind by the era's writers and journalists as the expression
of a vision that endures to this day. The "scratches on our minds"
that Isaacs detailed can still itch. It can certainly feel as though history is repeating itself. Few remain convinced that the Chinese discovered the Americas, but from Vining's time to ours, we continue
to rely on the same types of intuition when regarding a distant place
and its people. This book is filled with echoes across time, for we still
live in a moment when authority and identity are interlinked—and
where China remains the stuff of dreams. "You know the remarkable
thing about China," a Swedish friend remarked to the publishing
magnate Henry Luce at a cocktail party in the early 1940s, "is that
everyone who comes here becomes enchanted with the tremendous
possibilities for achieving whatever it is they want to achieve."[32]

In 1940, Tsiang was awaiting a hearing on his case to stay in the
United States. He had violated the terms of his student visa, though
he believed that he had been targeted for his revolutionary poetry.
For two years, Tsiang was a resident of what he playfully called "Ellis Island Hotel"[33] and he passed the time by writing letters—many,
many letters. He wrote letters to anyone he thought could help his
case. He wrote follow-up letters in case these letters were lost in
transit. He wrote flirtatious, pun-filled letters to secretaries and ap-
prentices in the hopes that they might speed up their boss's replies.

He poured his heart out to Rockwell Kent, a well-connected proletarian artist and writer, on yard-long strips of toilet paper, and he
would seize on any name casually mentioned in one of Kent's letters
and bombard them as well. He wrote to Vico Marcantonio, a famed
New York labor lawyer sympathetic to the immigrant cause and, in
a misguided attempt to endear himself to this stranger, made fun of
Marcantonio's name.

At this point in his life, the forty-year-old Tsiang realized that his
literary ambitions might never be fulfilled. None of his letters mentioned *A Floating "Chinaman"* or anything resembling the sprawling,
global novel he had outlined a decade earlier. Yet he still held out
hope for some small measure of validation. And so he kept sending
out letters, ever hopeful for some good news.

1

Theoretical China

IN AUGUST 1941, Rockwell Kent sent a letter to Bennett Cerf, the founder of Random House, heralding the peculiar insights of a Chinese writer he had befriended named H. T. Tsiang. Kent was a painter and printmaker best known for illustrating the edition of *Moby-Dick* that introduced Herman Melville's then-obscure novel to a wider audience in the 1930s. On the eve of the United States' entry into World War II, Kent had become deeply committed to progressive political causes, acting as a connector of sorts between activists and artists, particularly those who shared his enthusiasm for international friendship and cooperation. Maybe this was how he viewed Tsiang—as someone who might have interesting things to say about transpacific solidarity. Kent promised to help the Chinese writer find an audience for his books, most of which Tsiang had self-published and peddled out of a suitcase around lower Manhattan. Tsiang showed his appreciation by sending Kent—who he frequently addressed as "The Artist"—a steady stream of manic, aggressively chummy letters filled with poems, recipes for chop suey, twisty double-entendres, and desperate appeals to help him find a publisher.

A few weeks later, a representative from Random House politely declined on Cerf's behalf. As per Kent's letter, Tsiang had delivered a parcel of his self-published books to the Random House office. An editor had read them, mostly out of deference to Kent, who had designed the publishing house's colophon in the late 1920s. He told

Kent that the process of massaging Tsiang's works into publishable shape was one of potential "futility."[1]

With Random House uninterested, Kent tried the John Day Company. In September, he mailed the same letter to Richard Walsh, the publishing house's founder and chief editor. "I am always interested in anybody who interests you," Walsh replied a few days later. "We publish a good many books about China and some by Chinese authors, including Lin Yutang, therefore I should be particularly interested in looking at Mr. Tsiang's books."[2] But where were the books? Had they been lost in the mail? Or maybe Walsh had misunderstood—maybe Tsiang was going to come deliver the books personally?

In reality, Tsiang was petrified. Kent was forwarding him copies of these letters and the Chinese author was unsure how to respond. Though Walsh had no idea who he was, Tsiang knew a fair amount about the publisher and his wife, Pearl Buck. The couple exercised an astonishing degree of influence over how Americans imagined China in the decades leading up to the cold war. The success of *The Good Earth* in 1931 had established Buck as the most prominent American spokesperson on all things Chinese. Walsh had a keen interest in Asia and used the John Day Company to introduce the American reading public to Buck as well as Asian thinkers like Lin Yutang and Jawaharlal Nehru. Walsh and Buck oversaw *Asia* magazine's transformation from a lifestyle rag about the exotic elsewhere into a forum for international affairs. As a Chinese writer shut out from the publishing establishment, Tsiang resented their influence.

Still, Tsiang thought to himself as he read and reread Kent's letter to Walsh, he had been on the sidelines for too long. What if Walsh agreed to publish him? Maybe this was the break he had been waiting for. The break he deserved.

In order to appreciate H. T. Tsiang's anxieties in this moment, we must first understand the broader histories that gave rise to America's interest in China, as well as the forms of expertise this fascination eventually demanded.

To know China: it was an ambition older than the nation itself. The colonies had been barred from trading directly with China, but the importation of tea and porcelain via England engendered a deep curiosity about the distant land that had produced these goods. The imagination was nourished by figures like John Ledyard, an American sailor who returned from a trip through Asia in 1782 with fantastic tales of ships cutting across the seas, sagging with goods and profits.[3] Practically the moment the colonies declared independence, ships set sail for China armed with ginseng and the sort of self-effacing deference that ingratiated foreigners to the Chinese. In 1784, the *Empress of China* left New York for Guangzhou, returning one year later. The cargo was sold for a modest profit and the attendant excitement of this successful maiden voyage across the Pacific inspired author Philip Freneau to pen a poem titled, "On the First American Ship That Explored the Route to China and the East-Indies, After the Revolution." In 1786, Congress attempted to formalize relations by appointing Samuel Shaw the first American consul in Guangzhou, although the post had little clout behind it.

The early China trade not only allowed America new access to a coveted foreign market, it was also a symbolic, confidence-building expression of the young nation's global aspirations. This relationship would take on a more complicated character in the next century, as the United States expanded its sphere of influence throughout the Pacific world. If the notion of esteem can ever be applied to nations, then the nineteenth century might crassly be described as a period when China and United States traded places. For ancient China, these would be the last days of dynastic rule. The Opium Wars (1839–1842 and 1856–1860) were the most significant of the various foreign incursions that essentially forced China open to the West. Even more significant than the damage wrought by the wars were the uneven treaties and forfeited territories that followed. China's rude introduction to the global economy was exacerbated by internal challenges to imperial authority, sporadic rebellions, and famine. With China in seeming decline, the lure of work opportunities abroad—such as those across the Pacific—eventually drew thousands of young men desperate for work overseas.

For the United States, this was a period of growth and maturation, one guided by the promise of "Manifest Destiny." The young, upstart nation's westward expansion created a need for cheap, abundant labor. A half-century after the *Empress of China*'s initial foray across the Pacific, ships full of impoverished Chinese "coolies" completed the circle, arriving on America's western shores to mine gold and build the railroads. By the end of the civil war, however, the need for Chinese labor had subsided and grassroots nativist organizations like the Supreme Order of Caucasians fomented for their expulsion. A century after the *Empress of China* announced America's modest intentions abroad, the passage of the Chinese Exclusion Act of 1882—the first American immigration act targeting a specific ethnic group—dramatized the two nations' reversals of fortune. Entering the twentieth century, China's internal stability and international prestige were both in shambles.[4]

And yet—all of this just served to enhance China's allure, at least within certain intellectual circles. China always provided a useful surface upon which to project American anxieties and hopes. Economic and political realities notwithstanding, China remained a point of civilizational comparison. The spiritual crisis of the Gilded Age resulted in a spate of turn-of-the-century books and articles pondering America's future. In 1905, the educator and politician Seth Low published "The Position of the United States among Nations," an exemplary specimen of this genre. "It is not an uncommon thing," Low begins his essay, "to hear men say that 'the future belongs to the United States'; or, that 'the United States is the country of the future.'"[5] But where might the nation look to understand the complexities and contours of this awesome responsibility? In contrast to the open, inviting United States, he invokes the sad example of China, which "has never been a world-power in the modern sense of that phrase because their ideal has been to keep the world out of China, rather than allow China to come into living contact with the rest of the world."[6] China's failure to adapt to these times of greater interdependency, Low continued, left it at a great disadvantage. "A nation cannot live to itself alone, and continue to be either great or strong. The law of life of a healthy nation is that it shall do its share of the world's work as well as its own, precisely as the law of life of a healthy man is that he shall live for others as well as for himself."[7]

Ultimately, Low concluded, China's massive size and history meant that it still had a significant part to play in the coming century. For many observers, this came down to the fact that there were fortunes to be gained by looking across the Pacific. Even in its weakened state, China, as I will discuss in Chapter 3, would become known as the land of "four-hundred million customers."[8] The language and outsized imagery used to describe China's potential as a market communicated how Americans perceived their place in the emerging constellation of world powers. It also recalled the providential visions first applied to China by the Christian missionaries, who began arriving as early as the 1830s. The movement blossomed in the years of secular overseas expansion after 1890, when American colleges sent as many as 6,000 missionaries abroad per year.[9] As Horace Pitkin, a prominent figure in the nineteenth century missionary community, would later recall: "China was the goal, the lodestar, the great magnet that drew us all in those days."[10] Irrespective of one's spiritual inclinations, it became commonplace to speak of China in such elevated terms. The missionary's zealous language of imminent change became indistinguishable from the rhetoric of economic and political imperative. It was up to the "Young Giant of the West" to command a greater influence over China in the coming century, former diplomat James Angell told graduates of the University of Michigan in 1900.[11] Our return to China had been preordained. As the scholar and diplomat Stanley Hornbeck put it, America's penetration of China's untapped markets would be "as inevitable as has been the migration to our western prairies."[12] In a commencement address at the University of Washington in 1914, Frederick Jackson Turner offered an addendum to his observation that "the frontier has gone." There remained a *tabula rasa*, far beyond the Pacific Ocean:

> Across the Pacific looms Asia, no longer a remote vision and a symbol of the unchanging, but borne as by mirage close to our shores and raising grave questions of the common destiny of the people of the ocean. The dreams of Benton and Seward of a regenerated Orient, when the long march of westward civilization should complete its circle, seem almost to be in process of realization. The age of the Pacific Ocean begins, mysterious and unfathomable in its meaning for our future.[13]

Turner's remarks capture the paradoxical mystique of China. It was an "unfathomable," strange riddle. Yet its solution was inevitable, predestined, as obvious as tracing the edge of a circle.

This was a shape that flattered all who shared in its circumference. Consider "The Cycle of the Civilization," a speech that C. Y. Tang, a Chinese student at Wisconsin's Beloit College, delivered at various Midwestern oratorical contests throughout 1917. It was an impassioned plea for the international powers to recognize the plight of China, locked in what he termed a "backwards" trajectory. Taking the longest view possible, Tang posited that all Western civilizations were actually "born in the Orient" and that the ideas fundamental to the West had traveled across the globe, birthing modern Europe and producing "this new America." With China gingerly entering a new global configuration founded on national powers, it was the lessons of America's rise that the old republic desperately needed to remaster. By looking eastward and lending a hand—completing the cycle, so to speak—Tang felt that the United States would begin to understand the crisscrossing flows of ideas and ideals encoded in its own creation. Together, Tang wrote, China and America were in a position to "strive for a brotherhood of nations" that might produce "a new and better life for all humanity."[14] This question of a shared humanity would take on a sharper focus following World War I.

In Chapter 6, we will further examine the perspectives of Chinese students like Tang. But suffice it to say that it was rare to hear Chinese voices like Tang's during these American discussions about civilization, progress, and international cooperation. This is what made *Whither Mankind: A Panorama of Modern Civilization*, a 1928 volume edited by Charles Beard, a bit unusual. "Anxiety about the values and future of civilization is real," Beard observed in his introduction. Astutely, Beard cautioned against a growing tendency among Americans to invoke the hyperbolic "guise of Oriental wisdom"—to offer Asia as the "sharp antithesis and challenge to the West" purely as a way to "assail the evils of capitalism at home."[15] In order to combat this fetishizing attitude and give texture to this distinction between the "Orient" and the "Occident," Beard's volume opened with an essay by Hu Shih, a Chinese writer and reformer who had studied under John Dewey at Columbia University in the 1910s.

"The difference between the Eastern and Western civilizations is simply a degree of success or failure in the process of breaking away from the medieval ideas and institutions which once ruled the whole civilized world," Hu wrote.[16] Instead of the self-defeatism and "medieval" superstition at the heart of "Oriental wisdom," he welcomed the new religions of the West: democracy, machine-age innovation, pragmatist philosophy.

We can begin cataloging the common themes Americans relied upon when they told themselves stories about China. The American impressions of China had been shaped by the earliest communities to make contact: missionaries and businesspeople, both of whom retained faith in China's size and population. It was precisely China's underdevelopment that made it such a welcome market for Western ideas or goods. As America's stature grew, however, the need to reckon with China shifted accordingly. Opportunities still awaited the adventurous and enterprising. But China, which seemed to be frozen in premodernity, also became a surface against which turn-of-the-century Americans could project their own hopes and anxieties. Interestingly—and as we will consider in subsequent chapters—their sense of curiosity rarely extended to the actual Chinese people living in urban Chinatowns or along the West Coast—populations affected by the Chinese Exclusion Act in 1882. Even as Americans romanticized China's potential, the Western complicity in China's decline was often left unexamined.

By the 1920s and 1930s, then, a desire had emerged for new perspectives on the transpacific future. The opportunity was there for someone who might illuminate the wondrous possibilities that linked the two nations.

The distance between the well-circulated myths about China and the realities of the American experience there represented a particularly vexing issue to Pearl Buck (born Pearl Sydenstricker). She was born on June 26, 1892, in Hillsboro, West Virginia, while her missionary parents, Absalom and Carie Sydenstricker, were on furlough in the United States. Absalom and Carie were Southern Presbyterians who had been stationed in China in 1880. Pearl was the fourth of seven children, but one of only three who lived to see adulthood.

She was three months old when her family returned to China, where she would spend most of the first forty years of her life.

There was no single reason why young Americans committed themselves to missionary work abroad. While spiritual yearnings were always central, some missionaries were simply drawn to the prospect of an exciting and unconventional career in an unusual place.[17] The Sydenstrickers, however, were clearly steeled by the word of God. From Buck's perspective, this did not necessarily mean that they were enlightened. Years later, in a memoir titled *My Separate Worlds*, Buck would reminisce about "the small white clean Presbyterian American world of my parents and the big loving merry not-too-clean Chinese world, and there was no communication between them."[18] To Buck, the missionary enterprise was profoundly flawed, peopled by so-called believers who were "so lacking in sympathy for the people they were supposed to be saving, so scornful of any civilization except their own, so harsh in their judgments upon one another, so coarse and insensitive among a sensitive and cultivated people that my heart has fairly bled with shame."[19] Many speculate that she was slyly indicting her father, often described as a grim, thoroughly oblivious man.

Instead, in the formative years of her adolescence, Buck and her siblings aspired to be "bilingual little beasts,"[20] developing sympathies for the plight of the native Chinese, particularly the laboring classes. As she would later recall: "When I was in the Chinese world I was Chinese, I spoke Chinese and behaved as a Chinese and ate as the Chinese did, and I shared their thoughts and feelings. When I was in the American world, I shut the door between."[21] It seemed as though the country was different each time her family returned from a furlough abroad. In the immediate aftermath of the Boxer Rebellion, Buck sought out a former teacher, who explained that the international response to the uprisings had so damaged the spirits of the native Chinese that the nation lay powerless to the intrusive international indemnity demands.

Within decades, though, this feeling of relative weakness gave way to a new and hopeful post-Boxer attitude about the nation's future. The younger generations of China, unencumbered by feelings of inferiority, viewed the West as a model for their own modernization.

Military schools flourished and there were reforms to improve the army. The judicial system was overhauled and international trade slowly gained support.[22] Literature began to show Western influences as well, thanks largely to translators like Lin Shu—famous for his widely read 1901 translation of *Uncle Tom's Cabin*, renamed *A Black Slave's Cry to Heaven*.

When Buck left for college in 1910 it was "with a sober heart and a mind too old for my years."[23] As a student at Randolph-Macon Women's College in Lynchburg, Virginia, she had a difficult time following the events back home in China: "Sometimes, I felt as I read the papers that I was a juggler trying to keep a dozen balls in the air at once."[24] She was known to many of her American classmates as "the freak who could speak Chinese."[25] She was a sensitive, reclusive young woman slowly coming to understand her bicultural heritage, occasionally exploring her Chinese roots through writing.[26]

Though Buck had intended to remain in the United States after graduation in 1914, the illness of her mother compelled her to return to China. In 1917 she married John Lossing Buck, a notable agricultural economist who was quickly becoming an expert on Chinese farming practices. Her interest in representations of China was rekindled, partly because of growing tensions at home. From 1920 to 1933, the Bucks were based in Nanjing, on the campus of Nanjing University. Lossing Buck's fieldwork required the couple to travel through the bleak farmlands of the north so that he could collect data and deliver talks on the wonders of Western farming techniques.

"At this period of my life," Buck would later recall, "I was keenly aware of the Chinese peasant—his wonderful strength and goodness, his amusing and often alarming shrewdness and wisdom, his direct approach to life."[27] This was in stark contrast to her husband, who held firm to the belief that the Chinese were a "queer people (with) many things to learn from Western agricultural experts."[28] His time in China convinced him that the scientific, rational West had little to gain from the exchange. This dynamic of a foreign expert touring the Chinese countryside and dispensing Western know-how had played out earlier in Buck's life with her missionary father and his "small white clean" world. Decades later, as Buck accompanied her own "young American" on his agricultural research trips, she continued to cultivate a sympathetic, if not idealized, image of the underestimated Chinese peasant. "I must confess," Buck would later write, "that I had often wondered secretly what a young American could teach the Chinese farmers who had been farming for generations on the same land and by the most skillful use of fertilizers and irrigation were still able to produce extraordinary yields and this without modern machinery."[29] She began to contribute stories and essays for publications such as *The Nation, The Chinese Recorder, Asia,* and *Atlantic Monthly.* In 1930, after several rejections, the John Day Company published her first novel, *East Wind, West Wind.*[30] While it was a modest success—the *New York Times* praised her flexibility in dealing with both Chinese and Western concepts of family and clan—Buck was still a literary unknown as she worked on her second novel.

Buck's next book was tentatively titled *Wang Lung.* It told the story of a Chinese peasant family as they persevered through famine, revolution, and crises of faith. We begin in the waning days of dynastic rule, as the modest, hard-working Wang Lung marries O-lan, the homely but loyal former slave of a wealthy household.[31] Through hard work, thrift, and a canny understanding of the value of land, they build a modest estate. But when the entire region's crops suffer after a spell of horrible weather, Wang Lung, O-lan, and their three children leave the countryside behind, fleeing to a nearby city in search of work. Importantly, they sell everything but their farm.[32]

The family's experience in the city is a transformative one. Relegated to poverty, the children are forced to beg. Wang Lung, once a proud paragon of self-sufficiency, resorts to the somewhat demeaning work of pulling a rickshaw. In the city, the family encounters the various challenges facing a suddenly modern China: political turmoil following the end of dynastic rule, the presence and authority of Westerners, and rumblings from nascent Communist agitators. Through it all, Wang Lung and his family resist the temptations of revolutionary politics or Western religion; they only desire to return to their precious land. They ignore the overheated passions of everyone around them, choosing instead to scrimp and save. Fate smiles upon Wang Lung when he is swallowed into a rampaging mob and somehow makes off with a small fortune.

Eventually, Wang Lung and his family return to their beloved soil. They have been rewarded for their steady humility in the face of change and tumult. The household where O-lan was raised in servitude has fallen into ruin and they buy her now-impoverished master's estate at a steep discount. Despite the machinations of his jealous uncle, the ruinous influence of his concubine, the death of O-lan, and the general instability of the Chinese countryside, Wang Lung prospers, thanks largely to his unyielding faith in his land. The novel ends on an intriguingly vague note, with Wang Lung on his deathbed and two of his children hatching plans to liquidate their fortune.

Wang Lung remained the title of Buck's manuscript until her agent, David Lloyd, sent it to the John Day Company. Named after a renowned Elizabethan printer, John Day had opened in 1926. In its first few years of operation, there was nothing particularly noteworthy about its list; there was certainly nothing to suggest that it would become a political force, shaping American perceptions of Asia.[33] When Lloyd had set out to find a publisher for *East Wind: West Wind,* John Day had been their twenty-ninth choice, after twenty-eight rejections.

Lloyd described *Wang Lung* to Richard Walsh, the publishing house's founder and chief, as "a direct yet delicate portrayal of the conflict between the old and the new in China. I think it may interest you." Walsh replied directly to Buck:

Dear Mrs. Buck:

I wish you were not so far away because I am afraid it is going to be impossible for me to express adequately in this letter our enthusiasm for *Wang Lung.* The beauty of style which attracted us to *East Wind: West Wind* is only one of its great merits. Your characters are drawn with such fidelity that the reader has no difficulty in forgetting that they are not of his own race and in sharing their emotions as human beings . . . By your choice of incidents you have somehow succeeded in making us believe that we are seeing almost the whole of the life of the plain people of China in all its details, from birth to death. Over and above all this, I believe that you have written a book of permanent importance, one that will rank with the great novels of the soil.

There are just three points I want to take up with you. One: the title. We feel that *Wang Lung* is quite impossible. The sound comes unpleasantly from the American tongue . . . and is subject to facetious parody. 'One lung,' for example, but also because of the immediate effect—that is, typing the book as Chinese. We have to present this book not as a story of Chinese life, but as a novel of the soil. The only title I have been able to think of is *The Good Earth*.[34]

Soon thereafter, Walsh received an enthusiastic reply from Buck agreeing on all counts—this was no longer a book about old China in the throes of great change; it would be a "novel of the soil." This was, after all, in line with her longstanding aim to render a version of China free of exotic frills. For Buck, the point was to write as plainly as possible, to contradict "all those writings about the Chinese which make them strange and outlandish."[35] From Walsh's perspective, this was clearly a novel about China; but could it be marketed to Americans as a book about more relatable experiences as well?

The Good Earth was published on March 2, 1931. Henry Seidel Canby, chairman of the Book of the Month Club, seemed to draw directly from Buck and Walsh's private discussions when he announced the novel's selection in the organization's influential monthly newsletter:

The Good Earth is China. In this story the West is a distant and unimportant phenomenon . . . The people in this rather thrilling story are not "queer" or "exotic"; they are natural as their soil. They are so intensely human that after the first chapter you are more interested in their humanity than in their novelties of belief anad [*sic*] habit . . . You go Chinese in this book, and after reading it can never again think of the Chinese struggle and the Chinese people as drab, far away and incomprehensible.[36]

What does it mean to "go Chinese"—to, in Walsh's phrasing, forget that these characters are not of your race? It is certainly a peculiar and brusque form of flattery. But it helps explain how many American readers processed Buck's work. Buck's prose was spare, unadorned, and utilitarian. She was writing against the tradition that always cast China as strange and unknowable. She tried to use the common dignity of Wang Lung and O-lan to introduce readers to new, Chinese archetypes deserving of our admiration.

But did Buck's admiring version of China merely flatter the American reader's sense of self? As the literary critics Peter Conn and Colleen Lye have argued, Buck offered a multifaceted kind of realism. The book brought China into clearer focus by appealing to the questions and struggles facing most Americans during this time.[37] "Quietly and almost unnoticed," Canby observed, "the art of skillful realism has passed beyond our own people, beyond our own civilization, and has begun to deal with strange cultures, which we have never even tried to know from the inside, as they see themselves." Now that advances in transoceanic transportation were "tying all the world together," it was important to revisit what we *truly* knew about places like China, "the mysterious cloud on the horizon for all of us." But Canby picked up on the novel's universal appeal as well. "Wang Lung is a Chinese symbol of every man who has ever worked his way up in the world," he proclaimed. He described it as a more gripping version of "a like story laid in Dakota" and compared Wang Lung's sense of honest virtue to that of a Puritan. Americans, Canby was suggesting, would have no difficulties associating with this book's landscape and characters. By rendering her characters as plainly as possible, Buck's readers began recognizing their own story.[38]

While much of this period's popular fiction concerned with China trafficked in a leering otherness, Wang Lung comes across as *Ragged Dick* with a cup of tea and a queue. Buck's rags-to-riches tale of virtuous struggle was published in the same year that the Dust Bowls began.[39] For many Americans, the story of an honest family trying to tame the unforgiving land was a familiar one. Read this way, *The Good Earth* became the timeless story that Walsh had envisioned, its characters tied to the soil, persevering through great changes to the social, political, and natural landscape. Early in the novel, as the earnest farmer Wang Lung carefully maps a path toward fortune, he grows fixated on the possibility of owning his own fields. His obsession begins to consume him, dwarfing any responsibility he might feel toward his wife or family. It is the only reliable aspect of his life: "At least I have the land—I have the land."[40]

After Wang Lung's own, spiteful uncle inspires a town raid on his household, the farmer finds philosophy in the permanence of his most prized possession—"They cannot take the land from me. The labor of my body and the fruit of the fields I have put into that which cannot be taken away. If I had the silver, they would have taken it. If I had bought with the silver to store it, they would have taken it all. I have the land still, and it is mine."[41] When the family decides to move to the city to wait out a nasty drought, O-lan convinces Wang Lung that he is foolish to even consider selling the land, arguing that they can sell the house's table, beds, bedding, and cauldron, but never the land itself.[42]

Everyday things come and go, but their relationship to the land evolves into something far deeper—it is a metaphor that sustains them, both "a sign and a symbol."[43] As the novel progresses and their harvests grow fickle, Wang Lung's dependence on the land becomes literalized. In the midst of the drought that pushes Wang Lung and his family to the south, he threatens to ingest it: "I shall never sell the land! Bit by bit I will dig up the fields and feed the earth itself to the children and when they die I will bury them in the land, and I and my wife and my old father, even he, we will die on the land that has given us birth!"[44] It is the land to which Wang Lung constantly returns for meaning and solace. He laments the idleness of his pampered son, who never learned the humbling lessons of barren fields.[45] Later, as he frets over the troubles his concubine has brought to his house, wandering through his estate restores his perspective. Instantly, he was "healed of his sickness of love by the good dark earth of his fields and he felt the moist soil on his feet and he smelled the earthy fragrance rising up out of the furrows he turned for the wheat."[46]

Wang Lung's land becomes a way for him to understand the narrative arc of his life. On the one hand he is a by-the-bootstraps entrepreneur whose life aspires toward a larger, grander *telos* of his own choosing. But on the other hand, he is a farmer subjected to the predictable, natural cycles of the Earth. The land will outlast him. "Some time, in some age, bodies of men and women had been buried there, houses had stood there, had fallen, and gone back into the earth. So would also their house, some time, return into the earth, their bodies also. Each had his turn at the earth."[47] As they turn the soil over and over, they are humbled by the totalizing magnificence of the natural world: the land's permanence gives perspective to the ambitions and whims of its owner. It is always true, whether it is in China or the Great Plains. After all, it was the land, the fertile soil, the earth itself that was prized—never China. Nearly one hundred pages pass before Buck locates her novel in Anhwei, located in eastern central China.

While there are enough markers to fix *The Good Earth* to Chinese history and geography, there is also a universalism that feels intentional. Initial readers and reviewers echoed Canby's enthusiastic framing, noting the many resonances between Buck's windswept prairies and those of the United States. Writing in the *Christian Century* in 1931, P. S. Hutchinson connected *The Good Earth* with the tragedies of the Great Depression: "As far as the spiritual content of Wang Lung is concerned, it would not have differed greatly had he toiled on the Nebraska prairie rather than China."[48] A notable review from the *New York Tribune*'s influential book review described *The Good Earth* as a novel about "soil anywhere":

> When Mrs. Buck's *East Wind: West Wind* appeared a year ago I wrote that it was the first mature novel in English dealing with China. Now with *The Good Earth* she is entitled to be counted a first-rate novelist . . . This is China, China as it has never before been portrayed in fiction. *The Good Earth*, however, is much more than China. This is the elemental struggle of men with the soil anywhere, a struggle more stark and heavier with drama in China only because there men fight with the will alone, unaided by mechanical devices.

On one hand, *The Good Earth* is commended for its verisimilitude— "This is China," the critic declares. But the review ends with praise for the novel's presentation of a *timeless* human drama—it is not only a novel about China, it is a rumination on the human will that is set, the reviewer underscores, in a premodern environment. The review continues:

If there is some straining for effects of Biblical poesy, more often there is poignancy In the simple narrative . . . Most of all there is verity. The undramatic horror of famine, the mute suffering of the peasant wife displaced by a flowerlike concubine, the primitive struggle for survival—these are the life of a race. Wang Lung is his people and his kind, but he is not only a Chinese and a peasant, he is an individual understandable apart from his race . . . She has succeeded also in conveying a sense of the dignity of this life, however primitive it may be.[49]

A now-familiar refrain: the Chinese—*they're just like us.*

But what did actual Chinese people think?

The Good Earth offered the possibility of transpacific harmony, with the American reader's sympathetic self-identification completing the circle. Buck encouraged such readings of her work. "When I come to America," she told a reporter in 1932, "I do not stay in the cities any more than I can help." Echoing one of the book's themes, Buck refused the din and squalor of American cities. Instead, she sought out the serene, undeveloped regions of the country that reminded her of home. "I have felt that the good earth is the good earth no matter it be China or America."[50]

Critics in China thanked her for offering a corrective to all the books and movies casting the "Chinaman" as "dirty, mean, and cunning." One Chinese reviewer praised her as "undoubtedly a friend of the Chinese nation," expressing gratitude for her attempts to correct these longstanding stereotypes.[51] Another extolled Buck as Chinese in "spirit and soul."[52] As the literary critic Liu Haiping has noted, the Chinese reception to Buck's novels tended to be quite positive. Throughout the 1930s, her novels were wildly popular, with one translation of *The Good Earth* going through twelve editions.[53] Shortly after *The Good Earth* was published, Buck received a letter from the nephew of Lin Yutang, a Chinese writer and inventor with whom she would later collaborate. "As a little Chinese writer myself," Lin's nephew remarked, "I have devoted my attention to our peasants, and I found your novel tells more truths than any famous foreign professors, who have written several volumes of books dealing with Chinese peasant life. Your novel, I am sure, will be largely appreciated by Chinese readers."[54] Chinese American readers agreed. The *Chinese Digest*, the first English-language Chinese American newspaper, praised *The Good Earth* as "one of the great novels of our time."[55] For these growing and often misunderstood young Chinatown communities, Buck represented a hero of sorts, someone who could teach American readers that the Chinese were honest, dignified, and hardworking.

Of course, not everyone considered the modest, thrifty Wang Lung a representative man. Some even preferred cities to the countryside. In 1933, Kiang Kang-Hu, a left-leaning Chinese politician and scholar, took Buck to task in the pages of the *New York Times*. Kiang saw himself as a true cosmopolitan, fluent in English and capable of mingling in American and Canadian intellectual circles. His resume suggested a bold, intrepid spirit: he had founded the Socialist Party of China before the formation of the Republic; he was the first Chinese in Beijing to establish a modern public school for girls; and he was a staunch advocate of "freedom and absolute equality" between Chinese men and women.[56] Still, throughout his travels, Kiang was constantly confronted with the same question, for which he had no answer: what did he, an actual Chinese person, think of Pearl Buck? "I must admit that I never cared much to read Western writers on Chinese subjects and still less about their novels about China," Kiang explained. But the amount of interest in Buck's novel could not be ignored. He eventually "picked up *The Good Earth* glanced it over in one evening."[57] Suffice it to say, he hated it.

Kiang wrote a piece for the *New York Times* registering an array of objections large and small. Kiang attacked Buck for romanticizing the life of peasants and misrepresenting the particulars of Chinese funeral processions.[58] She had exaggerated the Chinese appetite for beef and fumbled the details of how a rural commoner prepares tea.[59] "Very often I felt uneasy at her minute descriptions of certain peculiarities and defects of some lowly-bred Chinese characters," Kiang confessed, criticizing Buck's sensational depictions of the sex lives of Chinese peasants. "A natural and sound free sex expression is much to be desired for our younger generation but not the pathetic and unhealthy kind that is chiefly presented in Mrs. Buck's works."[60]

Despite Kiang's purist nitpicking, even he had to admit that Buck's novels succeeded in bringing attention to an oft-ignored segment of the Chinese population. It was just that Kiang himself had little interest in these people. "They may form the majority of the Chinese population but they are certainly not representative of the Chinese people," he protested. By fixing on these lower classes, Kiang argued, Buck was offering a narrow impression of the nation that was "far less true to Chinese life as a whole."[61] His quibble was with representation—not just who was allowed to speak on behalf of China but what image of the growing nation those representations highlighted. Why not focus on the Chinese whose influence and ideas would guide the nation? As he remarked in a related essay on China's image in the world, "misrepresentation is even worse than nonrepresentation!"[62] Buck issued a polite, measured reply to Kiang, insisting on the veracity of *her* China and reiterating her more general belief that the nation's future would be shaped by the masses, not pompous elites.

Kiang's seeming animosity toward the lower depths of Chinese life only bolstered Buck's sense of moral authority. But his skeptical dismissal of Buck's yeoman farmers might be seen as a proxy for larger concerns with how Americans received their impressions of China. In the preceding decades, Americans rarely saw fit to gaze across the Pacific. Now that an opportunity to educate Americans about China had emerged, Kiang was frustrated that the most acclaimed tales trafficked in a kind of premodern backwardness. "The great harm is that the reader would naturally be led to imagine China from this picture and to form his judgment upon it accordingly; the writer has thus consciously or unconsciously rendered a most unwelcome service to the country in which she was born and still lives."[63]

Let us momentarily ignore Kiang's fussy petulance and consider the substance of his objection. While Kiang's perspective was actually one of elite privilege, his main point was to remind American readers that a range of Chinese lives existed beyond *The Good Earth*'s "coolies and ammahs." In a roundabout way, Kiang was lobbying for a diversity of perspectives on the China question. After all—how often did a Chinese byline like his appear in the *Times?* Kiang's accusation that Buck had relied on these "coolies and ammahs" as her "first-hand translators" of China proved to be misguided—unbeknownst to him, she was actually bilingual. But he was raising an important question about the responsibilities facing those who sought to "translate" China to those incapable of accessing the country directly.[64] For Kiang, Buck's work as a cultural go-between ignored the contributions of the "intellectual minority" that would lead China into the future. The nation clearly cherished its common folk, Kiang clarified in a follow-up piece for the *Chinese Christian Student*, "but we do not like to see them being made our representatives by a Western writer."[65] He continued to skewer Buck's fixation on a limited segment of the Chinese population and the extent to which their uniquely "queer practices" would, as a result of her success, come to define China in the American imagination. What if Kiang himself were to write a tale of America based on the strangest experiences he had collected on his travels: "the speakeasies in New York, the gangland in Chicago, the Kentucky mountaineers and the Southern Darkies; all full of queer practices. With my respect and love of America and the Americans, I can simply not write a book like 'Uncle Sham,' even if the 'regions' supply my material."[66]

In this way, maybe Kiang was right. While we can recognize the slippery, "timeless" quality of *The Good Earth*, it was still, as Kiang and Buck both noted, marketed as a novel about China. The paucity of readily available and reliable books on China and Chinese culture elevated *The Good Earth* to the status of a guidebook, with Buck assuming the position of the United States' chief interlocutor of all things Chinese. While Buck ambivalently shrugged off these duties as an unfair imposition, many of her books trafficked in a kind of modest authority. These were books self-consciously *about* China.

It is understandable why others queued up for the opportunity to attack her, especially when *The Good Earth*'s popularity meant that its version of China began circulating as hard fact. In China, a scholar named Wu Lifu published a skeptical, twenty-eight-page introduction to one translation of the novel. He was dubious about the "wide-reaching impact of her version of China upon the world" and ran its details through a rigorous session of fact checking.[67] No less an authority than Lu Xun, China's preeminent modern writer and critic, took Buck to task for her skewed, "superficial" perspective on China: "It is always better for the Chinese to write about Chinese subject matter, as that is the only way to get near the truth. Even with Mrs. Buck, who was given a warm welcome in Shanghai, what her books reveal is no more than her stand as an American missionary woman who happens to have grown up in China . . . Only when we Chinese come to do it, can we expect to reveal some truth."[68] When Helen Foster Snow arrived in China in 1932, she would later recall that everyone from American missionaries to young Chinese intellectuals loathed *The Good Earth*, all for different reasons.[69] "Western-educated Chinese hated [*The Good Earth*] because they didn't want foreigners to learn anything unpleasant about China."[70]

Then again, it is not as if Buck categorically deferred to Chinese writers. Their birthright did not protect them from her criticism. Maybe it blinded them from seeing the bigger picture. In a letter to a classmate about Lao She's 1936 novel *Rickshaw Boy*, which had just been translated into English, she questioned Lao's perspective on the common laborer. "That is, I think a Chinese intellectual who is very far from the common people has written what he thinks a rickshaw boy thinks and feels. But I do not believe it is the way the true rickshaw boy thinks and feels."[71] Buck saw herself as someone forcing these young elites to face up to the "unpleasant" realities they had chosen to ignore.[72]

All of these questions took on more urgency when the title of resident expert was at stake.[73] Kiang's quibbling, nagging tone notwithstanding, it is important to consider the context of his grievances. His petty accusations shaded a larger concern about China's status in the broader world, something he encountered firsthand with every new city he visited. He had a different perspective from the Chinese critics in China, who could admire the effect of *The Good Earth* from a distance. What Kiang desired was for outsiders to respect and admire China, not pity or condescend to it. American readers disillusioned with the prospects of modern industry may have been attracted to *The Good Earth*'s homespun themes and rural setting, but critics from a still-developing China were sensitive to what they perceived as a condescending, anti-urban undercurrent in Buck's writing. This certainly came through in how she represented herself. During a promotional stop in New York, a *Times* writer described Buck's "quieter and more leisurely" manner as a product of "the static solemnity of an older nation." (To the writer, this was all in stark contrast to the American manner, all "clanging cars," "tooting automobiles," and the "roar of jazz.")[74]

Both Buck and Kiang had agreed that the United States (or, in Kiang's terms, the West) had something to learn from China. But where Buck saw the potential for interrelatedness and cooperation, Kiang fixed on the discreteness of cultural ways. Most of Kiang's published articles and speeches harped on the ultimate incommensurability of Chinese and Western cultures. "Chinese ways of thinking and action are different from, and often contrary to, Western methods," he writes. "By trying to understand the Chinese viewpoint your scope of life will be enlarged and enlightened. It is the only means to rid of prejudice and ignorance."[75] In a different speech, Kiang expands on this point. Perhaps it is not China that should be looking for American help; perhaps Chinese philosophy and values would be the best corrective for the social and political decadence that accompanied the West's material growth: "Western culture, with all its victory and splendor, shows some imperfection and weakness, while Chinese culture, with all its drawbacks and unfashionableness, indicated the possibility of being rejuvenated and utilized as a remedy for the defects of others."[76] Kiang did not oppose the project of modern progress. He, like many of the Western observers who seemed to fetishize the East, simply believed that China could figure out a way to accomplish its ends without incurring what he saw to be the West's modern excesses.

To Kiang, Buck's preference for what he termed "common people" suggested an ambivalent, if not outright hostile, attitude toward the urban. Buck's attitudes are exemplified in an extended sojourn that comprises the middle third of *The Good Earth*. When droughts and poor harvests force Wang Lung and his family south, they end up in the city of Kiangsu, face-to-face with modernity. Kiangsu bustles with contact between new technologies and timeworn superstitions; young nationalists and old traditionalists; and hope-starved Chinese workers and oblivious, wealthy Westerners. Wang Lung is unable to find stable work, so the family is forced to settle in a dingy shantytown of beggars and menial laborers, which is cut off from the city center by a wall.

Wang Lung tries to maintain belief in the rags-to-riches modesty that propelled him to wealth in the countryside, but the structures and shaky morality of city life make this difficult. Buck portrays the city as a zone that maintains and exploits class difference, with its immodest cosmopolitanism founded on the backs of the laboring classes: "Day by day beneath the opulence of this city Wang Lung lived in the foundations of poverty upon which it was laid." A fellow slum dweller observes, cryptically, that the classes are arranged symbiotically. The vanity of the rich is served by the desperation of the poor, and vice versa: "When the rich are too rich there are ways, and when the poor are too poor there are ways."[77]

This tension between the classes in Kiangsu initially echoes the caste consciousness of Anhwei, where the peasantry and the elites depended on each other as well. But where the cycles of the simple, rural life reward modesty over hubris—they are all ultimately dependent on cooperation from the physical world—the markets and services of the urban economy expand unchecked. In the city, class disparity is a naturalized phenomenon. There is no equivalent of living humbly off the land; there is only currency and exchange.

He begins to recognize these factional distinctions upon taking a job as a rickshaw driver shuttling wealthy passengers throughout the city. He encounters "a creature the like of whom he had never seen before. He has no idea whether it was male or female, but it was tall and dressed in a straight black robe of some rough harsh material and there was the skin of a dead animal wrapped around its neck."[78] A passing rickshaw driver explains to Wang Lung that this is a white foreigner. In Anhwei, there was no consciousness of a national identity; there was no "other" to define what one was or was not. In Kiangsu, where exotic Westerners and Chinese of all classes mingle freely, Wang Lung finally realizes that foreignness is a relative value. He finds this somewhat reassuring: "Then Wang Lung knew that this was indeed a foreigner and more foreign yet than he was in this city, and that after all people of black hair and black eyes are one sort and people of light hair and light eyes of another sort, and he was no longer after that wholly foreign in the city."[79] Though there are practical benefits to acquiring this understanding of foreignness— Wang Lung quickly learns that the quick-tempered yet foolish white passengers give better tips—he is ambivalent to the enterprise of solidarity.[80] One day, Wang Lung happens upon a crowd gathered on the corner of a Confucian temple that is enraptured by the charged words of a young Chinese man: "[H]e said that China must have a revolution and must rise against the hated foreigners." Thinking that he, the peasant migrant, is the despised foreigner against whom the young man rails, Wang Lung slips away quietly. Soon thereafter, he hears another young man exclaiming that "the people of China must unite and must educate themselves in these times," though it does not occur to Wang Lung that he is himself Chinese.[81] He loses interest in the men on the streets peddling their revolutionary rhetoric—this city "was full of young men speaking," he dismisses.[82] All this "speaking" just makes him nostalgic for his land.

All throughout the city, there are young zealots trying to illuminate a path toward hope. A foreigner—presumably a missionary—hands him a slip of paper depicting "a man, white-skinned, who hung upon a crosspiece of wood."[83] The image hypnotizes Wang Lung; he is at once fascinated by its inscrutability and stricken with fear by its unabashed goriness. He totes the slip around for the next few days, carefully avoiding the part of town where he first encountered the Western missionary. His curiosity soon passes and thoughts return, predictably, to his land. O-lan sews the paper into the soles of a shoe as reinforcement. Rather than dithering over the question of spiritual redemption, Wang Lung and O-lan concentrate on practical use. He accepts another slip of paper depicting a gruesome execution, only this time the poor, bloodied victim is "not white-skinned and hairy but a man like Wang Lung himself, a common fellow, yellow and slight and black of hair and eye and clothed in ragged blue garments. Upon the dead figure a great fat one stood and stabbed the dead figure again and again with a long knife he held."[84]

A young orator—praised by a passerby as a "young teacher"—warns that the "the dead man is yourselves," suffering at the hands of "the rich and the capitalists."[85] For the first time, Wang Lung finds himself sympathetic to the message: "Now that he was poor Wang knew full well" that the illustration had some element of truth.[86]

But instead of joining this incipient Leftist insurrection, Wang Lung falls back on his modest, yeoman-like aspirations. He asks the speaker if the oppressive rich can make it rain, so that he and others can return to their land and work in peace. The young speaker laughs at Wang Lung: justice will not come until the rich share their money and food. "Yes, but there was the land," Wang Lung thinks to himself, unsatisfied. He immediately turns from the scene and resolves, again, to return to Anhwei. Even as talk of class overthrow seduces the downtrodden laborers, Wang Lung remains steadfast—although he is conscious that he, too, is little more than the capitalist machine's grist, he desires "nothing but his land under his feet again."[87] Even as poverty drives his children to become street thieves, Wang Lung finds comfort in the fact that his land was "waiting for him."[88]

Surviving their urban trial, Wang Lung and his family cobble together enough money to go home and begin anew. The city has only strengthened their resolve. They have seen the brutish pace of modern life, and they have chosen to return to a life of subsistence and constraint. Tempted by the promises of class-based revolution, national uplift, and metaphysical redemption, Wang Lung rejects it all. Allured by the fashions and foods of cosmopolitan city life, Wang Lung chooses temperance.

The fact that Wang Lung has a choice at all is at the heart of the book's appeal—for readers of the 1930s or even today, there is no "retreat to Anhwei." Rather, Buck negates the city because its worst elements—poverty, jingoism, restlessness—are universally undesirable. For Kiang, this view of urban China was troubling. The issue was not whether to modernize, but how. In attacking Buck, he had unconsciously picked up on an interesting facet of *The Good Earth*: it is a referendum on the issue of modernity—in China, the United States, or anywhere. In the face of urbanization, markets, and a world expanding, Buck's novel indulged in a weepy nostalgia for the land, idealizing the countryside as a defense against the unfeeling city. Her vision of the transpacific may have portrayed China and its culture in a deeply flattering and almost virtuous light. But it was an unrealistic response to the new pressures of the global order.

The Good Earth earned Buck a Pulitzer Prize in 1932. Six years later, she was awarded the Nobel Prize for Literature. The Swiss Academy commended Buck's works—particularly *East Wind, West Wind* and *The Good Earth*—as "rich and truly epic descriptions of peasant life in China."[89] Critics in the United States immediately protested that the prize had not gone to a more erudite figure, such as Theodore Dreiser, Willa Cather, Carl Sandburg, T. S. Eliot, or Ernest Hemingway.[90] Many accused the awarding process of being unnecessarily politicized. It is presumed that the committee sought to highlight the plight of China, which had just been invaded by Japan, but rather than bestowing the prize upon an actual Chinese writer, the committee chose Buck as a "surrogate."[91] Some Chinese writers felt she idealized the peasant classes and ignored the nation's urban intelligentsia, while others felt that her overly conciliatory representations of rural China did a poor job of capturing the proto-Communist passions of the laboring classes.[92]

If Buck found few friends in the American and Chinese literary scenes, her own behavior did little to appease her critics. She was a prodigious writer, producing over one hundred novels, short stories, articles, and children's stories, nearly all of which drew on some fac-et of her own life. Her strange mix of activism—she rarely refrained from trumpeting the various social and political causes that moved her—and practicality—her writing career supported her children and various charities—also set her apart from the idealists and aesthetes that constituted the American literary scene. She became the perma-nent property of the middlebrow, in part because of this illusion of political autonomy and flexibility.[93] *The Good Earth* offered different appeals to different audiences—even those who dislike her do so for divergent reasons. Some posit Buck's novels of Asian life as a portal into foreign lives from a distant past, while others just as legitimately harp on her books' timeless themes of perseverance and hard work. It is this purposeful vagueness that makes the 1930s such a fascinating and, in retrospect, politically powerful moment of American contact with China, a time when American readers could see themselves in the thrift and underdog innocence of prerevolutionary China. It was as though, in response to the gap between Chinese myths and realities, she decided to craft the most painstakingly mundane work possible.

A stray anecdote: I was introduced to *The Good Earth* when I was in middle school. It was the high point of 1990s multiculturalism and we were required to take a class called "Global Issues." One day, our well-meaning teacher asked everyone to pair up with a member of the opposite sex. She led us outside and instructed us to walk to the bleachers and back, only the boy—playing the role of the husband—was to remain ten paces ahead of the girl—the wife. We did as we were instructed. That, our teacher explained once we were back in our seats, is what it is like in China. She began passing out copies of *The Good Earth*.

Despite the varied criticisms of Buck's work, no individual played so significant a role in shaping American views of China. Besides the national and international awards, it also established Buck as a global advocate for the Chinese people. In 1935, she and Walsh divorced their spouses and married each other. Together, they managed Buck's career and oversaw a range of political and philanthropic interests. Buck helped Walsh oversee *Asia* magazine and exerted considerable influence on the range of authors that the John Day Company considered for publication.

The Good Earth became a cultural phenomenon. Buck's tale made its way to Broadway and then a successful 1937 film adaptation.[94] Wang Lung and O-lan's legacies provided the foundation for two sequels. In the coming decades, Buck would publish over seventy novels and receive over a dozen Book of the Month Club nods. She became a sought-after lecturer on everything from human rights to women's rights to segregation to the prospects for war.[95] She helped overturn the Chinese Exclusion Act in 1943. Succeeding generations—my middle school teacher among them—continued consulting *The Good Earth* as an introduction to Chinese civilization.

According to an October 1938 Gallup poll, Americans considered *The Good Earth* the sixth-most interesting book they had ever read.[96] In 1958, Harold Isaacs published *Scratches on Our Mind*, a landmark study on American attitudes toward China and India. Surveying a cross-section of Americans about their impressions and interest in these two countries, Isaacs observed the long-standing effect Buck's works had on China's place in the American imagination. Nearly one-third of respondents credited Buck's *The Good Earth* "as a major source of their own impressions of the Chinese and these were almost uniformly impressions of a wonderfully attractive people."[97] Even as Buck's perspectives came to seem anachronistic after America had "lost" China to communism, her work still resonated throughout the Cold War. A 1966 Gallup poll ranked her among the ten most admired women in America; a similar poll conducted that year by *Good Housekeeping* ranked her second only to Rose Kennedy.

Most importantly, Buck helped popularize the figure of the China expert. Because of her comfort speaking and advocating on behalf of the Chinese, Buck herself became a character in the drama evolving along the transpacific circuit. Her popular celebrity and political influence coalesced into a rare kind of authority. The mammoth success of *The Good Earth* helped create a new audience for books about China and, in the subsequent decade, fellow authors like Carl Crow, Alice Tisdale Hobart, and Edgar Snow would benefit from the heightened stature given to those who could comment on China. It is often argued that the only true rival to her influence was publishing magnate Henry Luce—and, compared to Buck, he had an entire fleet of magazines at his disposal.

When Americans thought of Buck, then, they unconsciously invoked a bygone version of China. Even those who loathed her influence still had to reckon with the shadow she cast. In 1941, Columbia University Press introduced the Chinese philosopher Lu Xun to American readers with a volume of his translated stories and essays. The collected works, the introductory note suggests, renders China in all its complexity—in contrast to the "sympathetic writers" who have "superimposed a sentimental montage of a land where peace and tradition reign, where every earth-turning peasant is unobtrusively a philosopher."[98] When Frank Chin, Jeffrey Paul Chan, Lawson Fusao Inada, Shawn Wong, and a collection of likeminded writers began mapping out the politics of the emergent "Asian American" identity in the 1970s, they decried *The Good Earth*, with its demure, by-the-bootstraps message, as the product of a "racist white supremacy passed off as love and acceptance."[99] More recently, interest in *The Good Earth* has been rekindled among both Americans—thanks in no small measure to Oprah Winfrey's book club—and Chinese—where a reevaluation of Buck's role in representing China abroad has resulted in conferences, the restoration of her old home, and even a statue.[100]

Let us return to 1941, where H. T. Tsiang is pacing his uptown apartment, awaiting word about the fate of his books from Richard Walsh.

Buck's rise to prominence had not escaped Tsiang's attention as a graduate student in New York.[101] He had lived through much of the tumult described in *The Good Earth*; he knew the cities of China and the United States firsthand; and, as an apostle of New York's proletarian arts movement, he found Buck's passive political views intolerable. Most of all, Tsiang was baffled by Buck's success: her version of China was wholly unfamiliar to him—yet readers could not buy enough of her books. Tsiang had been composing his own stories, which described his own transpacific circuit and celebrated the modern spirit of young China. Dreams of overtaking Buck's influence sustained him.

When Rockwell Kent wrote his friends in the publishing world on Tsiang's behalf, he praised the Chinese writer's "extraordinarily genuine" voice and authenticity. He praised Tsiang's tenacity, his willingness to continue publishing and selling the books himself in the absence of any interest, the optimistic vibe he maintained during his brief incarceration on Ellis Island. In Kent's estimation, Tsiang deserved his "deserts" [*sic*]: a publisher and a public.

> We want to find him a publisher not only for the poetry that Tsiang wrote on Ellis Island, for the novel—the story of a coolie's life—which he has planned but not yet written—but for those still-born works which, brought out under his imprint and marketed in restaurants and on street corners, can still be said to have not been really published.[102]

To have not been really published. Kent probably meant no offense in brushing Tsiang's street corner hustles aside. Tsiang was working so far outside of the publishing establishment that Kent could be forgiven for exaggerating the "still-born" nature of Tsiang's self-published novels. But this friendly banter between friends *within* that establishment also captured Tsiang's sad, peripheral position. Despite the intense curiosity in China, only certain perspectives on the transpacific future circulated. It was up to people like Buck, Walsh, or the publishing magnate Henry Luce to define the terms of these forecasts to the American public. When figures like Lin Yutang or Hu Shih entered the fray, it was often due to the patronage of American thinkers and writers.

Tsiang only had Kent. And, given that Kent thought Walsh and the John Day Company might actually be interested in Tsiang's work, it seems likely that Kent only gave the Chinese writer's books a cursory skim. At the very least, Kent had missed the moment in *China Red* when Tsiang's characters likened Buck's work as America's favorite China expert to prostitution, or the passage in *And China Has Hands* when Tsiang's characters skewered their "cousins" over in *The Good Earth*. He even went out of his way to attack Buck's "publisher"-turned husband.[103]

Tsiang had waved his arms and named the menace. But nobody had paid attention. Now, of all the people who might be willing to give his old books a fresh read, it just had to be Walsh.

2

Naïve Melody

A FEW YEARS AGO, I bought an original copy of H. T. Tsiang's out-of-print 1931 novel *China Red* from a rare book dealer. Having failed to convince any respectable (or semirespectable) publishers to issue this novel—it was, after all, a transpacific epistolary romance about Communism—Tsiang decided to go it alone. There were few opportunities for Chinese writers in New York and Tsiang's strange, verbose wit and radical politics probably didn't help his case. All told, he had about 7,000 copies of *China Red* printed independently, though one imagines that many of these paperbacks, with their relatively cheap binding and cardstock covers, were discarded or destroyed in the decades that followed. I could only find a copy that was so frayed and weathered, bits of the spine and back cover would flake off each time I opened or closed it. One day, while searching for clues about the book's publication history, I noticed that Tsiang had signed the title page for its previous owner. What luck! It was amazing to think that Tsiang had once held this book in his hands—that a man named Bob had bought it and asked the author to sign it before gifting it to a woman named Ruth. It felt humbling to enter into this semiclear lineage of ownership, to glimpse the provenance of these old things around us, things that survived the twentieth century by equal parts luck and negligence.

Like many of the Chinese students who lived in the United States in the 1910s and 1920s, Tsiang was deeply invested in the political future of the transpacific. But unlike many of his classmates, Tsiang had witnessed the establishment of China's republican government firsthand. His participation in this new regime had earned him the scorn of rival nationalists, who preyed on China's instability and waited for their turn to lead. Tsiang's departure for the United States represented more of a cautious, self-imposed exile than an earnest desire to forge a life somewhere across the Pacific. But once he arrived, something about American culture seized him. He was seduced by the possibilities of the American voice, with its slangy, idiomatic expressions and coarse, sarcastic wit. He was enchanted by the world-changing promise of proletarian art. And he saw the novel as an eminently elastic form that he could remake for his own use. His arrival also coincided with a renewed interest among American writers and readers in his former home, China. Having already had a brief career in politics, Tsiang now devoted himself to becoming an artist. The journey would begin with self-published pamphlets of revolutionary poetry and end years later in Hollywood. Somewhere in between, he created some of the most ambitious and, at times, bizarrely self-aware works of modern American literature.

Months later, I found a first edition copy of Tsiang's next novel, *The Hanging on Union Square*, which he self-published in 1935. It was signed as well—an astonishing coincidence! I searched online for more early printings, and it seemed that every one of these first editions bore a signature or some kind of friendly inscription. The sense of mystery I had attached to Tsiang, an obscure writer and thinker tracing his own orbit, thickened. It was hard to imagine that the person who had written these radical, irony-drenched books might have been affable, even charming—that Tsiang had literally touched so many of those around him.

Tsiang was born in 1899 in a small village in the Kiangsu province of China, not far from where Pearl Buck had set *The Good Earth*.[1] He suffered through a rough upbringing—his father passed when Tsiang was nine and his mother died four years later. Despite growing up in poverty, Tsiang excelled academically. He earned a scholarship to study at the Jiangsu Tongzhou Teacher's School and then Southeastern University in Nanjing, where he took courses on political economy and acquired a relatively decent grasp of English. He demonstrated a keen, eclectic interest in politics. He was jailed for antigovernment activities after protesting Chinese president Yuan Shikai's concessions to Japan, only to be released at the behest of his schoolmaster. Upon graduating in 1925, he took a post as aide to the secretary of Sun Yat-sen, the revolutionary leader who had overthrown the Qing Dynasty in 1911 and established the Republic of China in its place.[2]

Tsiang's arrival to national politics came at an inopportune time. Sun's prestige in China was at its nadir, with many members of his own nationalist Kuomintang Party questioning his authority. The early years of the Chinese republic were bedeviled by political instability, and the passing of the forceful Sun in 1925 resulted in a tumultuous power struggle within the party. Tsiang began working for another left-leaning Kuomintang official, Liao Zhongkai. When Liao was assassinated, Tsiang and others grew fearful that the increasingly powerful conservative wing of the Kuomintang would continue to purge the party of any left-leaning sympathizers. In 1926, following an unsuccessful bid to emigrate to the Soviet Union, Tsiang fled to the United States.[3]

So began Tsiang's itinerant, decade-long tenure as a graduate student.

What kind of America was Tsiang entering? At the time, the United States still adhered to the Chinese Exclusion Act of 1882—to this day one of the most restrictive pieces of immigration legislation in the nation's history. The act had been prompted by a nativist backlash to the mid-century surge in Chinese migration, particularly along the West Coast. In a broader context, these Chinese laborers had been the unwitting pawns of an evolving global economy. The vast majority of these immigrants hailed from China's southeastern port cities, which had been wrecked by the Opium Wars and then impoverished by the subsequent, postwar treaties, which institutionalized Western dominance. The Exclusion Act made the qualifications for immigration by nonlaborers from China unreasonably high, essentially freezing Chinese communities in America. The Johnson-Reed Act further tightened restrictions around immigration and immigrant rights, passing with overwhelming Congressional support in 1924.

It was within—and against—this context that the new, hybrid identity of the Chinese American was born. While the initial waves of Chinese laborers rarely arrived with aspirations to settle permanently, most were locked into unfair contracts that had exploited their desperation, making it difficult for them to earn enough money to return. The rough outline of a Chinese American community begins to emerge in the pre-Exclusion era: the formation of Chinatowns, the arrival and settlement of Chinese missionary students and the rise of anti-Chinese sentiment compelled many to begin drawing on the language of rights and citizenship. An early proponent of self-determination was the radical writer and activist Wong Chin Foo, often cited as the first person to use the term "Chinese American" to describe this new category of identity.[4] Wong, who had been educated by missionaries in China, arrived in the United States in the 1870s. He tried to start a Chinese American political party and rallied Chinese communities against the Exclusion Act. In 1883, he founded a newspaper uniting various American Chinatowns titled the *Chinese American*.

Conversations around this new Chinese American sensibility were gradual and decentralized, engaging everyone from Chinatown youth to visiting students. While few Chinese were admitted entry during the Exclusion era, various treaty provisions had made allowances for students like Tsiang. In the early 1900s, Chinese students had created their own transpacific circuits of knowledge, using college and church newspapers to discuss issues of identity and inclusion, civilization and capitalism, drawing freely from both Chinese and American traditions of political thought. The literary historian Chih-ming Wang has argued that much of this student writing embodies a "self-reflexive and self-referential transpacific imagination"—the students were conscious, he explains, of their unique position between and beholden to Asia and America.[5] Their distance from the actual sites of political contestation back in China allowed them to engage in more imaginative debates about their homeland's future, borrowing strategically from a range of ideas and philosophies.

The students who oversaw papers like the English-language *Chinese Students' Monthly* returned to China and imported ideas like pragmatism and progressivism to the Chinese intellectual scene. Many of the student leaders would return to China and become ambassadors, bankers, and government officials. A famous example of this transpacific loop was the Chinese debate around humanism pitting the ideas of John Dewey against those of Irving Babbitt—a debate that originated in Cambridge and Manhattan but migrated to China, thanks to Dewey and Babbitt's elite disciples.[6]

Tsiang enrolled at Stanford University, spending most of his time studying and writing about Chinese politics. At first, his experiences were fairly typical. While Chinese students arrived under radically different circumstances than the laborers of the previous century, they were still concerned with the treatment of their countrymen, if only because the abject status of the Chinese under American law affected the prestige of China. They also sought alliances with local Chinese American students in the hope that they would see themselves as part of a larger Chinese diaspora. But Tsiang's exposure to America and the proletarian arts scene radicalized him further, as the politics of the Chinese mainland shadowed his interactions with fellow "overseas Chinese" living in the United States.

Tsiang was only nominally a student, and his interest in bringing these new ideas back to China loosened by the year. His experiences in California were a reminder that Chinese political animosities respected no borders. He eventually left *Young China*, the Kuomintang daily where he served as associate editor while at Stanford, out of frustration with the party's increasingly conservative turn. (Or maybe, as a writer for the *New Yorker* guessed, he simply realized that "being anti-Communist didn't pay.")[7] He began editing an independent weekly called the *Chinese Guide in America*. One of their frequent targets was Chiang Kai-shek, who was purging the Chinese establishment of any traces of Communist influence. In 1927 Tsiang formally broke from the Kuomintang, publishing an article eviscerating the party for executing members who leaned too far toward the left. He organized rallies against Chiang along the West Coast. But the ocean separating Tsiang from the conservative mobs in China could not protect him. Angry pro-Chiang sympathizers in the Bay Area assaulted Tsiang and the staff of the weekly, spelling the end for the *Chinese Guide in America*.

In the fall of 1927, Tsiang moved to New York. He enrolled at Columbia University, taking courses in law, economics, and history. He

wrote op-eds and gave speeches on China's conservatism. At night
he washed dishes at a Greenwich Village nightclub.[8] Encouraged
by professors like the Shakespeare scholar Ashley Horace Thorndike and the philosopher John Dewey, Tsiang began writing poetry
about the Chinese revolution and its relationship to the working
class movement stirring in American cities.[9] In the next few years,
his work would begin appearing in the *Daily Worker* and the *New
Masses*, leading left-leaning journals of the day.

With unflagging energy, he used the directives of proletarian literature to pursue some of the moment's contradictions. How had he
been shaped by his experience as an itinerant Chinese in New York?
Did one choose to be Chinese, or was it merely an identity foisted
upon the individual from without? Did the fact of shared national origins mean anything essential, or were the floating proletariat
free to forge new alliances, beyond contingencies of race, nation, or
class? Proletarian art rested on structures of affiliation and empathy,
so what could be done to expand the reach of these works beyond
familiar contexts? How could one convey to the American working
class that a nation of comrades awaited, across the Pacific Ocean,
and that only together could the laboring masses forge the just, new
world of their dreams?

In Chapter 4, we will track Tsiang's critical engagement with the
tenets of proletarian art, particularly the movement's philosophical
discomfort with the form of the novel. At this early point in his career, though, Tsiang seemed perfectly comfortable parroting the basic harangues of working class art. After composing poetry in his native Chinese, he began experimenting with English-language poetry,
submitting his work to radical newspapers and journals. In 1929—
only six months after he had penned his first poem—in English *or*
Chinese—Tsiang self-published his first book, *Poems of the Chinese
Revolution*, with a run of 7,000 copies over three printings.

In the foreword to the second printing, he explained that he was
printing the poems in "various languages so as to let millions of readers become more familiar with the Chinese revolution." It is unclear
whether Tsiang ever succeeded in this strikingly ambitious multilin-
gual, multinational project, though the sentiment speaks to his grander
vision of a "world-revolution"—as well as his own vanguard position.[10]

The first few pages of *Poems* reprinted letters from supportive readers. Minnie Davis, a "young worker in Canada," complimented Tsiang for his unadorned style: "I am glad to see the old flowery way of writing thrown into the waste-basket; for that style has only the capacity of lulling people to sleep. Your poems breathe the spirit of rebellion."[11] The *Daily Worker* and *New Masses* note the revolutionary vigor of Tsiang's work, though their praise was a bit more measured: his poetry was "readable" and, thankfully, "facile."[12] The most distinctive commentary for *Poems* came from the Jewish daily *Freiheit*, which Tsiang reprinted as an inscrutable block of untranslated Yiddish.[13] The progressive writer and activist Upton Sinclair offered a reluctant note of encouragement in his introductory statement:

> This is a voice to which the white world, the so-called civilized world, will have to listen more and more as time passes. I do not mean to this particular young Chinese poet, but to the movement which he voices. The exploited races of the world are awakening and demanding the rights of human beings. Here is a young Chinese student whom the American authorities sought to deport and deliver to the executioner's act at home. What he has written is not perfect poetry, but it is the perfect voice of Young China, protesting against the lot of the under-dog.[14]

This would not be the last time Tsiang bravely reprinted his readers' tepid reactions to his genius, though it would be years before he returned to the straightforwardly polemical style that animated his poetry. As Sinclair notes, there was something unique about Tsiang's perspective, not just as an outsider to the "white world," but as an observer from abroad as well. If proletarian art was notable for foregrounding the structures and shared injuries of class rather than the artist's individual psyche, then Tsiang's work, which described those relations in a global context, introduced his fellow travelers to a radical new scope of experiences.

How could a poet grasp something so vast, a chain of effects separated by geography and language? Tsiang's book collects eight poems, five of which had been previously published in the *Daily Worker* and *New Masses*. Three of the poems—"Shantung," "May 30th," and

"Gum Shan Din"—were originally written in Chinese and subsequently translated into English. The book constantly shifts perspectives, as a way of reminding his fellow, would-be revolutionaries of their common bonds. It is as though he wanted to offer *Poems* itself as a model for a kind of collective consciousness, as an occasion to come together, whether as workers scattered around the globe or as poems fixed on an array of lives, written in different languages.

One example of this is "Shanghai." The poem conjures a working class panorama, the stanzas leaping from "Rocky Mountains" to "Shanghai" and from "Nanking to Nicaragua."[15] There is a dizzying procession of causes and symbols, from Sacco and Vanzetti, who had been executed a year earlier, to the plight of the "Negroes." He regards the on-looking Statute of Liberty and asks:

> Why don't you turn your face
> And look at the eastern Asiatic land,
> Where four hundred million toilers live?
> They are thirsty for you!
> They are hungry for you!
> They are fighting for you!
> They are dying for you![16]

"Shanghai" was one of the poems Tsiang wrote in English as an "appeal of the Chinese workers to the American Labor movement." In what would become a constant theme throughout his works, Tsiang begs, on behalf of China's "four hundred million," to be recognized by his American comrades. For Tsiang, adhering to national identities obscured the global scale of the struggle. This vision of solidarity animates "Shantung," a poem set during the pivotal 1928 clash between Japanese forces and the Kuomintang's southern army in China. The poem's subject is a laborer toiling in "far away" Shanghai, pondering the situation in Shantung and concluding that he probably shares more in common with the typical "toiler of Japan" than his cruel Chinese boss.[17]

"Rickshaw Boy" is another poem in the collection that expresses his skepticism toward the notion of "countrymen."[18] It is an account of a weary and mournful rickshaw puller, not unlike *The Good*

Earth's Wang Lung. His constant grief is underscored by Tsiang's liberal use of exclamation points, as he wallows in his loneliness: his father, a penniless farmer unable to provide for his family, committed suicide; his mother was kidnapped and possibly raped by marauding soldiers; his "firm-breasted sister of fifteen" is now a concubine; and his exhausted grandparents await death.[19] But where Buck's hero saw rickshaw pulling as a temporary trial, Tsiang's driver grows desperate as he hustles about, wedged between the horse and the automobile on the city streets. Even his horse leaves the driver envious, for at least it receives a master's care. His self-pity evolves into rage, much of it directed at his fellow Chinese, who happily exploit their own kind. They serve as middlemen in the oppression of the toiling class: "Pulling rickshaw! International park, no dogs nor 'Chinese' admitted," Tsiang writes, alluding to the signs dividing Chinese land from international territories. "None but rich 'Chinese' may be permitted!" The poem ends with a call for the workingmen to be "nobody's tools."[20]

Tsiang's resentment toward his fellow Chinese was not in itself unusual—factional conflict was rife in early twentieth century China. But Chinese visitors to the United States like Tsiang usually enjoyed a degree of privilege that buffered them from the plight of the Chinese American working class. Instead, Tsiang gravitated toward the experiences of the Chinese American proletariat, particularly the lowly Chinatown laundryman. Tsiang's poem "Chinaman, Laundryman" is believed to be the first attempt by an Asian American writer to recuperate the image of the long-derided Chinese laundryman. The poem opens broadly, the subject lamenting his lot in life: "'Chinaman'! / 'Laundryman'! / Don't call me 'man'! / I am worse than a slave." Some of the metaphors are hackneyed, as when he asks: "Why can I smooth away / The wrinkles of others' dresses / But not the miseries of my heart?"[21] But the laundry worker's dissatisfaction isn't merely aimed at the mystical "almighty 'Dollar'"—a symbol that would resurface in Tsiang's second novel, *The Hanging on Union Square.*

Instead, the laundryman hates his boss, a fellow Chinese who shares the same family name. His boss reminds him that he is free to return to China, where "unlimited hours of toil" are rewarded with meager wages. The choice, of course, is illusory. "'Thank you, Boss! / For you remind me. / I know / Bosses are robbers / Everywhere!'"[22] His boss preys on their shared heritage, assuring the laundryman that he is actually helping him navigate an inhospitable system:

> Chinese boss says:
> "You Chinaman,
> Me Chinaman,
> Come work for me—
> Work for your fellow countryman!
> By the way,
> You 'Wong,' me 'Wong'—
> Do we not belong to same family?
> Ha! ha!
> We are cousins!
> O yes!"[23]

The laundryman chooses the identity of "workingman" and "Worldman" over "Chinaman." With a brush made of Marxism and soap rendered from Leninism, the workers of the world will "clean" this world.[24]

It was the precariousness of the drifting, floating worker's position that made him susceptible to exploitation by his own countrymen. But what of their prospering bosses? What appeal could be made to them? Tsiang seems to address them directly in "Gum Shan Ding," a dialogue between Tsiang and a Chinese migrant worker who lives in relative comfort. "Gum Shan" translates as "Gold Mountain," the name given to the United States because of the mid-nineteenth century legends of easy American riches used to attract foreign laborers. "Gum Shan Ding," Tsiang explains in a footnote, is "a sarcastic nickname given in China to those Chinese workers who return from America."[25]

Tsiang calls out to this unnamed worker who seems to embody the promise of the "Gold Mountain." But he implores him to scrutinize the conditions of his prosperity. Something still nags at him, even as he amasses his fortune:

Don't talk about China!
"I am a rich merchant.
No more 'fatherland'!
I am an American citizen."

Yet there *are* worries.
That is too bad.
Face not so white,
Nose not so high.
When I pass by
All men call me,
"Chinaman!" "Chinaman!"

Wealth has not saved him; in the eyes of America, he remains a mere "Chinaman." Despite this epiphany, Tsiang remains unsympathetic, poking fun at his creation's naïveté before admitting that he is just giving him a hard time: "Pardon the sarcasm / You are not alone." Tsiang offers this unfulfilled Gum Shan Ding's empty successes as universal; all men should rise up and "kill all who are not fools!"[26]

To whom was Tsiang addressing his screeds and cries? *Poems* was animated by spectacular ambitions, a collision of scenes, experiences and, ultimately, audiences coming together within and because of these pages. Audience would become a defining question for Tsiang in the years to come. In a way, that is what makes his reference to "sarcasm" so strange—a sly confession, given that the rest of the book trades on the straightforward, sentimental rabblerousing of the proletarian artist. It suggested a new direction his work might take: ironic, self-referential, bitter, an inside joke with himself.

In 1932 the composer Ruth Crawford Seeger adapted two of Tsiang's poems, "Chinaman, Laundryman" and "Sacco-Vanzetti," as part of a commission she received from the Society of Contemporary Music in Philadelphia. Crawford Seeger was herself in the midst of a shift toward music that could be a "weapon in class struggle."[27] As an ideal example of a "worker's recitation," Tsiang's poems possessed the "exclamatory commands, exhortations . . . and addresses to the reader" that Crawford Seeger hoped to incorporate in her rather confrontational composition.[28]

Crawford Seeger's version of "Chinaman, Laundryman" sounds both sparse and frenetic. The poem is tracked in a crazed, antilyrical sing-song, more fitting for "angry oratory" than the stage, while the accompanying piano ranges chaotically, striking at the vocals with an almost mocking dissonance. It produces a deeply disorienting sensation, as voice and piano follow their own separate lines of rhythm and melody, colliding and canceling each other out.[29] It is repetitive and brusque, particularly the piano, its keys banged, chords clattering against one another, the stifled noise conveying the dull, predictable rhythms of the immigrant worker's life. The song comes with a built-in sense of antagonism, a set of yearnings trapped within a thicket of spitefully hammered notes. As Crawford Seeger's husband, the composer Charles Seeger, observed, the two parts—piano and voice—only needed to begin and end together.[30] The couple would perform their musical adaptations of Tsiang's poetry frequently in the early 1930s, as they sought to merge the aims of modern composition and the proletarian art movement.

There is no record of communication between Crawford Seeger and Tsiang. It is likely that she came across his poetry in the *Daily Worker* or *New Masses* and felt its repetitiveness suited the musical demands of her commission. But perhaps we can hear something prophetic in Crawford Seeger's radical adaptation of Tsiang's poetry. His words, spare and direct on the page, take on an urgent, new strangeness stretched and splayed atop her arresting din. They transmit a secondary layer of meaning that forces the listener to confront something opaque, even inscrutable, a feeling of dread. The jagged brutality of the piano signals ironic mockery one moment, the heights of heroism the next. Crawford Seeger seems to complete Tsiang's vision of disquiet, or at least point toward new possibilities of how one could provoke, confound, and baffle an audience into recognizing a shared struggle.

Whether Tsiang was stirred by these performances is unknown. After *Poems*, his work began to stray from proletarian art's call for a lucid polemics. Instead of straightforward invective, his later writings would traffic in a similarly unnerving, almost manic energy.

Tsiang's sense of voice as a writer and poet was still immature in *Poems*, though there are moments that anticipate his eventual turn toward quirkier delivery systems for his leftist politics. His sarcastic jab at the haughty worker of "Gum Shan Ding" suggested a move away from the more literal-minded precepts of proletarian art. Why add a niggling footnote identifying the gesture *as* sarcasm? Did Tsiang fear that his exaggerated furor would strike no blow?

Neither acute sarcasm nor mocking condescension seem like particularly effective tactics for leftist proselytizing, especially given proletarian art's preference for plainness and clarity. For Tsiang, this was a moment of emotional transparency—the truest rage he expressed throughout the book. His personality could not be suppressed. Tsiang's work would only grow stranger, for at least the bulk of *Poems* can be taken at face value. Seeded in his minor dig at the worker of "Gum Shan Ding" was a radical turn away from earnest, literal language, toward a more playful, erudite, and self-aware style. Tsiang had internalized the lofty aims of proletarian art: as a citizen of the transpacific, he embodied them. But he realized that proletarian art's faith in empathy and persuasion was limiting. The masses did not need slogans and simple parables; they needed new forms.

Perhaps, in the years to come, it was precisely Tsiang's inability to assimilate into a community of either proletarian artists or Chinese expatriates that frustrated him, pushing his art toward strange, new directions.[31] He was able to work in the margins, free of the expectations placed upon his literary heroes, men like Sinclair or Theodore Dreiser. And so he inflicted injury upon proper English and hectored his fair reader, discovering something productive in his ignorance of literature's decorum.

Did H. T. Tsiang care about assimilation? Had he any use for the promise of Chinese American identity and the sense of belonging it proffered? Or was he driven to ask a different set of questions entirely?

Within this loose community of Chinese students and Chinatown youth, the 1930s was a period of intense debate around questions of allegiance, cultural tradition, and whether one's future lay in China or the United States. But Tsiang, who expressed but a notional interest in such things, continued to float away from any established paradigms of identity and community. He was Chinese, yet he felt estranged by what was happening at home, as well as the unusual ways in which Chinese identity could be deployed from afar. He had lived in America long enough to understand its charms; he had also lived in America long enough to recognize the inequalities that underwrote its bogus, "Gold Mountain" dream.

Transcendence, it seemed, came in the promise of art. Following the minor success of his poetry, Tsiang pursued other creative outlets. In 1930, he joined Manhattan's Theatre Guild for its production of Sergei Tretiakov's *Roar China!*[32] The following year, he wrote a novel titled *China Red*. He published 7,100 copies over at least three print runs, and portions appeared in *New Masses*, the *Daily Worker*, and the *Daily News* of New York University. But this time—perhaps emboldened by the praise he had received for *Poems*—at least he considered it praise—Tsiang had first submitted the manuscript to various New York publishers, who all turned it down.

Tsiang did something curious. He reprinted excerpts from these rejection notes on the back cover of his book. A sense of bemusement runs through the letter from Jonathan Cape and Harrison Smith's representative, who found *China Red* "most unusual" and "well written" but unsuitable for publication. An agent from Alfred Knopf agreed. Despite the book's intriguing politics, it would have a hard time finding an audience: "We doubt very much its popular appeal because of the political discussions we realize are necessary to the book." A note from Theodore Dreiser appears inside the book, though it is hardly enthusiastic: "'China Red' contains much that is moving and colorful. The idea of presenting both sides of an argument is always interesting."[33] (As discussed earlier, these words were actually written by Dreiser's secretary.)[34]

So Tsiang decided to go it alone. At the bottom of the back cover, a statement of self-determination: "Now published by the Author."[35] There is something playful about this chorus of boos sounding the reader's approach. It is a strange and abject thing to do as a writer, yet it also feels defiant—this was a book Tsiang fought to bring into this world, the condescension of the publishing establishment notwithstanding. One approaches *China Red*, then, not just as a jumble of language, a curious collection of ideas, or even a story. Instead, the reader is instantly reminded that this book is, foremost, a physical object. It possesses weight and heft: it is a commodity.

By the 1930s it was not unusual for authors to publish their own works. What's more, small presses proliferated during the interwar years, giving unproven or experimental authors opportunities to be read. But there is scant evidence that anyone else in the literary landscape of the time inserted themselves into their works quite the way Tsiang did: on the back cover alone, the level of self-awareness, if not outright self-deprecation, is striking. Perhaps he was lampooning the over-concern with marketing and audience that afflicted the major publishing houses, blinding them from the stories of the street; perhaps the excerpted praise was the final act in a performance of proletarian resistance to the dominant mores of culture and industry.

Or perhaps the problem was one of vision. The moral authority of proletarian writing rested on an assumption that it exposed capitalism for what it was: a justification for class exploitation. But these were merely indictments of local effects. Little of this writing succeeded in drawing further back and recognizing that urban America was the product of an even greater global process; of circulations of capital and labor across oceans; of boundaries jutting haphazardly against boundaries. In Tsiang's view, proletarian literature needed to consider the displacements that resulted from transatlantic and transpacific labor. The complexities of the moment defied the clean, succinct style of realist writing most critics, proletarian or otherwise, sought. In response to a social reality too large for traditional narrative, perhaps traditional narratives were impossible.

What Tsiang seems to suggest is that *China Red* is more than a mere story. Its pages call attention to its status as a material object that needed to be printed, bound, and exchanged in a marketplace. Even the world of proletarian art, predicated on notions of solidarity and community, was not immune to these economic imperatives. So there is *China Red* and the story of political awakening and class revolution that plays out within its pages. But the book itself implies a separate, real-life narrative, with Tsiang cast as the charmingly hapless author negotiating the snooty dictates of the publishing industry. Tsiang's lukewarm blurbs may have been an ironic gesture of self-mockery or a novel act of self-promotion. But printing them also suggested a new tactic for convincing the reader of the artist's position as a luckless laborer. It reminded readers that books were commodities and authors were fellow laborers, beholden to the same bosses, gatekeepers, and power structures as everyone else. With *Poems*, Tsiang had hoped to write sentences powerful enough to stir readers into recognizing their shared struggle. It presumed that the truth would set its readers free. In contrast, *China Red* hailed its readers with a furious aggression. Even if its words and characters failed, the reader would still be left pondering the plight of its hard-working author and all the publishing house politics and industrial machinery he had overcome in the name of free expression. What better way to begin communicating this than by implicating the reader directly— by forcing him to ponder this commodity in his hands?

Tsiang paid for the publication of *China Red* himself. Operating outside of the traditional publishing business infrastructure, his distribution network consisted of wherever he could drag his suitcase full of paperbacks in his spare time. He peddled copies anywhere he could find a concentration of fellow travelers: Greenwich Village, Times Square, college campuses, cafeterias. This was why so many of the surviving copies of his first-edition works bore his signature: it was probably part of his sales pitch as he badgered passersby into supporting his dream.

China Red didn't exactly sell itself. The paperback opens with a brief, almost jaunty poem about Vladimir Lenin's influence on the political climate of the 1930s. "'Lenin! / Who is that guy?' 'He is not big / Neither is he high; / He has two hands, / And a pair of eyes; / Just as human / As you and I." The tone is light and whimsical, as though it is a playful riddle describing some mysterious organism to a child. Tsiang explains that Lenin is leading a world revolution that will make the "Czarists" and "capitalists" cry: "'Oh me! Oh my! / Lenin—that guy!'"[36] Breezy and irreverent, the poem introduces readers to the central conceit of *China Red:* it is a novel about ideas, political possibilities, and revolution, played for laughs.

China Red borrows its format from the genre of epistolary romance. It consists of thirty-four letters written from Chi-Ku-Niang to her betrothed, Sheng-Chin-Yeu, though her dispatches rarely convey the kinds of affectations shared by young lovers. Instead Chi recounts the political struggles in China, recites newspaper clippings, transcribes conversations, inserts her own poetry, and makes catty observations about the lives of the working class.

We never access Sheng's letters directly, only Chi's responses to them. Chi is initially offered as the blissfully innocent woman, given to wild sways of emotion and maudlin prose. The first letter carries the date of June 26, 1926, and the saccharine title "Echoes of Farewell." "My heart was sore. My tongue was stiff," Chi writes of the day she saw Sheng off. "Oh Siren of the ocean steamer, I wish I could break you into pieces! Moving! Moving! Your ship . . . At first I could see your face, then only the outline of your figure. At last I could not even see the ship clearly. I was very sad."[37]

She helpfully recaps the lovers' last evening together, spent discussing politics at a friend's home. The guests—many of whom spent time studying overseas—agree that China must become a modern nation, and in order to achieve this, the Chinese need look and learn beyond their own borders. While Chi's observations are conveyed with a childlike awe—she describes herself as "a pessimistic Petty Bourgeois"[38]—they carry traces of Tsiang's own cheeky, knowing wit: "It is very important for one to go to American even if only to see how nicely the American people use their forks and knives, and how carefully the gentlemen comb their hair, and how beautifully they shave."[39]

Their guests embody the privilege of the Chinese students who trained at elite American institutions, hailed as young visionaries and experts upon their return home. Their friend "Mr. Hu"—the Columbia University-trained "secretary of the Foreign Commissioner at Shanghai"—sounds suspiciously similar to the real-life Hu Shih, a Columbia-educated philosopher and educational reformer who became China's ambassador to the United States in the late 1930s. The fictional Hu muses on the pleasures of debating and Chi is left dizzy with wonder. In America, Hu explains, anything is subject to debate: capitalism, literary convention, marriage, even the deliciousness of milk and the tastiness of coffee. "That spirit, debating for debating's sake, is really what we Chinese need. With such a classical debating spirit used on subjects like Coffee with Cream or Coffee without Cream . . . the western countries have produced modern civilization!"[40] It all sounds like hot air.

A villager at Sheng's going-away party recounts a well-circulated myth about the United States, only it is slightly askew: "'Is it true that in America the roads are paved with gold and that you can pick up as much of it as you can carry? Is it because of this, that the American government has made so many regulations to keep people out?"[41] The villager refers to "Gum Sang," the myth of America's gold-paved streets and gold-bearing trees that Tsiang had previously referenced in *Poems*. They trade tall tales of American largesse, spinning a naïve, alternative interpretation of the Chinese Exclusion Act. Given all this abundance, the villager wondered why Chinese students abroad still wrote home asking for money—"Everybody laughed at his innocence."[42] When Chi learns of San Francisco's Angel Island, the processing center for new immigrants, she marvels at the array of services awaiting the migrant laborers:

> When they arrived in America, a commission was already waiting to take them to Angel Island to be entertained. The "Angels" on the island entertained our poor brothers there for many weeks and months and made them forget to go ashore to pick up the gold. Sometimes the "Angels" were so hospitable that they even gave some free tickets for the home voyage, much against their will. American capitalists are surely men of justice![43]

There is a delightfully nonsensical quality to *China Red*, the way its characters' longwinded explanations, clumsy poeticism, and mistranslated metaphors result in a bizarre, pidgin form of English, as well as a trippy misapprehension of the American Dream. When Sheng leaves, Chi assures that she will not consider him a "pocket-book or tooth-brush," though she is positive he regards her as "a taxi-cab or an automobile"—references to a story she had read in something called "American True Story."[44] Her romantic yearnings fail to find shape in English, instead dissolving into non sequitur.

Over time, Chi's letters grow stranger and stranger. One letter, titled "Impressions of America," opens with Chi in the deep, spastic throes of love: "[W]hen I take my pen in hand I suddenly forget what I wanted to write. Isn't that strange? Oh, I know. This mystery is called love."[45] The letter leaps from her long-distance doting to a question about the linguistic inner-workings of American racial epithets:

> [W]hile we Chinese students study English grammar very hard, it seems that Americans do not care very much about it. The word "China" is a proper noun, just the same as the word "America," so why should not the man who lives in China be called "Chinese"? I see so often in print, "Chinaman," "Chinaman"! Somebody said that this word is used to make fun of us. If they want to make fun of us, they should call us "Chinese Devils," as the most ignorant Chinese do; these, when they see a fellow with a pale face and light hair, call him "Foreign Devil."[46]

Of course there is no satisfactory answer to Chi's question, for one imagines that most racists speak with little regard for the rules of grammar. But her point is well taken: why, exactly, is the term "Chinaman" offensive, other than the hostile intentions that forged it? After all—and here is where Tsiang's coy sense of humor arises—it lacks the blunt efficacy of "foreign devil," the slur that the Chinese lob at Americans. She continues her letter by poking fun at another odd condition of the Chinese American experience: "Maybe you can tell me in your next letter how to make Chop Suey or Chow Mein? Many American friends ask for these dishes, but nobody here knows how to prepare them. Yet they insist that they are our national dishes."[47] Chi's innocent questions about racial slurs and "chop suey"—one of Tsiang's enduring fascinations—make America seem strange and unfamiliar, as though it is the clueless Americans who do not understand what they are saying.

These moments call attention to Tsiang's utter powerlessness when it came to influencing the construction of China within the American imagination. Perhaps the only recourse Tsiang could imagine was to write, forcefully and playfully, against the existing orthodoxies and mythologies. At one point, for example, Chi is given a leaflet featuring a poem titled "On the Road up Hankow Way," which spoofs Rudyard Kipling's "Mandalay." Whereas Kipling's romantic original waxes nostalgic for a sleepy, exotic Asia, this version features "Chinks" who can "flight like blazes," setting the famed poet's imperial fantasies ablaze.[48] Tsiang was writing on behalf of the characters these canonized stories ignored or belittled; in this case, he was turning the gaze back upon the British interloper. Elsewhere, Chi draws on Kipling's "The Ballad of East and West" in order to convince Sheng that the status of the Chinese was improving:

> "East is east, west is west, and never the twain shall meet." Many Chinese buy western straw hats that do not fit their heads. Westerners have long heads and easterners have round heads. Since the World War, many western philosophers condemn their own civilization and try to prescribe our oriental medicines for their own people. You wrote me before that in San Francisco many Chinese herbists are making good money. Is this not proof that the Westerner attempts to become more easternized?[49]

Is this what it means for the proverbial East and West to meet—straw hats and herbs, hairstyles and a thirst for debate? Perhaps Tsiang felt that he himself inhabited the "twain" where East and West converged. The back page of his previous book, *Poems*, reproduced political cartoonist Robert Minor's 1926 illustration "Workers of the World Unite!" A line of proud Soviets welcomes a cluster of soldiers and workingmen representing China, India, and the African continent. At their feet, a smaller drama plays out, as a tiny capitalist labeled "Kipling" chides an ant: "The East is East and the West is the West and Never the Twain Shall Meet." "You're a liar," the ant replies. For Minor and Tsiang, once the revolution came, the meeting of East and West would be inevitable—and unstoppable.

Tsiang was interested in what else could circulate this space of the "twain." *China Red* fills it with goods—books, magazines, razors—and ideas—capitalism, communism, democracy, Christianity. The East and West encounter one another through newspaper clippings, rumors, anecdotes, and promises. In tracing Chi and Sheng's letters back and forth between China and the United States, *China Red* embodies the kind of transpacific discourse that complicates traditional notions of national or racial identity, dramatizing the larger discussions of the 1930s about the "Eastern spiritual civilization" and the "Western mechanical civilization."[50] In one letter, Chi visits Sheng's former village and witnesses a public squabble about the spiritual future of China. She comes upon two peasants sitting in front of a churchyard, debating the presence of Christian missionaries in their country, eventually concluding the "Blue Eyes" have the best "cakes and pies." A passing Buddhist reprimands them for their meager greed:

Those "Blue Eyes" are not coming to China to preach heavenly God but to advertise their earthly, fancy goods. They take away our disciples by tempting them with chewing gum. They make Christians by entertaining them with moving pictures. They put up western schools in our country to preach the God of Dollars. Our government, imitating them, confiscates our Buddhist temples and uses them for school buildings. The students though that they could learn better English in the Christian Sunday schools. But they read Christian bibles and lose their souls. They are told to join the Y.M.C.A. where they will have a better place for bathing. By reading foreign bibles, the students come out of the bath with clean bodies but dirty souls.[51]

For the Buddhist, though, the solution was merely to replace one form of worship for another, a view echoed by a passing Confucian disciple: "If we really want a religion," he remarked, "we should worship Confucius. He is a Chinese. China for Chinese!"[52] Next on the scene was "a short skirted coolie with a Red Flag," offering a different version of "paradise."[53] It was the "earthly lures" like chewing gum and motion pictures that had helped Western missionaries overtake Confucius and Buddha. But it did not matter. They were all "religious dopes."[54]

You are all opium peddlers. We workers now need nothing of these religious dopes. We do want chewing gum. We do want moving-pictures. We do want all the earthly goods. But we want to make them ourselves. We don't want these foreign imperialists to come to China to exploit us and use these goods to induce our peasants and workers to become baptized. Fellow workers! Brother peasants! Send these dope peddlers to their damned heaven![55]

Naturally, the complacent and comfortable Chi remains unmoved; she loathes the Communist impulse "to fight all the time," claiming that it "disgusts the intelligent person."[56] Befitting her position of privilege, her desire is for Sheng to give up politics and pursue an untroubled life in the middle: "You can remain just a sympathizer with the working-class! That will be enough. No more, no less."[57] She retreats from the grim realities around her. "I think I had better not read any more newspapers, had better read poetry only."[58]

Why, Chi wonders, does Sheng change? Her letters track his zig-zagging politics, which eventually drift leftward. He relinquishes his nationalist ways and begins referring to Communism with a burgeoning curiosity. He has squandered his good fortune and chosen a difficult and unlikely path. "With your family background," she writes, "you would have become a farm slave getting ten dollars a year; or become a worker getting ten cents a day. Now you have had the chance to go to grammar school, high school, college and even to be in America for your education. Still, you are not satisfied. What do you want?"[59]

The question, of course, might actually be for Tsiang himself. *What did he want?*

Politics had lighted his path—but, like his character Sheng, his actual beliefs proved to be quite malleable. In 1935, he told a writer from the *New Yorker* that he had originally abided by the Kuomintang's anti-Communist wing. While at Stanford he served as the associate editor of *Young China*, a Kuomintang daily, and wrote anti-Communist editorials. But with the emergence of the party's new leader, Chiang Kai-Shek, his views began to drift. "While I go right to reft [*sic*], he go reft [*sic*] to right," he explained, punctuating his joke with what the writer termed "an Oriental giggle."[60]

What kind of intervention did he hope to make? *China Red*'s letters presumably crisscross the Pacific, though it would suit Tsiang's bizarre sense of humor to create a wide-eyed character who pens letters to an imaginary lover. The drama animating *China Red* happens elsewhere, not in Chi's letters but in Sheng's off-screen drift from grounded, mild-mannered student to political radical. Slowly, the reader learns about Sheng's life. It is revealed that his departure

from China was hastened by threats he received for his politics—
he is described as a "Right Wing Nationalist—a reactionary."[61] He
flees because of his extreme anti-Communism, ending up at Stanford, where he works for a pro-Kuomintang newspaper called *Young
China*,[62] all biographical details that allude to Tsiang's own life. At
one point, Chi begins discussing Sheng's views on dishwashing, purity, and imperialism, revisiting the imagery of Tsiang's old poem,
"Chinaman, Laundryman."[63]

Of course, as a dramatization of his life, there was some embel-
lishment as well. As Sheng's activities in the Bay Area grow more
radical, Chi receives a newspaper clipping about his potential deportation. The article describes Sheng as "one of the most brilliant
young Chinese to be found in an American University. He writes
better English than the average American student, and is generally
well informed on world-affairs as well as history."[64] John Dewey,
Tsiang's real-life professor, defends Sheng from the immigration bureau and his supporters liken him to Upton Sinclair. "The decapita-
tion of young Sheng-Chin-Yeu would be of no benefit to anyone,"
the article concludes. "He has a brilliant mind and a fine education.
If his head is allowed to grow older it might be useful to the world."[65]
These are perhaps the most fantasy-filled pages of the entire novel.
In the end, Sheng becomes a martyr. The penultimate page of *China
Red* features a crudely drawn pool of blood and a note that Sheng
was, indeed, deported and then executed. Facing this page is the epi-
logue, a poem rousing the "coolies" of the world to rise up against
Andrew Mellon, Rockefeller, Wall Street, Chiang Kai-shek: "Come
on, you Hungry of every nation!"[66]

Maybe the union *China Red* envisions is not between Sheng and
Chi but between the reader and an imagined comrade-in-arms. The
image of letter writing suggests a kind of exchange between a sender
and a recipient, a chain of exchanges that depict a relationship as it
changes and grows. An epistolary novel draws attention to the transformative possibilities of reading by making the act central to narrative progression. Maybe you, the reader, are the one being wooed.
When Chi learns that Sheng has decided to relinquish his anti-
Communism, she suggests that her letters have been part of a seduc-
tion plot—and that it worked. "You see what a skillful propagandist I

was. I mixed up politics with the sentimental nonsense and the Chinese Antique. That is why you read what I wrote you with joy and why I have finally stopped your Anti-Red activities."[67] Unfortunately for her, she had only hoped to transform him into someone who was apolitical. She did not foresee how this would eventually push him toward an embrace of actual Communism.

In acknowledging her own "sentimental nonsense," though, Chi reveals herself to be wiser than her letters would suggest. Perhaps this was Tsiang's way of asserting his own intellect, as well. Despite his deference and seeming humility, his spare prose obscured violent political intentions and a sense of irony. These moments of self-awareness, when the author steps out of the shadows to assert his presence, remind us of what we are holding in our hands. It is a book, a commodity, maybe even a weapon. Its back cover names all who found its ideas uncomfortable or dangerous. When Chi dissuades Sheng from politics and encourages him to immerse himself in his studies, she explains: "If some day you should want to be a successful writer, your success will not depend upon how good your writing is, but upon how much it meets with the approval of the mediocre tastes of your readers. Then you will get a publisher. Don't tell too much of the truth. The truth will not earn profits for the publisher."[68]

These were truths Tsiang knew all too well.

A decade later, Tsiang was on the verge of deportation. He had overstayed his student visa; his work as a political agitator didn't help his case, either. He had spent much of his free time in the early 1930s walking the streets, entreating strangers to buy his books. Awaiting his hearing on Ellis Island, he sat in the corner with a typewriter balanced on his knees and began writing letters.

Forthcoming chapters will consider the cache of poems and letters Tsiang produced during his incarceration. Many of his dispatches were addressed to the progressive artist and activist Rockwell Kent, who, as we saw in the first chapter, had volunteered to help Tsiang find a proper publisher for his works. Kent would explain to his friends that Tsiang merited their consideration for he was still an unknown, unshaped talent. He had spent the early 1930s publishing his own strange tales and selling them in restaurants and on street corners. These books, Kent explained, "can still be said to have not been really published."[69]

Maybe Kent was simply exaggerating Tsiang's bad luck to prospective publishers. But it is more likely that this would have been the common attitude among artists of renown and privilege toward Tsiang's self-published, self-distributed works. Without the sanction of a recognized publisher, he would never be taken seriously. Tsiang's books had "not been really published"; they had never had the chance to compete in the marketplace. He had saved, toiled, and dreamed against reason, and it was as though these books, full of daring insights about a transpacific future, did not actually exist.

China Red's epistolary form might have dramatized Tsiang's own growing sense of despair. At one point, Chi recounts a story she heard about Sheng's obsessive "oratorical practices." He hoped to become a skilled orator, not unlike C. Y. Tang, the Chinese student whose "Cycle of Civilization" speech had made him a minor celebrity throughout Wisconsin. Sheng practiced his speeches in front of anyone who would listen. "You kept on talking to them with your unmusical tone and drove them crazy! They ran away!" He kept searching for an audience, until his friends eventually grew tired of his lifeless performances. "You forced people to listen to your speeches and time you. Once, twice. When they got tired and wanted to go, you pulled their sleeves."[70]

Tsiang probably pulled the sleeves of a lot of passersby as he tried to sell copies of *China Red*. We never hear from Sheng, and we can only infer his responses to Chi's letters. She continues writing him, even though we are never sure whether he is inviting her affections or floating away. Sheng's trajectory mirrored that of Tsiang's own life. But Sheng is also an opaque, imaginary recipient, somewhat like the potential readers his creator, traversing Manhattan with his suitcase of books, aspires to find. Tsiang might as well be sending letters into the ether, for nobody ever writes back.

3

Four Hundred Million Customers

In 1910, Carl Crow was working as a reporter at the *Fort Worth Star-Telegram* covering homicides, small-time robberies and the occasional story from south of the border. He was twenty-six years old, acquiring important life skills such as how to tame hard liquor and hustle the unsuspecting at poker.

The life of the itinerant, adventuring journalist had always appealed to Crow. He was born in 1884 and raised in Missouri, acquiring his passion for newsprint and ink at a young age. By the time he was 19, he had started a weekly newspaper and sold it for a profit. He used the money to head north to Minnesota to attend Carleton College, eventually returning home to finish his studies at the University of Missouri. After a friend bilked Crow out of his life savings, he dropped out of college altogether and decided to work fulltime. He had begun to string together a fairly successful livelihood as a reporter in Fort Worth when he received a telegram from Tom Millard, a fellow Missourian working as a war correspondent in Asia. Millard offered him a job in Shanghai. Crow was interested, though he knew next to nothing about China. Whatever knowledge of the country he possessed had been gleaned from the lurid, "throat-slitting villains" that populated the movies and novels of the time. He didn't even know whether you sailed by way of the Atlantic or the Pacific to get there.[1]

By the following summer, Crow had moved to Shanghai to assume the position of associate city editor for the *China Press*, an English language morning newspaper founded by a loose federation of China-watching Americans and overseas-educated Chinese. Given the local dominance of British newspapers, the *China Press* was an ambitious operation. It was modeled after the *New York Herald Tribune* and its founders had registered it in Delaware to avoid issues with local censors. While the British papers reported on the minutiae of life back in London—English-language papers were largely for the expatriate class—the *China Press* sought to foster a sense of community among those living in Shanghai's international quarters and the local Chinese. It was not unusual for Europeans or Americans in Shanghai pass their days with little sense of what was going on just beyond their compounds, let alone the political upheavals a few cities away.

Crow did not suffer from his thin grasp of Chinese history and culture. He arrived just in time to witness the fall of the Qing Dynasty, one of the frequent twentieth century upheavals when China seemed to reboot itself. The Republic of China was installed in 1912 and Crow, a tireless writer and editor, quickly won the confidence of figures like Wu Ting-fang—an early backer of the *China Press* who went on to serve in the provisional government—and Sun Yat-sen—who became the republic's first president. Crow chronicled China's changes for readers in Shanghai as well as the United States. At one point, his close friendship with Sun earned him a commission to ghostwrite a book about the politician's life for North American readers.

After a passing stint as a farmer in California, Crow returned to China during World War I. In 1918, Crow opened Carl Crow Inc., the first Western-style advertising and merchandising firm in Shanghai. In a way, this work built on the challenges and questions that had animated his reporting. Where his journalism had been pegged to large questions of political change and Chinese civilization, his work in advertising focused more on the hopes, anxieties, and self-image of those just outside the political elite. His business brought him into even closer proximity with the everyday life of Shanghai, compelling him to understand a new kind of Chinese citizen, one with the resources and ambition to do exotic things like wear lipstick and buy imported luxury goods. Crow employed a staff of expatriates and locals, and the success of his shop gave him an unusual authority as a kind of interpreter of Chinese whims for American readers.

Crow's unlikely career arc embodied the strange possibilities of the time. Despite his initial ignorance about China and its political culture, he had become an influential local journalist, a trusted confidante of the rising nation's young leaders, and a visionary businessman. He had become an authority on China and all he had done, it seemed, was go there. As discussed in Chapter 1, America's emergent fascination with China in the 1920s and 1930s took on a variety of shapes and trajectories. Across disciplines and worldviews, looking toward China offered a sense of possibility. For scholars and philosophers, China was the surface upon which questions about civilization, progress, democracy, and modernity were projected—it was the next frontier, a *tabula rasa*, a completion of civilization's cycle. For Christian missionaries who had been in China for over a century, China continued to represent a land of heathens awaiting salvation. And for those in business, China held the key to our economic future: it was the land of "400 million customers." If only someone could figure out how to reach them.

This is the puzzle that Crow was helping Americans solve: entering the long-elusive China market. The Treaty of Nanking had forcibly opened China's ports in 1842, and representatives from various European powers arrived soon thereafter, eager to engage a world that had been closed for centuries. "Let me say this to the businessmen of America," Representative William Sulzer announced in an 1898 speech to Congress, "look to the land of the setting sun, look to the Pacific! There are teeming millions there who will ere long want to be fed and clothed the same as we are. There is the great market that the continental powers are today struggling for."[2] Despite the new opportunities presented by China's initiation into a new global order, it took decades for foreign firms to figure out how to penetrate this tantalizing market. "When I landed in China," John Thomas, a prominent and pioneering American tobacco exporter, explained in a 1923 article for *Asia*, "I felt that some one had taken me by the heels and thrown me into the Pacific Ocean. I had to swim out. The thing was overwhelming. Here was a country of four hundred million people extraordinarily true to their civilization."[3] The secret to his success, Thomas explained, was "adaptability"— the willingness to tailor his approach according to another people's whims. As China's commercial landscape matured, intermediaries like Thomas and Crow became central decoders of this distant land's desires and tastes.

Of course, others believed that the early twentieth century China market only ever existed as an overheated myth.[4] As an American diplomat remarked at the turn of the century, "When the magazine writer refers in glowing terms to the 400,000,000 inhabitants of China, he forgets that 350,000,000 are a dead letter so far as commerce is concerned."[5] But it was the persistent elusiveness of the myth as well as that mouthwatering number—a four trailed by eight zeros—that produced the demand for these new authority figures: cultural translators and go-betweens, writers and journalists, interlocutors capable of making China comprehensible to the average American. Consider the success of Pearl Buck's *The Good Earth* in 1931. On one level, it was a novel full of characters whose virtues and struggles made them instantly relatable to the American middlebrow readership. Readers and reviewers at the time recognized Buck's yeoman farmers as distant relations; her novel brought China closer. But *The Good Earth* also made Buck herself a character in this evolving drama between China and the United States. Its success created a lane for Buck—the best-selling author who had been raised in China as a "mish-kid," or child of missionaries—to become a public authority on all things Chinese.

Crow wandered into a similar fate. In writing about his firsthand experiences courting China's colorful new consumers, he gained recognition as a kind of transpacific explainer. He played a direct role in the circulation of goods between China and the United States, profiting from these newly manufactured desires. But his background as a journalist and his keen understanding of how the Americans and Chinese imagined one another gave him a broader kind of influence as well. Buck had been able to transcend her status as a mish-kid-turned-novelist, using her writing to become one of the nation's most trusted voices on China. Crow came to embody a new type of character: he was the frontier businessman, here to share the secrets of the Chinese market.

In this chapter, we will consider the new forms of expertise that emerged in the 1930s. For the typical American, China was first understood via compassionate, relatable stories like *The Good Earth*. As the 1930s drew on, however, Americans turned their attention to a new crop of books about China—ones that depicted the Chinese not just as a focal point for American sympathy but as a subject for our commercial ambitions as well. These were tales by and about experts here to make China seem comprehensible, most notably Crow's breezy, triumphalist profiles of China's "400,000,000 customers." Just as *The Good Earth*'s parched farmlands and genteel sensibility had given solace to Depression-era readers, these new works mapped routes of global commerce that helped American readers imagine a brighter economic future. Buck had brought China closer. Now, China was a destination—a place where Americans could actually go. But what effects would the arrival of American engineers and businessmen or the needs of mammoth corporations like Standard Oil have on China itself? What new generations of Chinese and Americans would come of age along this new frontier? These were the questions that haunted Alice Tisdale Hobart, another American writer living in China, bearing witness to the nation's new economic realities. Her novels offered a much darker perspective on the American experts making these Pacific crossings.

Looking back on the riotous 1930s, Malcolm Cowley argued that "almost all the books published after 1932 belonged to the literature of the depression," regardless of whether they tried to reckon with its causes or flee "to the ends of the earth and the depths of time."[6] For Cowley, the decade's literature could be reduced to three tendencies, each of which bore some relationship to the economic crisis. There were stories about the political and social struggles that had directly resulted from the Depression. There were stories about the growing prominence of America abroad and an attendant awareness of international networks in general. And there was literature that depicted the "closing of the business frontier."[7]

Books about China served various purposes. Buck had encouraged Americans to look beyond their borders; now they were being told what to see. The books of Crow and Hobart—as well as the prominent success story of Standard Oil—helped forestall the end of the "frontier," offering readers some measure of hope for the country's economic future. What could American readers—few of whom would ever go to China, let alone do business there—learn from the exploits of businessmen abroad? What version of the Chinese populated these stories? What possibilities of transpacific exchange emerged in Crow's courtship of these new consumers and Hobart's dramatization of global trade's penetration of inner China? How did the logistics of doing business in China—local taste and consumption habits, language barriers and translation—take on a metaphorical value? What types of individuals were best qualified to navigate this emerging space: would it be the Chinese or the Americans?

And what consequences could these questions have on the everyday lives of the kindly American reader, holding these books in their hands?

Carl Crow would later remark that Western journalists at rival newspapers merely saw the Chinese as "400 million guinea pigs who could live a hundred years without one of them doing anything interesting enough to get his name in the paper."[8] It says something about the era that Crow's comparatively sympathetic treatment of the Chinese so distinguished him. His varied work experiences afforded him a unique perspective on China, and he capitalized on the American reading public's inexhaustible appetite for books about the young republic, then under threat from Japan. He wrote a series of affable yet authoritative books like *The Chinese Are Like That* and *I Speak for the Chinese* that helped typical Americans form their mental images of our friends the Chinese. In 1937, Crow published *Four Hundred Million Customers*, a book he had been working on for years about his experiences selling things in China. Tales of a faraway market seemed to provide American readers hope as the country slowly recovered from the Great Depression. The book was a best seller, winning a National Book Award in the category of "Most Original Book of 1937." It became an essential guidebook for anyone looking to do business in China and, to this day, Crow's title survives as a figure of speech—a shorthand description for the Chinese multitudes waiting to be shaped. American military leaders, politicians, and publishers consulted Crow for advice.[9]

At the time, Crow merely saw *Four Hundred Million Customers* as an opportunity to collect the stray lessons, anecdotes, and images he had acquired while doing business with the Chinese: the fickle, occasionally obstinate profile of the Chinese consumer; their peculiarly lax approach to the workday; their elevation of thrift to art; the importance of saving face. Crow detailed the inner workings of his office and his process for motivating employees. He described the campaigns he launched to hawk everything from soap to pills. Every decision was made with an awareness of the seeming immovability of Chinese traditions. His prose is casual and warm, befitting his sympathetic feelings toward the "interesting, exasperating, puzzling, and, almost always, lovable" people of China.[10]

Lovable or not, these were people that Crow, as the go-between linking Western merchants with the Chinese, was actively working to change. Visitors to China had always projected their own desires onto this possibility-rich population. But the Chinese people that emerge in Crow's account are not the tradition-bound sages or wayward heathens populating most of the China-watching books of the time. Instead, new characters emerged in this evolving story of global trade: the local workers he trained were heirs of a new China, beholden to both Chinese decorum and American business practices. The same applied to the Shanghai officials and elites with whom Crow did business. In reimagining China as a land full of prospective customers, Crow was unlocking a series of mysteries about desire, self-expression, the potential emergence of a Chinese consumer ethos on the cusp of modernity.

What kinds of Chinese people would American readers encounter in Crow's stories? They are unusually healthy and robust given their occasionally dingy living conditions. The typical Chinese mind "has distinct feminine traits," prizing feeling and intuition over rational deduction. "Statistics bore them to the point of resentment."[11] In meetings, Crow's trusted staff of local Chinese could be "evasive and non-committal," polite and fearful of all controversy and confrontation.[12] All the same, they could haggle and bargain within an inch of their lives. The Chinese women, Crow claimed, "are the most perfectly groomed in the world and, everything considered, enjoy the greatest measure of luxury."[13] Even those hailing from modest backgrounds always kept talcum powder, rouge, creams, and perfumes nearby. "The Chinese women undoubtedly spend—and have spent for many centuries—a greater proportion of the family income on cosmetics than is spent by any other national group."[14] The almost cartoonish cheer of Crow's Chinese suited his motives. They were people, like Crow himself, who had grown comfortable with the circulation of ideas and goods back and forth across the oceans.

Consider the Chinese barber. In the opening pages of *The Good Earth*, the earnest, rough-hewn farmer Wang Lung decides to get a haircut. It is his wedding day. As he takes his seat, the barber thinks to himself: "This would not be a bad-looking farmer if he would cut off his hair. The new fashion is to take off the braid."[15] The braid that the barber refers to is commonly known as the queue. Worn with a smoothly shaven scalp in the front and a single, slender pigtail in the back, the history of the queue[16] in China spans all the way back to the Tang dynasty (618–907). The custom was largely a regional one, coming and going over the next few centuries. In the mid-seventeenth century, the conquering Manchus reinstated the hairstyle, forcing all Chinese men to shave their heads clean except for a queue. As such, Chinese immigrants to the United States in the mid-nineteenth century arrived with readymade markers of foreignness. (There was no reason to shave it off upon arrival, since many laborers assumed they would return home.) The image of the Chinese man with his long, unnecessary queue would become a fixture in xenophobic political cartoons and advertising cards.

By the time Pearl Buck wrote *The Good Earth*, few Chinese wore queues. In the 1890s, young Chinese scholars saw the ancient custom as symbolic of the nation's resistance to modernization. Their protests continued through the next two decades, as "hair-cutting tides"[17] swept the nation's urban centers. Crow witnessed this movement firsthand when Chinese staffers at the *China Press*, the newspaper he edited, held a ritual queue-cutting day.[18] By December 1911, the outdated Manchu codes had become useless; a decree from the prince regent proclaimed that the Emperor of China's subjects were no longer required to wear queues. Two months later, the Emperor abdicated and the Republic of China was established.[19]

The end of the queue would seem like a fairly minor moment in the history of modern China. But allowing Chinese men the choice to wear their hair in whatever fashion they desired offered new possibilities of self-expression and privilege. As Crow observed in *Four Hundred Million Customers*, these whims resulted in new businesses that boasted fashions, technique, and equipment imported from Europe and the United States. "Soon after the Republican Revolution caused the cutting of millions of Chinese queues, and made barbering a more serious business than it had ever been before, an enterprising Chinese who had lived in San Francisco established a *pucka* barber shop in Shanghai, with reclining chairs and a sign which looked like a giant stick of striped candy."[20] Previous to this, the usual practice among Chinese barbers had been to set up shop on the side of the road or make house calls. Recreating something he had seen in California, though, was just the beginning. In Crow's telling, this well-traveled entrepreneur also insisted on using Sheffield-style razors manufactured in Japan rather than the cheaper Chinese razors that had been fashioned from old horseshoes imported from Hamburg.

Contemplating something as basic as how Chinese men wore their hair brought a new map of relations into view. For Crow, the introduction of these physical, San Francisco-esque barbershops traced some of the emerging lines of exchange involving people, things, and ideas among the United States, Asia, and Europe. *Four Hundred Million Customers* fixes on these moments of encounter. Elsewhere, he muses on the effects of perception and hearsay on the global trade of Chinese eggs. "Eggs are very cheap in China, compared to the price which prevails in most other countries, and in 1919 there was a roaring business in Chinese preserved and cold storage eggs which were exported to England and America."[21] The importation of Chinese eggs never occurred at such volume to challenge local farmers. "But for some reason there sprang up, in each country, a tremendous and bitter propaganda against Chinese eggs, which were alleged to harbor innumerable dangerous germs, to say nothing of other and more spectacular creatures."[22] One farmer in England wrote to his local newspaper about a Chinese egg that hatched a snake. Although there was no proof that this actually happened, dozens of papers throughout the country republished the farmer's story, seriously denting the import market for Chinese eggs. Crow stops short of naming the evil that impelled the farmer's anecdote; racism is the most likely "reason" such tales "sprang up." Instead he fixes on the transitive properties of reputation and the ways in which it can be invoked, even through circuitous allusion. Crow's company, in turn, devises a campaign to sell a specific brand of soap to the Chinese by drawing associations between their local movie stars and those of far-away America. "It happens to be the same soap that is used by all the Hollywood stars, so, in our newspaper advertising, we picture one Hollywood and one Chinese star together, but we devote more space to the Chinese star. In our world, she is the more important, though the Hollywood star earns more in a week than she does in a year."[23]

Crow's book implies two sets of consumers. There are the hundreds of millions of Chinese, inhabitants of this mythical market prized by America. But there are also the Americans themselves—a mass of readers consuming tales of China, populating the Western "elsewhere" imagined by their Chinese counterparts, participating in the buying and selling of things on a global scale. They are customers of a different sort. This mutuality—as well as the possibility of misapprehension—was captured in a chapter on Chinese food, as Crow made light of the American fascination with "chop suey," the dish that had become synonymous with the Chinese even though, as we saw in Tsiang's *China Red*, few people in China had ever heard of it. The invention of Chinese immigrants in California, "chop suey"—a hasty scramble of leftovers doused in "Chinese sauce," essentially—had become "a culinary joke at the expense of the foreigner."[24] Though Crow glossed over the tumultuous lives of these nineteenth century immigrants, the effect of this brief aside was to put the Chinese and Americans on equal footing—they could both occupy the position of the foreign "other." Here, it was the Chinese who condescended to the strange, clueless Americans, the butt of a decades-old joke. Crow's interactions with the Chinese were sufficiently enlightening that he would later spearhead an effort to have the derogatory term "Chinaman" removed from American and English dictionaries.[25]

Crow's book—as both a description of the market and an object circulating within it—embodied the ways ideas traversed the Pacific. In other words, Crow was introducing his American readers to a new cast of characters—Chinese customers, salesmen, Western go-betweens like himself. But, more importantly, he was also implicating the readers themselves, making them aware of their participation in the far-away encounters his book detailed. It was their American tastes and preferences, after all, that were dissected and judged by the Chinese market. It was their barbershops that were being emulated in far-away Shanghai. They were the masses holding up the standard of Hollywood celebrity invoked in a distant soap ad. It was their appetite for something called chop suey that amused their neighbors across the Pacific. They were as curious and exotic a population to Crow's Chinese customers as curious, exotic China was to them. It just took someone—a lone driver of change, like the barbershop entrepreneur or the rumor-mongering farmer—to see the connections. That is what *Four Hundred Million Customers* did for Crow: it established him as an intermediary between America and a new China—as someone capable of seeing new forms of desire or identification that stretched across the ocean. His company had sold everything from textiles to perfume to the Chinese. It had offered Western clients campaign strategies, translation services, and pseudoanthropological reports on the Chinese.[26] It had linked this awakening nation to America, England, Germany, France, the Netherlands, Belgium, Australia, Japan, and Canada.[27]

This was the vision of the new Pacific world that Crow was selling to his readers. He opened *Four Hundred Million Customers* with a quick note about the healthy, cluttered marketplace for China books. "With the vast number of books on China which have already been published and are being constantly produced, the advent of a new volume on this very interesting country places the author on the defensive," he acknowledges.

> The reading public is quite within its rights in asking him to explain why he thinks a new book necessary and why he has written it. With the shelves already crowded with books by writers on religion, by travellers, statesmen, humourists, philosophers, economists, and representatives of dozens of other branches of highly specialized knowledge, what hope have I, they may ask, to add anything to what has already been written and published, and why should I be audacious enough to attempt it?[28]

Put another way: why would you possibly buy this book about China over someone else's? In the wake of *The Good Earth* and the rise of general interest books and reportage about China, what could Crow offer? Weren't there already enough books depicting China from every possible angle?

For Crow, trade was the best way to understand and access the Chinese. He took the widest possible approach, studying their character, history, institutions, language, anything that provided insight into what the Chinese were becoming. He likened the work of the businessman to that of an "anthropologist."[29] But what ultimately distinguished Crow from his competitors was his ability to involve the average American in this evolving drama. The closing chapter of *Four Hundred Million Customers* traced the unlikely geopolitics behind the common toothbrush. The best toothbrushes in the world, Crow explained, are made with bristles from a certain kind of white pig now almost exclusively raised in China's war-torn regions. These pigs had previously been raised in Russia as well. But their numbers dwindled after the ascension of the Communists—"a grand Soviet gesture of contempt for capitalism and all its bourgeois refinements," Crow joked.[30]

"It probably never occurred to you," he continued, to recognize the influence a conflict thousands of miles away might have on the quality of your toothbrush. This was Crow's value: he was blessed with the vision to see and describe this new, "neighborly" world.[31] The China experts of the 1920s and 1930s had worked to make distant China seem more approachable—it powered the condescending fascination of the missionaries and travel writers, the humanitarian yearnings of journalists and politicians, the relatable sentimentalism of Pearl Buck. Crow brought China closer by pointing out that we were all connected: Americans and Chinese, customers all, tracing the circuits of global trade. "Consider your tooth brush," Crow's book ends, "and reflect on the smallness of the world, which makes you a neighbor of the 400 millions of China."[32]

During his time in China, Carl Crow acquired a functional grasp of Chinese: he was capable of basic haggling and skilled at cussing. Language was an everyday concern for Crow and the wave of

Americans and Europeans seeking to do business in China. When Crow was building his Shanghai advertising firm, one of his great challenges had been recruiting and training a reliable staff of local Chinese. Despite his affection for his workers, he found them to be too diffident and risk-averse. They needed to be guided—and he needed their access. Though countless merchants throughout Europe and the Americas had been lured to China by the promise of its enormous market, the question of how to effectively reach these masses continued to vex one and all. The nation was too vast and its population, from cosmopolitan Shanghai to the undeveloped interior, was too diverse. Size lent China its narrative mystery—the unfathomable reaches of this massive nation teemed with the "400 million customers" prized by Crow and others. The question was how to reach them. A figure like Crow might have been able to coax and decode the whims of those in the cosmopolitan, coastal cities. But China's infrastructure and uneven development presented immense challenges to those hoping to penetrate deeper.

Stretching back to the 1840s, foreign enterprise had relied on Chinese "compradors" to act on their behalf. The term "comprador" originally applied to Chinese servants working in European households who would go to the local markets and barter on behalf of their employers. The demands of late nineteenth century trade created a need for a more sophisticated and better educated class of helpers. Companies began recruiting local Chinese who had traveled abroad or studied English in missionary schools. More important than mastery of formal English, though, was fluency in pidgin or "business English," a mixture of Portuguese, Chinese, and English that was the international language of the ports.[33] Some compradors essentially managed the Chinese branch of a multinational operation, others operated as freelancers. But while the compradors that emerged during this decades-long "opening" of China were empowered to act on behalf of foreign companies, anxieties over the mellow Chinese character, too conservative and shortsighted for the world of modern business, still nagged at people like Crow. Nor were the compradors universally respected by their countrymen, who criticized these marginal figures for their association with the "parasitic" practices of foreign merchants, their relative privilege, and their embrace of

Western culture and commerce. Decades later, the accusation of being "compradorial" became a slur for Chinese too willing to betray the nation's integrity to foreign interests.[34]

The history of migration and encounter is a history of these oft-overlooked go-between figures. It is history of possibilities, forms of hybridity and mixture thwarted as false starts. Crow, for example, had ventured to China on a whim. The era of the compradors was ultimately brief and geographically confined; they are minor figures, for example, in the major histories of American trade with China. But one might also place the comprador within a looser orbit of figures that collectively brought the transpacific into focus. After all, it was missionaries and visionary businessmen who first helped America reach China, decades before the nations had established a robust diplomatic relationship. The historian Yen-Ping Hao has argued that the compradors participated in a vibrant "hybrid culture" in China's port cities. Their proximity to Western traders affected every aspect of their lives, from their style of dress and feelings about architecture to their attitudes toward religion, family structure, or jurisprudence.[35] They were not merely economic middlemen; they played a role in rethinking cultural mores as well. The comprador class introduced new notions of status and success, and the sons of compradors were often encouraged to attend Western-style schools or venture abroad to America or Europe.[36] Hao notes that the compradors helped business thrive while the missionary movement stalled, since the presence of Chinese faces—as well as an impression that new economic practices could supplement rather than replace preexisting systems—helped ease the Chinese toward modern ideas.[37]

In other words, the comprador helped both Chinese and Americans imagine what it would be like for someone to travel back and forth, between not just businesses, but cultures and belief systems as well. Lingering on the comprador reminds us of the scattered networks that made encounter between American and China possible—how dependent these exchanges were on translators, servants, brokers, and assistants; students and disciples of American missionaries; coolies, migrants, engineering businessmen with a passable grasp of English. It is a history of contact that includes writers fascinated with

China as well as the readers eagerly consuming those stories. While these Pacific crossings might have been energized by a variety of purposes—trade, God's word, a taste for adventure—their collective effect was to introduce a vision of a shared, transpacific space. Before the Chinese American existed as a discrete category of identity, these figures carried forth the seemingly minor exchanges that commingled East and West.

Claims of identity are always commentaries on the social world—what society condones, what individuals ask of it. In a way, then, the figure of the comprador foretold the possibility of these new forms of belonging somewhere in between. The new configuration of world powers had created a need for people like Buck and Crow to essentially explain China to the American masses. It had also created the need for "John Comprador," as one 1878 article called him, so that Western interests could be executed remotely.[38] Like the Chinese staffers of Carl Crow Inc., "John Comprador" was a new archetype. He embodied unprecedented forms of status and desire; he was conscious of Western innovations and Chinese tradition, yet strictly beholden to neither belief system; most importantly, he was capable of mediating between these two radically different worlds. Still, these new possibilities of acculturation—of achieving some balance between Asia and the West—were not the compradors' reason for being. They existed to promote trade and commerce.

Eventually, the question was asked: was there a more efficient way to set up shop in China? How could businesses bypass the comprador system? As early as 1867, a British consular report wondered about the long-term viability of relying on so many intermediaries: "The most hopeful permanent remedy will be an increased knowledge of the (Chinese) language on the part of foreign mercantile employees, to which the necessities of the times and their future altered position are both pointing."[39] Throughout the 1860s and 1870s, British and German trading firms began offering language courses to their employees. Around World War I, the modernization of the Chinese banking system and the introduction of credit would further reduce the long-standing dependency on "John Comprador's" personal guarantee.

In 1940, Crow published *Foreign Devils in the Flowery Kingdom*, another book reflecting on the penetration of China by the West.

In a chapter on American successes in China, Crow highlighted the unprecedented advances of John Rockefeller's Standard Oil Corporation. The company was founded in 1870 and, within a decade, held a virtual monopoly on the American oil trade. But Standard Oil's aspirations far exceeded the domestic sphere. It had grown so rapidly that its executives soon began looking abroad for new "spillways" for its surplus production.[40] By the 1890s, Standard Oil was responsible for 90 percent of American kerosene exports and over 70 percent of the world market.[41]

Standard Oil's foray into China required some deliberation. As Crow explained, the use of artificial lighting "was associated in the Chinese mind with a certain amount of moral turpitude because only gamblers, prostitutes and drunkards habitually stayed up all night."[42] In order to sell kerosene to the Chinese, then, Standard Oil had to change local attitudes toward artificial illumination. As one advertisement reasoned, "If a person wishes luck, longevity, health and peace, he should live in a world of light . . . If there is a child who studies at home, he will work harder in the light. Who would not want a child of his to progress?"[43] In 1882, the company dispatched William Herbert Libby to China to study the market.[44] The following year, Standard Oil entrusted the entire Chinese operation to a local merchant named Ye Chengzhong. Despite Ye's great successes, he and his staff were fired in 1893 amidst accusations of fraud.[45]

At the turn of the century, Standard Oil initiated a more aggressive approach to China, building a physical plant for bulk distribution. Most importantly, they began dispatching Americans to China rather than relying on middlemen, introducing a more hierarchical structure to a field that had previously been dominated by looser and more localized social networks.[46] In 1907, the company began selling cheap, efficient, and safe kerosene "mei-foo lamps" which could provide up to 240 hours of light.[47] The lamps were essentially sold at cost, making the company very little money. But, by aggressively distributing the mei-foo lamps far and wide throughout China, Standard Oil had successfully manufactured a nationwide need for kerosene. They gave away branded promotional items like mirrors, hammers, and pliers to those who could not afford to buy them.[48]

What made Standard Oil's approach to China so radical was its workforce. As Crow explained, the company "reversed the usual procedure and discharged the compradors. The comprador staff was replaced by American salesman and Chinese assistants who could be trained to follow American methods."[49] In order to represent Standard Oil abroad, salesmen had to apply for a rigorous training program in New York. Admission was competitive—most hopefuls already held college degrees—and the course of study was demanding. Those who graduated were then given three-year appointments in China, with the possibility of renewal. Upon arrival in China, the new salesmen were mentored by more experienced managers before being assigned small stations of their own.[50] Instead of relying on Chinese middlemen, who could be unreliable agents of corporate strategy, Standard Oil trained thousands of Americans and dispatched them to the far corners of China to oversee the oil trade directly.[51] Once they had mastered the language and local customs, their responsibilities included traveling about their territories, appointing and managing a stable of local dealers, even studying regional politics and crop conditions.[52]

Standard Oil salesmen became a new and highly visible type of transpacific intermediary. For example, there is a moment in Pearl Buck's 1948 novel *Kinfolk* when a young, idealistic Chinese American character named James sets sail for China. Born in China but raised in the United States, Buck offers James as a symbol of "East and West." Though he has not been back to China since leaving as a small child, he dreams of helping his spiritual homeland rediscover its greatness. His fellow passengers chart a range of strategies for approaching and understanding China. There are journalists, businessmen, missionaries, and a Standard Oil executive—all representative go-betweens bridging China and the United States. Crow remarked that, for many years, every American steamer arriving in Shanghai seemed to have a few graduates from the corporation's training school.[53] The rigors and challenges of life abroad gave these positions a unique kind of luster. A sense of glamour attached to the hard work of providing, as one of Standard Oil's first slogans declared, "oil for the lamps of China."[54]

In 1913, a Standard Oil executive in New York remarked that the company's Chinese strategy rested on three pillars: "Superior

manufacturing and distributing methods. But most importantly—
superior men!"[55] That year, a young Standard Oil employee named
Harold Sheridan wrote a letter to his parents crowing about his
plush, princely life in Shanghai. The short of it: he was being paid a
handsome salary to delegate work to local Chinese agents and translators. "Four hundred million yellow people look up to you and respect you as a superior being because you are white, and are pleased
to render you services of any description befitting what they consider your fitting position. It's great out here."[56]

Again, that number: four hundred million. The American in-
fatuation with China's wondrous population dated back at least
to the 1890s. But it was in the 1930s that the number took on a
new charge. Four hundred million: an astronomical, almost mythic
number. A beacon and a lure. An untapped world of four hundred
million "guinea pigs," "yellow people" looking up to the white man,
sickly people "who ignored the laws of health."[57] For H. T. Tsiang,
they were "four hundred million toilers," thirsting for revolution.[58]
For Carl Crow, they were four hundred million customers, full of
a different, upwardly mobile kind of desire. In 1935, an American
writer named Mary Nourse published *The Four Hundred Million:
A Short History of the Chinese*. There were the four hundred million strivers persevering through poverty and foreign invasion, as
depicted in Joris Ivens's 1939 documentary *The 400 Million*. One
of the film's chief fundraisers was Luise Rainer, who had won an
Academy Award for her performance in the big screen adaptation
of Pearl Buck's *The Good Earth*—a novel that had helped humanize
this inscrutably large number.[59]

There was a darker side to these euphoric tales of America's global
conquests. Standard Oil's gradual replacement of Chinese compradors with young Americans, for example, brought a more hierarchical structure to bear on Chinese business.[60] Many of these "young
griffins"—a term used to describe white newcomers—imported a
sense of smug superiority with them. As an internal bulletin crowed,
there was a "civilizing effect" to Standard Oil's international business
as well. Giving the Chinese the gift of kerosene "extended aid to millions of people in the very best way that aid can be given: It made it
possible for those people to help themselves by increasing their own
efficiency."[61] Providing oil for the lamps of China became a way of

merging commercial imperative with a vague, almost providential sense of international duty.

There was a toll to be paid for this rush to court China's four hundred million—to bring them enlightenment. Even the most sensitive accounts trafficked in a light air of condescension. As the historian Jerry Israel would later remark, a more apt title for Crow's exceedingly cheery book might have been "Four Hundred Million Number One Boys." These new systems of exchange aggravated the imbalance between China and the West. But they were also built on the ideals and ambitions of young Americans who viewed themselves as new pioneers. From "four hundred million customers" to "oil for the lamps of China," the call to head abroad had become part of the American language: these were the new clarion calls that sent young Americans like Harold Sheridan across the seas. What most young griffins eventually discovered was that life in China fell short of Sheridan's effervescent accounts of obedience and respect. For Standard Oil's New York-trained agents, stints in China were marked by extreme isolation. They were prohibited from marrying or leaving the country during their first contract.[62] There was the occasional infestation of bedbugs. Even those stationed in quieter regions had to suffer the fate of a different, dingy Chinese inn each night, a one-thousand-day buffet of Chinese food.[63] In the anarchic 1920s, the Standard Oil salesmen and their local employees were responsible for keeping the supply lines open, often at great personal risk. Crow claimed that more than one-third of the young men who returned to America after their three-year assignments chose to stay home.

A famous example was Earle Tisdale Hobart, a faithful employee who frequently put his life in harm's way to insure that Standard Oil's kerosene could flow freely. He was a hopeful young executive when he and his wife Alice had married in Tientsin 1914. The company posted them in Manchuria, where they lived through civil war and bandit raids, all in the hopes that he would earn a transfer to a much-desired position in Shanghai. In 1927, Hobart was managing Standard Oil's storage facility in Nanking when the National Revolutionary Army arrived during their Northern Expedition. After the nationalists vanquished the local warlord—dubbed China's "basest warlord" by *Time* magazine—their soldiers began targeting the port city's foreigners. The Standard Oil facility was especially vulnerable and Hobart sustained a broken ankle during the evacuation. Order was restored after a few days of rioting and looting but it was the most serious challenge in decades to Standard Oil's position in China. Hobart resigned when it became clear that the company intended to reward his bravery by reassigning him not to Shanghai but a town directly in the path of the Communist troops. The Hobarts returned to the United States shortly thereafter.

Hobart's wife Alice was far from a passive observer. She was born Alice Nourse in 1882. Her childhood was marked by stretches of poor health. After graduating from high school, she enrolled at Northwestern University, though she never completed her degree. A stint at the University of Chicago went unfinished as well. She moved to China in 1910 to join her sister Mary, author of the aforementioned *The Four Hundred Million*, who was working as a teacher at a girl's school in Hangchow. Four years later, she married Earle Tisdale Hobart.

It was in China that Alice Tisdale Hobart began writing about her life. She contributed firsthand accounts of her life in China for magazines like the *Atlantic* and *Harper's*. Though literary historians have largely forgotten Hobart, she was a successful travel writer and novelist throughout the 1930s whose career bore many similarities to Buck's. Both Hobart and Buck's China writings were shaped by the experiences of their husbands, who were each engaged in work that—broadly speaking—required them to challenge Chinese traditions. Buck began writing while accompanying her husband, John Lossing, on agricultural missions through the Chinese plains. He tried to impart the wisdom he had attained at Cornell University to Chinese farmers. But his ideas rarely gained traction. As Pearl would later recall, part of the problem was that nobody had bothered to ask the farmers what they thought: "One worrisome evening when there seemed no solution to this problem, I suggested that perhaps the wisest plan would be to discover first the facts about Chinese farming and rural life."[64] For Buck, this kind of expert-driven chauvinism, where the flow of information between the sage Westerner and the backward Chinese always traveled in one direction, recalled the paternalism she had witnessed during her missionary childhood.

"I must confess that I had often wondered secretly what a young American could teach the Chinese farmers who had been farming for generations on the same land and by the most skillful use of fertilizers and irrigation were still able to produce extraordinary yields and this without modern machinery."[65]

Hobart was far more sympathetic toward her husband's travails, particularly the psychological strain of working for Standard Oil. In Hobart's view, the true villain was a system of thinking that implicated all under its spell. In 1917, she published her first book, *Pioneering Where the World is Old*, which drew from their bandit-filled experiences in Manchuria. Her next book, 1926's *By the City of the Long Sand*, was based on her perspectives as the wife of an oil executive. Their harrowing adventure in Nanking was recounted two years later in *Within the Walls of Nanking*. Buck and Hobart were acquaintances from a brief moment of overlap when they both lived in Nanking in the 1920s.[66] It is perhaps inevitable that Hobart's China novels were frequently compared to *The Good Earth*.[67]

In 1929, Hobart published *Pidgin Cargo* (herein: *River Supreme*), the first of what she envisioned to be a four-novel examination of "the impact of West upon East."[68] *River Supreme* is set during the introduction of steam navigation to the upper reaches of the Yangtze River in the 1910s.[69] It tells the story of an American sailor and engineer named Eben Hawley who becomes obsessed with conquering the Yangtze. His manic determination affects everyone around him, from his family to the local Chinese, indifferent to his strange ambitions.[70]

Hobart's intention was for her four China novels to offer an indictment of the "blind drive of machinery into a civilization stocked with man power" as well as "the forcing of impersonal business organization" upon a people whose traditions had served them quite well.[71] At the center of each novel is an idealistic American driven to near madness by his commitment to modern ideals of progress and expertise. Each man sets foot in China presuming that his ways of knowing are superior to those of the Chinese. For each man, a central question becomes the role China might play in its own civilizing process. While these characters are charged with executing a vision of which Hobart herself seems skeptical, she remains sympathetic to their powerlessness. In a formative moment of *River Supreme*,

Hawley dines with a character named Archibald Little, who bears a close resemblance to Archibald John Little, an English sailor and travel writer who had aspired to open the Chinese market in the nineteenth century. Little introduces Hawley to the prevailing attitude of Western chauvinism: "The future of China and of foreign trade lies on the Yangtse . . . resources untouched . . . enormous population in the Yangtse Valley . . . needs outlet . . . ought to be one of the great markets of the world . . . wealth in it for all three, China, England, America . . . We cannot let these people go their own way."[72] Despite the protestations of a missionary at the other end of a table ("Machinery will change their whole lives. You are killing an enormous industry.") Hawley has chosen sides, spellbound as he is by the lure of uncharted waters: "Aren't we giving something in its place? Aren't our steamers better than their junks?"[73] When Hawley's beleaguered wife wonders why he has become so fixated on exerting his will over the river, he invokes a pioneer birthright. "My family have always done things like this. My great uncle went out to settle Kansas . . . I don't know; in the blood, I guess."[74]

Despite Hawley's drive, Hobart casts him as the victim rather than heir to this imperial lust. Control remains just beyond Hawley's grasp, for there are great, invisible hands underwriting his actions. Over the course of *River Supreme*, it becomes apparent that neither Hawley nor China itself will survive this collision of the proverbial East and West unscathed. Hawley grows increasingly delusional and the river eventually destroys him, while China begins changing at a pace that threatens to undermine its values and traditions. "They are of a different genius," a sympathetic American consul laments, praising the "passive, gentle" immovability of the Chinese.[75] Perhaps Hobart's sentimentality, then, is tinged with paternalism: *River Supreme* becomes a case for the recognition and preservation of that "different genius," of the Chinese perspective on these changes wrought from without. Though the novel is powered by Hawley's whims, the bemused Chinese onlookers provide a running commentary on the American's peculiar obsessions. Hawley's sailors conspire to fleece their boss and his Chinese servant begins questioning his loyalty to these "outside barbarians."[76] They smuggle opium—the titular "pidgin cargo"—aboard Hawley's ship. Chinese neighbors gossip about the "white residents" living in their "glass-houses." All the while, Hawley and his family "knew nothing of all this," going about their business in ignorant bliss.[77]

From the opening pages, failure seems inevitable for Hawley, a man who feels the winds of change without recognizing where they may carry him. Instead, the novel's most intriguing characters become the ones who embody this contact between China and America. It infects the young Chinese, raised during the chaos of the early twentieth century. They are the sons of the sailors, traders, translators, and compradors who recognize a new array of opportunities. "They sailed for America, England, avid to know what made the West so strong."[78] Meanwhile, Hawley's son, Eben Jr., develops a keener sensitivity to China, describing himself as "a man with two countries."[79] He remains inspired by his father's crazed quest, even as he himself grows ambivalent toward this historical moment. "If only, thought young Eben, East and West were not so suspicious of each other and would enter into mutual respect and confidence! [. . .] If only both could forget and start over!"[80] But the son's idealism is impossible. Like the elder Hawley's trek up the river, it is too late to turn back. There is no starting over.

Hobart's next novel expanded on this possibility of the invaders' despair. In 1933, Hobart nicked Standard Oil's slogan and published *Oil for the Lamps of China*, a fictionalization of her husband's life in China. The novel was a best seller upon its release and, two years later, it was adapted for the big screen. It tracks the mounting disillusionments of Stephen Chase, an ambitious young agent for the American Oil Company, Hobart's stand-in for Standard Oil. In the preface to a later edition of *River Supreme* issued to capitalize on the success of *Oil for the Lamps of China*, Hobart noted the similarities between her two American protagonists. "Let [Hawley] stand beside Stephen Chase, dreamer of lamps who came to understand something of the dark struggle he had helped to bring about. Two men, themselves a part of the human cost of the advance of Western civilization; two dreamers crushed by the forces of civilization they espoused."[81]

As the novel opens, Chase reflects on the path that brought him to the northeast of China, a region then known as Manchuria. He had been unable to find work upon graduating from the College of Mines in 1908. With the mining industry stagnant, he enrolled in a demanding training course at American Oil's headquarters in New York, arriving in China two years later. An apprenticeship with a local American Oil executive in Manchuria was followed by a series of short trips on his own to settle accounts. After demonstrating his ability to work with the local Chinese agents, he was promoted to the role of inspector, exploring opportunities for regional expansion. Now, two years after arriving on Chinese soil, he was finally in a position to hire and oversee his own staff of Chinese agents for a new territory.[82] Chase's new managerial role within American Oil's foreign venture demanded a new form of responsibility: he could no longer rely on intermediaries. "He had no interpreter because the boss felt that any Chinese would feel it his inalienable right to arrange a commission for himself out of the deal. Therefore, with his limited knowledge of the language, he must handle the arrangements alone."[83] All of these details—the New York training courses, the terms of the apprenticeship, the trajectory toward management—drew on the experiences of Hobart's husband.

For all the hype surrounding China's new markets, there were few representations of the day-to-day logistics of Western corporations in China. While the compradors had been a powerful symbol of these new commercial endeavors, they are practically invisible in the era's fiction and reportage.[84] Perhaps this is why readers devoured the specificities and details of Crow's books. Hobart, on the other hand, was interested in exposing readers to another side of these overseas adventures: delusions of superiority, chaos, crushing isolation. Alone, casting about northern China, Chase struggles with the brutal tedium of his everyday life:

Two years had trained his mind and muscles to the slow even rhythm of primitive travel across gigantic distances. He kept his eyes on the road unwinding under the cart, flowing toward him, a rough red band of tangled hoof-marks between the deep ruts which heavy wheels had made. The modern world lay far, far away. He was lost to all but the vagabond days, the life of the inns, the rumbling cart.[85]

This had not been part of the job description. And yet Chase is energized by his sense of duty and obligation. Here, Hobart again draws on Standard Oil's outlandish sense of self-regard. Chase recalls his mornings spent "high up in the Oil Company's great building," taking classes and learning his trade. Despite the hardships of his current post, he remains steadfastly loyal now that "he had his place in the work of this great corporation. The corporation. After the assignments had been made, a director of the Company had spoken to them of what the corporation wanted. Cooperation, emphasis on the whole and not the individual, hard work and loyalty."[86]

A missionary's zeal sustains Chase through his rough period of acculturation. Just as Standard Oil claimed to be civilizing the Chinese, Chase begins to imagine a higher purpose to his work. "Enterprise brought these frontiersmen here. Progress should follow fast."[87] This was "a new land like our West,"[88] rich with untouched plains and "virgin forests."[89] The pace of change was dizzying: already, there were railroads, telegraphs. "Soon the country would be well lighted, too. Light had become Stephen's fixed idea of progress."[90] Eager to establish himself in the corporate hierarchy, Chase dreams up a device that will help American Oil rule the Chinese market: small, affordable kerosene-burning lamps.

> Why had no one thought of such a lamp—to be exported with oil? A tiny chimney, tiny bowl that could hold a few coppers' worth of oil! A lamp that peasants and coolies could afford to buy! . . . His dream expanded. In time the Company could put a lamp in every inn, every hut in Manchuria, in China! Four hundred million people, millions of lamps. He saw himself famed for the little lamps, important in the Company.[91]

As mentioned above, Standard Oil had indeed marketed mei-foo lamps to Chinese consumers, practically giving them away in order to establish a dependency on kerosene. The idea for the lamp is credited to William Bemis, a high-ranking executive.[92] "Just to show you what may be done in the way of selling goods to the Chinese and introducing new appliances," Bemis explained to the *New York Times* in 1925, "take a look at those lamps on the table there." While studying conditions in China, Bemis continued, he noticed that Chinese silk workers frequently went to bed in the late afternoon because it was simply too dark to do anything else. He returned to America and developed a cheap, easily mass-produced lamp that revolutionized the silk industry—in his benevolent retelling, he empowered the Chinese with the tools to help themselves. "In my opinion, there is no region on the face of the globe to-day equal to China in commercial possibilities. The Chinese need money. They are going to get it."[93]

In Hobart's fictional account of the mei-foo lamp's invention, Chase ends up deprived of the acclaim that attaches to his moment of genius. He presents the idea to his superior—one of many cold, impersonal authority figures who embody America Oil's logic of corporatism—and it keys their China strategy. But Chase's boss attributes the lamp's creation to "teamwork." Chase rationalizes the situation:

The other men went back to their work, but Stephen stood with a lamp in his hand. How he had dreamed of it—the Chase lamp—the honor, the individuality it would bring him. Anger flamed within him. It was his idea . . . he should profit by it. Lucy should profit by it. The Company was exploiting him in not acknowledging his rights in the lamp. Then, suddenly, his anger was gone. Let him be honest with himself, others had contributed. With a sigh, he set the lamp among its fellows, relinquishing his bright dream of personal aggrandizement, sinking his personality in the organization.[94]

While Chase's self-conscious sacrifice bears traces of the eternally elusive promotion that bedeviled Hobart's husband, *Oil for the Lamps of China* is clearly not intended as a faithful rendition of their actual lives. Chase, for example, struggles to maintain affection for his wife, Hester. For long stretches of the novel, he fails to recognize the degree to which he has internalized American Oil's imperial sensibility. "He could not understand the mind that did not desire light."[95] It is an affliction that captures his fundamental alienation from the people he sets out to assist: "The distinguishing lines of the faces of men of his own race were not in these faces. He was baffled by the strange sameness: the secrecy of the agate eyes, the lineless skins, the serene mouths. 'They all look alike,' he said to himself in despair, 'how shall I judge?'"[96]

As *Oil for the Lamps of China* unfolds, its sense of menace and despair begin to outsize anything the couple likely endured in real life. It is a dystopian vision of corporate machismo, something like *The Good Earth* crossed with Ida Tarbell's muckraking classic *The History of the Standard Oil Company*. There is Chase's manager, whose example suggests that the company demands a sadistic, ironman commitment from its foreign agents—he himself has not returned to America for forty years.[97] As Chase courts Hester—a marriage he initially pursues to maintain the appearance of a committed family man among his superiors—he warns her that life will not be easy. This is "a man's country," he explains. "There is something about this country, about this race that does swamp one alone . . . But we're backed by the biggest thing in America, men united in a corporation. We're safe."[98] During a brief return to New York, the couple is subjected to further indoctrination. China is their mission, American Oil their faith:

> To come into the director's office was like being taken up on to a high mountain—the riches of the world spread out at their feet. "See," said Mr. Swaley, leading Hester to the window, "the sun's going down, but it never sets on our business. Well, now, over in China," there was a flourish of his white manicured hands, "why, there's the sun and our business." There was also a flourish in his voice. "Doesn't it stir your patriotism, Mrs. Chase, America's economic empire? A rich empire. New citizenship of the world. Fine, isn't it?" he added.[99]

Hester is the first to grow skeptical toward the corporation's vision. "They ought to have put your name on the bottom of the lamps, like a Chinese chop," she contends. "Well, no," Chase replies, "not in a corporation. You learn to take pride in just fitting in."[100] Eventually, Chase's devotion to American Oil is supplanted by the promise of a healthful life with Hester. But even this modest goal remains out of reach. Hester suffers a miscarriage and, despite Chase's loyalty, the promotion he has long been promised never materializes. To make matters worse, a spell in America also ends in disappointment, sending them back to China. Throughout, American Oil remains a spectral presence, a "tenacious, unyielding will" that subsumes Chase's individual being. "Silently, the master will of organization strove with the little wills, subordinating them to its own use."[101] There are nameless, faceless directors and managers, supervisors mouthing words "as a puppet would speak."[102] There is no leader, just a kind of wicked inertia that collects those who were once so "jaggedly individual," preys on their fear of the unknown, and offers them a new identity as part of "the Company."[103] There is only business. As Chase himself comes to learn: "Trade never stops for danger."[104]

But what did corporations ever do to harm people? Reviewing *Oil for the Lamps of China* for the *Saturday Review*, Lady Dorothea Hosie, the wife of the British Commercial Attaché in Peking, bemoaned the sudden fashion for novels attacking global trade. "How they reconcile themselves to drinking tea or wearing silk, one cannot imagine."[105] Perhaps, like Crow alerting readers to the complex provenance of the common toothbrush, this was Hobart's point. The *New York Times* review of *Oil for the Lamps of China* rightly notes that Hobart's novel is as much about America as it is China. The reviewer praises her meticulously trenchant treatment of American Oil, born of her ability to "view Western civilization with the eyes of a detached observer."[106] As Chase grows more disillusioned with corporate life, he begins to revisit his chauvinisms. Where the "eyes of the Chinese" once terrorized him, he now finds America and its rhythms strange.[107] The company commands him to press further into China, leading him to lament the consequences of "China drawn into world trade. Her progress hurried, the delicate balance of the green valley disturbed; native peanut oil standing unsold, replaced by the foreign product."[108]

How did these disturbances manifest? A new China emerges over the course of Hobart's novel. Where *The Good Earth* treasured China's rough-hewn, folk spirit, *Oil for the Lamps of China* allowed that the future's transpacific crossings could bring the two lands near equal footing. At first, these moments of exchange and mixture baffle Chase: his budding relationship with his servant, the tradition-bound local merchants, the bizarre "Chinaman's conception of a foreign house" that his friend Boynton rents.[109] As the economy grows and local Chinese agents and compradors prosper, a new generation emerges. The younger Chinese begin to challenge Confucianism, believing that a "new Order will bring in the millennium."[110] His servant's son returns from school wearing Chase's old suit, speaking "in perfect English."[111] He begins to encounter Chinese business-men in tweed with stiff, finely sculpted hair. They, too, "spoke Eng-lish fluently. Altogether, they gave Stephen the sense of racial dif-ferences obliterated."[112] Those who ventured to America and came back to China begin pursuing "the good life, as they had seen it in the West."[113] This was the progress that Standard Oil's Bemis had prophesized: modern roads, amenities, Western enlightenment. But it has left Chase himself at a loss. Near the novel's end, he has no idea whether to regard these Chinese men who have been educated abroad as belonging to the West or the East. The truth is that they belong to neither—that both markers are pure projection. Chase, however, is incapable of recognizing this. "He was outside again."[114]

In her first two China novels, Hobart began identifying the Western ideals reshaping China, from the "blind drive" of machinery in *River Supreme* to the cold impersonality of modern business in *Oil for the Lamps of China*. In each case, the Americans themselves felt victim-ized by these endeavors. Much like Buck's anecdotes about her ex-husband's work struggle to teach American agricultural technique to Chinese farmers, Hobart's men discover that their blind faith in Western expertise has failed them.

Chastened by his father's failures, Eben Hawley, Jr. aspires to "start over." Stephen Chase is unable to reconcile his feelings of alienation—when he says that he feels "outside again" one wonders whether he was ever truly "inside" to begin with. In her next novel, Hobart would shift from the impact of industry and trade to the world of ideas. In 1936, she published *Yang and Yin*, the story of a missionary doctor named Peter Fraser who has arrived in China's backwards interior to practice and teach Western medicine. As with her previous two novels, Fraser, who opens the novel untroubled by the American presence in China, gradually loses faith. "Was the negative side of Christian civilization, with its keen grasp on revenue, always to thwart its positive aspects, its gift of mercy? Trade was trade, he pondered, as he rode home, ruthless and self-seeking, whether for opium or other projects."[115] Fraser eventually commits himself to acting as a one-man corrective for this deadly Western import, opening a clinic where he can nurse opium addicts back to health. He begins regarding his Chinese protégés as peers and, in a moment of pure selflessness, Fraser volunteers to carry a Chinese parasite back to the United States so the mysterious scourge can be studied in a modern laboratory.

What makes *Yang and Yin* so fascinating is the way it responds to Hobart's previous China novels. The opium that seizes Fraser's town has been smuggled upriver as "pidgin cargo" in ships like Hawley's. Lonely and in search of business advice, Fraser wanders into a local branch of American Oil and befriends Stephen Chase, protagonist of *Oil for the Lamps of China*. Hobart renders their friendship with tenderness and patience, as the pair chats amiably about their respective experiences in China—including a passing allusion to Hester's miscarriage[116]—and the warmth they feel for their Chinese advisors and disciples. Hobart had presented these protagonists—a sailor and engineer, a businessman, a missionary and doctor—as the experts paving the way for America's conquest of China. For all their experience and learning, however, each of them ends up disillusioned, swallowed alive by the forces of conquest.

They were leading men—not unlike Carl Crow, who managed to escape with his soul intact. In 1937 Alice Tisdale Hobart reviewed Carl Crow's *Four Hundred Million Customers* for the *Saturday Review*. "I have known many business men in my years spent in out of the way ports in China," she began. "From them I came to realize that if one wished to gain an insight into a foreign race, one could do no better than to associate with such men."[117] What impressed Hobart was Crow's sense of adaptability—his capacity to come out on the losing end of a deal with some clever Chinese merchant and allow himself to be changed by the experience. For Chase, however, it is too late. "There was no escape," Hester finally realizes. "The Company was too big to oppose. It filled the earth; it controlled the earth."[118] Chase's sense of authority evaporates. In all of Hobart's

China novels, it is the characters that seem peripheral, from perceptive wives and children to quietly engaged Chinese aides, assistants,
and compradors, who recognize the encounter of East and West for
what it is.

They were minor players blessed with the vision to see the game
for what it was—not unlike Hobart herself. So what did Hobart see?
An encounter between China and the West that would change all
who participated. A new regime of China experts tasked with executing impossible aims. Somewhere in the West's haughty treatment of
China, she saw the signs of what America itself would become. Hobart never completed her original plan of writing four novels about
America and China. Instead, her next novel was 1940's *Their Own
Country*, a sequel to *Oil for the Lamps of China*. Stephen and Hester
have finally returned to the United States from China, only to find
that Stephen is unequipped to navigate the politics and prerequisites
of modern American business. It is no different than the spectral
corporation that policed their ambitions when they were in China.

The only difference is that the cliffhanger on the final pages of *Oil
for the Lamps of China* is resolved. In the final pages, Hester reveals
that she is finally pregnant. "It's what you've wanted, a child," she
tells Chase as he prepares to leave for yet another mission. As with
Hobart's other novels, the child symbolizes faith, regeneration, the
possibility of a more ephemeral kind of progress, an alternative to
productivity that is measured in dollars and cents. But even as Chase
recognizes this—even as he grows critical of American Oil's expansion—he is inextricably a part of it. Duty requires him to leave them
behind. "Hester must have security, and his child must have security," Chase thinks to himself. "He was caught—the Company could
work its will with him."[119]

"Is there no other way?" she asks. His response, which stands in for
his entire worldview, corrupted by work and time: "I can't see any."[120]

4

Pink Flag

H. T. Tsiang wrote his second novel, *The Hanging on Union Square (An American Epic)*, at a Montclair, New Jersey "chop-suey palace" owned by his friend Kun Fong. Fong provided him with everything he could possibly need: "a typewriter, an occasional dish of chow mein, and plenty of Chinese brandy."[1]

Occasionally, Chinese friends proud of Tsiang's literary ambition would chip in fifteen or twenty dollars to help with costs. He was infinitely confident in his own talent, as anyone within his immediate proximity discovered. He was a tireless if misguided self-promoter, clotting the mailboxes of potential allies and editors with streams of playfully pompous letters. When nobody would publish his books, he simply printed their rejection notices in the place of blurbs. When nobody bought his books, he pounded the pavement both literally—in the streets of New York—and, as we shall see in *Hanging*, figuratively, as a presence in his own stories, trying to convince his own characters of their creator's genius. As Tsiang pressed a copy of *Hanging* into the hands of a writer from the *New Yorker*, he bragged that his next novel, *Shanghai-New York-Moscow*, would be about a coolie: "Somewhat like *The Good Earth* but much better."

Then again: who was Tsiang to challenge a cultural force like *The Good Earth*?

By the time Tsiang published *Hanging* in 1935, there was a crowd-ed field of American writers eager to share their opinions on China. While the American fascination with China stretched all the way back to the colonial era, a concerted effort to engage and understand the country and its people did not take root until the early twenti-eth century. In Chapter 1, we considered the long shadow cast by Pearl Buck and *The Good Earth*. Buck's tale of a noble farmer and his struggles against famine, political upheaval, and temptation was an immediate success upon its 1931 publication. But its influence went far beyond literary circles. It became a cultural phenomenon, introducing the American middlebrow to the enchantments of this distant land. Most importantly, *The Good Earth* established Buck as one of America's most prominent voices on all things Chinese, an informal position she would hold for decades. She carefully nurtured this authority through her political advocacy, an amazingly consis-tent output of novels and reportage, and her association with the John Day Company, a publisher that had begun prioritizing Asia after striking gold with *The Good Earth*. As a result of Buck's path-breaking success, she had helped to create and then grow an entire new market for authors with something to say about China.

To anoint an expert, though, is to draw distinctions between le-gitimate and illegitimate forms of knowledge. The case of Buck was complicated by the perception that her authority owed to her popu-larity. There were plenty of rival China experts who were rightly irritated by Buck's huge share of the market. As Helen Foster Snow, an American journalist who wrote frequently about China under the pseudonym "Nym Wales," later griped: "Nobody thought anything by or about China was interesting for the U.S. You couldn't sell it. Nothing sold but *The Good Earth*, which was the mystery of all time."[2] Anyone with an opinion on China had to at least reckon with Buck's presence, even if they had no interest in her work. We wit-nessed an example of this in Chapter 1, when the Chinese politician and critic Kiang Kang-hu arrived in the United States at the height of Buck's popularity. He had never heard of *The Good Earth*. Yet ev-erywhere he went, Americans bombarded him with questions and opinions about China drawn from their reading of the bestseller. He finally decided to read it for himself, if only to have a stock answer next time this happened. Predictably, he hated it. He wrote a series of articles meticulously listing her representational sins, eventually catching the attention of Buck herself, who publicly debated him in the pages of the *New York Times.*

It was powerful people like Buck and the publisher Henry Luce who shaped the China conversation. Both of them drew on the authority of having been raised in China as the children of missionaries. In the 1920s and '30s, the ideal intermediaries for this transpacific space were people of relative privilege: descendants of white missionaries, itinerant representatives of American businesses, journalists, and academics. But, as we saw in the last chapter, there were few additional prerequisites for becoming a successful author describing this emerging space. For example, when the journalist Carl Crow set sail for China in 1911, he had no idea whether he would be traveling via the Atlantic or Pacific Ocean. But thanks to his reportage and work as an advertiser, he soon became a trusted advisor to both American and Chinese businessmen and political leaders. China was a wondrous abstraction to all who approached it, an inscrutable assemblage of 400 million future Christians, consumers, or citizens, depending on your game. Promise on this scale required experts and explainers. It required prophets.

To the outside observer, this community of China experts could seem insular and one-sided. Buck and Luce oversaw powerful networks of influence, promoting the works of writers and thinkers with whom they mostly agreed. Luce proved his staunch loyalty to Chiang Kai-shek by regaling readers of *Time* and *Life* with a steady stream of cover stories and profiles sympathetic to the Nationalist leader. In Chapter 6, we will consider the Chinese writer Lin Yutang's success in America, the product of his close friendship with Buck and her publisher husband, Richard Walsh.

So, as Tsiang was preparing *Hanging* for publication, he, like most Chinese in America, could not access these frenzied, high-profile deliberations over the two nations' shared destiny. Even though communities of Chinese Americans eagerly debated the political future of their distant and increasingly abstract homeland in local Chinatown or student-run newspapers, they rarely breached these mainstream conversations. After decades of racist, xenophobic portrayals of the Chinese and Chinatowns, some within these communities lauded *The Good Earth* for its positive depiction of China. Others, like Kiang and Tsiang, loathed Buck's version of their lives. To register either viewpoint within the broader culture, though, was nearly impossible—unless, like Kiang, you could lob just enough spitballs to get someone's attention.

Tsiang watched from afar as the field of conversation took shape around Buck and her cohort. As detailed in Chapter 2, he had arrived in the United States in 1926 after a tumultuous career as a civil servant in the young Chinese republic. Tsiang edited an independent Chinese newsweekly while enrolled as a graduate student at Stanford University, publishing fierce criticisms of the nationalist leader Chiang Kai-shek. The ocean separating Shanghai and Palo Alto, however, did little to save him from the violent scorn of Chiang's supporters. He was chased out of the Bay Area, eventually ending up in New York a year later. While studying at Columbia University, Tsiang began exploring different outlets for his political enthusiasms. He wanted to help those around him see the larger struggle. "I sincerely hope that these poems are material from which to form some conception of the Chinese revolution," he wrote in the Foreword to his first and only poetry collection, "and in that, they will have served their purpose."[3] An artistic career might have seemed in the offing. But, as we shall see in this chapter, Tsiang never achieved the career to match his boundless self-confidence. He would self-publish his next two novels, *China Red* and *The Hanging on Union Square*, selling them to anyone who crossed his path in New York City. His frustrations as an author would spill into his novels, which would, in turn, grow more politically confrontational, stylistically experimental, and emotionally desperate.

What can Tsiang's ultimate obscurity tell us? On the rare occasion his path crossed with that of the China establishment, he was little more than a temporary irritant—a "pest," as he would describe himself in *Hanging*. His radical provocations were never allowed to disrupt the conversations that Buck, Luce, and others were having elsewhere. But there is something innately valuable, perhaps even inspiring, about paying notice to the unheralded and the forgotten, regardless of the tiny scale of their intervention. Failure always contains an alternative to the chosen path; at the very least, failure reminds us that some saw a choice to begin with.

Despite the blame Tsiang laid at the feet of establishment authorities like Buck, Walsh, or Lin, it would be an overstatement to say he was silenced by the powers-that-be. In an age when popular works about China were generally relatable, Tsiang produced books that were difficult and whimsically self-aware. Even so, he was not above pedestrian motivations like fame and approval. Whether by design or mere desperation, the body of work he left behind teems with desires and visions boldly and profoundly out of step with the world in which he lived and worked. Failure renders most to the dustbin of history. But it can also be generative. Tsiang came to embrace his position on the margin, free from the artistic or political systems that had rejected him. His failure compelled him to lash out at the orthodoxies around him, as he set out to challenge what a novel could do, where individuals turned to understand their identity. As fellow immigrants debated whether their futures lay in assimilation or a return to China, Tsiang rejected the very premise of the question. He aspired toward an identity that floated free of basic allegiances. He wanted to tear down the system: the system that had spurned him; the system that fooled us into thinking that our choices were limited to communism or capitalism, staying or going, assimilation or resistance, legitimate knowledge or pure madness.

The transpacific future demanded experts, explainers, and prophets, a call that Buck, Crow, Lin, Luce, and others gladly answered. It was a call that animated Tsiang, too. But he was constitutionally incapable of producing what the market demanded—and not for lack of trying. He had tried offering an earnest account of the Chinese revolution with his early poetry. Now, he aspired for something beyond status as a native informant. While his imagined rivals established themselves by publishing sentimental realism or sympathetic reportage, Tsiang drifted further away from the legible versions of how Americans imagined China. At once megalomaniacal and playfully self-effacing, he revolted against the dominant images of China and the boring machinery that had produced them. At a basic level, he was searching for more—both as a Chinese person making his way in America and as an artist zealous for new forms. He sought an identity that was far more flexible and contingent than what America's racial landscape allowed in the 1930s—perhaps now, too. It was a desire that mirrored his artistic frustration, for he desired a kind of freedom that few writers like him—Chinese, immigrant, non-white—enjoyed.

His failure only registers as such in retrospect. In the moment, he possessed an insatiable appetite for more than what America could offer him.

I am of the belief that anyone who self-publishes an "American Epic" is worth investigating, especially when they seem to luxuriate in their own marginality. One gets the sense that Tsiang's self-touting wit was a coping mechanism, a way to slow his drift toward cynical madness. Moments of absurd levity had given *China Red* a self-aware complexity unusual within the world of proletarian literature. But these moments when Tsiang invaded the page also suggested feelings of desperate, showy frustration, like someone whose grasp of the language could not keep pace with the wild sprints of his mind.

When Tsiang wrote *Hanging*, he had begun growing into the outer limits of his imagination. The novel recounts a hellish night in the life of Mr. Nut, an oblivious American dreamer wandering the streets of depression-ravaged Manhattan. When we first meet Nut, he is penniless but hopeful—he believes that it is only a matter of time before he somehow establishes a business of his own and joins the moneyed establishment that all the luckless leftists around him so desperately hates. But things only go from bad to worse, as he encounters the city's radiantly strange characters: housewives prostituting themselves to feed their children, slick-talking street urchins peddling Communist newspapers, sex-starved poets and book reviewers, con men working on their PhD theses, corporate bosses concocting a sinister plot to monetize surging suicide rates, a burlesque show involving desperate women, dollar coins, and magnets hidden where the sun don't shine. Tsiang himself even appears as a "pest" of a man selling copies of his previous, self-published book, *China Red*.

The New York of *Hanging* initially appears familiar, from the decadence of the wealthy to the desperation of the poor. Its settings and themes sit comfortably within the world of 1920s and '30s proletarian literature. But Tsiang populates this world with exaggerated caricatures of fat cats and revolutionaries, virtuous strivers and penny-pinching perverts, each one of them imprisoned by their rigid ideologies.

To make sense of all this—the bitterness, the sense of play, the self-awareness of writing himself into his novel as a "pest"—we might try to imagine Tsiang's relationship with the artistic communities that shaped him. In particular, let us ruminate on his initial enchantment with New York's proletarian arts community—and why he eventually grew restless within it. Examples of proletarian art first appeared in the 1920s, in the wake of international artistic movements such as cubism, Dada, and literary modernism. Collectively, these movements exploded traditional notions about art and its functions. For the loosely defined community of proletarian artists, the experience of living within an incomprehensibly large and ever-growing economic system in the 1920s and 1930s represented a challenging, hulking new muse, and it was to be conveyed directly, in language that factory workers and professors alike could appreciate. The moment called for stridency, clarity and confrontation. As the nation's financial markets plunged into depression, communities of artists emboldened by crisis set out to represent the psychic and physical ruin of the era, hopeful that their assaults on traditional forms and orthodoxies could resuscitate a culture that had rationalized itself into near-obsolescence. If humanity had doomed itself through its unflinching reliance on the language and logical structures of capitalism, then perhaps the aesthetic imagination could conjure an escape. Some leapt to their deaths from tall buildings, following the stock market downward; others plunged headlong into the artistic avant-garde, chasing for sense in a world gone mad.

How could one possibly create a work of art sensitive to these new scales of being? What would it mean to approach these ambitions with true faith and absolute diligence?

In the eyes of its practitioners, proletarian art was a warning to the masses, a promise of a better world, and a reminder of capitalism's noxious effects on the human imagination. As often happens with such movements, a great deal of energy was expended on the basic question of what the designation "proletarian" actually meant: was it the identity and background of the author or the content of the work that insured the text's properly proletarian values? Michael Gold's "Towards Proletarian Art," published in the February 1921 issue of *Liberator*, was an early attempt to address these concerns.[4] "We have been bred in the old capitalist planet, and its stuff is in our very bones. Its ideals, mutilated and poor, were yet the precious stays of our lives. Its art, its science, its philosophy and metaphysics are deeper in us than logic or will."[5] If only there were some way to excise that culture and its ideals from our worldview, to scrape it from our very bones. This idea of imagining a different culture altogether gained momentum in the 1920s, particularly in the world of the "little magazines"[6] and the self-published pamphlets and novels made possible by advances in printing technologies. Gold later described proletarian art in more concrete terms, explaining it as "taking many forms. There is not a standard model that all writers must imitate, or even a standard set of thoughts. There are no precedents. Each writer has to find his own way. All that unites us, and all we have for a guide, is the revolutionary spirit."[7]

Attempts to conjure this "revolutionary spirit" came in the form of massive tomes like *Proletarian Literature in the United States*. The collection was edited by Granville Hicks and published in 1935, by which time the spirit that had animated many of the proletarian artists had been rechanneled toward the broader cultural aims of the Popular Front.[8] The sweeping introductory note by the prominent leftist writer and editor Joseph Freeman offers a concise statement of the aims and techniques of the "literary class war."[9] Expanding on Gold's notion of proletarian inclusiveness, Freeman fixes on the artist's obligation toward "experience." In his view, the proletarian writer rejected the self-indulgent vagaries of a bourgeois universalism, instead rooting his or her work in the everyday struggles of the laboring classes: "No one says the artist should cease being an artist; no one urges him to ignore experience. The question is: what constitutes experience?"[10] Is the solution merely to broaden the range of available stories to include those of the self-identifying working class? Or could the experience of the working masses, too long ignored, avoid the effete fixations of bourgeois art?

Proletarian art, then, was more than an expansion of art's traditional subject matter; it was a call for new forms of expression as well.

To speak of beauty or timelessness or refined values—cornerstones of bourgeois taste—was to reveal one's decadent leanings. Rather than warmed-over abstractions, the works of *Proletarian Literature* aspired for a different expression of the universal, an art capable of capturing the diverse struggles that comprised our shared social reality and illuminating "the whole of the contemporary world from the only viewpoint from which it is possible to see it steadily and to see it whole."[11] The aim was to produce a "truly epic" art capable of encompassing the "tremendous experiences of a class whose worldwide struggle transforms the whole of human society."[12] For proletarian critics, the common sense instilled by capitalism had made our aesthetic imaginations unreliable prophets of revolutionary change. Art cultivated under the influence of the status quo set its sights toward a dull horizon of possibility. Freeman, Gold, and their comrades in the United States and Europe maintained belief that proletarian writing could disrupt our hardwiring.

Let us imagine, for a moment, H. T. Tsiang's perspective.

Tsiang had left the Bay Area after a series of run-ins with Chinese Americans sympathetic to the nationalist cause. He moved to New York, where his politics grew increasingly radical. Intoxicated by the proletarian arts movement, he took up their call to envision struggle on a global scale. Encouraged by his professors, he contributed to leftist papers like the *New Masses* and the *Daily Worker*. It is not hard to understand what drew Tsiang to the proletarian arts movement. By heeding its call for a "truly epic," international scale of analysis, he could contribute a genuinely new perspective to this predominantly American and European community. This was a movement predicated on solidarity, community, an expansive vision connecting the dots of a worldwide struggle—and he could connect them to brothers and sisters across the Pacific. Furthermore, Tsiang likely felt his rough-hewn work could find a home in a movement that prized passion and ideology over artistic convention or professionalism. It was a home for visionary amateurs. All of which is to say that the proletarian arts world seemed like a community of rebels, iconoclasts, and dreamers that would welcome the insights of someone like Tsiang.

In 1935 the critic Malcolm Cowley addressed the American Writers Congress on the topic of what the revolutionary movement could do for the individual writer. These new forms of panoramic, class-conscious writing, Cowley argued, would combat the banal "inward-ness" that ruled the American middlebrow. Instead, the writer would gain a new perspective—he would recognize himself as "part of a vast pattern," one among many flashpoints in this new and self-con-sciously global struggle.[13] Awareness of all this, Cowley continued, allowed writers to see

> human life not as a medley of accidents, but as a connected and continuing process. It ties things together, allowing novelists to see the connection between things that are happening to-day in our own neighborhoods, at the gates of factories, in backyards and street-corners, with the German counter-revolution, with the fight for collectivization in Russia, with the civil war now being waged in the interior of China; and it connects all these events with the struggles of the past. It gives the values, the uni-fied interpretation, without which one can write neither good history nor good tragedy.[14]

Perhaps this new art, for example, would be sensitive to the geo-graphical distribution of wealth versus poverty. It might document the harsh anonymity of city life, the remoteness of the rural, and the obscene riches of the city as points on the same map. It would bring the systems and structures of the status quo into clear focus. When Cowley surveyed the literature of the 1930s at decade's end, he argued that almost anything published after 1932 "belonged to the literature of the depression," whether it was a tale of unspoiled nostalgia, grimy muckraking or intercontinental escapism.[15] In fact, he pointed to the faddish popularity of books about life elsewhere as a sign of the reading public's exhaustion with the American scene. For the revolutionary movement, the emergence of international perspectives provided more opportunities to connect the common reader with their beleaguered counterparts elsewhere. Ultimately, Cowley acknowledged, one was not going to prosper grinding away on these kinds of underdog tales. But the hunger for revolution was strong and it offered the firebrand writer an audience—"the most eager and alive and responsive audience that now exists."[16]

One imagines this is all Tsiang ever craved—a part to play in the "vast pattern" and maybe an enthusiastic audience savvy to what his books were trying to convey.

In his address to the Writers Congress, Cowley pointed to two examples of authors who had recently attempted to capture this international perspective. Pearl Buck and Andre Malraux had each written novels set in China that featured the persecution of revolutionary heroes. But where Malraux invoked this setting to embolden and inspire his readers—to foster a "sense of unity with his comrades"—Buck's "not very exciting" version of revolutionary martyrdom failed to rise above melodramatic gimmickry.[17] What the movement needed, Cowley suggested, was a rousing, penetrative novel like Malraux's capable of conveying the "tragedy" of the present. A novel that could theorize the excesses and inequities of global capitalism and make these harsh truths accessible to the average reader. The movement had no use for Buck's sentimental tales of China.

One of the aims of this emerging community, then, was to capture their world in motion—to follow Gold's "revolutionary spirit" as it was taking hold anywhere and everywhere. The flourishing of market capitalism worldwide had created a web of interconnectedness that challenged the fortitude of national borders. Recall the histories of far-away change and conflict that converged in the modest toothbrush that Carl Crow described in Chapter 3. Economic crisis reshaped the horizons of everyday existence, from the urban to the rural. But these tumultuous changes reshaped the boundaries of the human imagination as well, altering our very notions of time and space. It was a moment of both promise and anxiety. On one hand, global capitalism represented a potentially destructive and at the very least destabilizing force. On the other hand, it made the world much smaller, facilitating the circulation of heretofore-unseen styles, modes of expression, and ideas of justice back and forth across the oceans. For the proletarian artist, the turbulence of the moment demanded a new scale of question. How could one grasp the possibilities of a global age? What new artistic forms or configurations of political energy could this moment produce?

On the sidelines, H. T. Tsiang waited his turn.

To hold *Hanging* in your hands is to acknowledge a distant cry. The object begs you to scrutinize its surface, all bold-faced exhortations and half-riddles; it challenges the prospective reader not to study its surface for clues as to what awaits inside. The khaki-yellow cover consists of three blocks of red and blue text which resemble a madman's conversation with himself—"YES *the cover of a book is more of a book than the book is a book*," "*I say*—NO," "SO." Flip it over and this last word stretches itself out and colonizes the entire back cover. Why is the cover "more of a book?" Is Tsiang spoofing our ready-made instinct to judge books by their covers? What of the "SO"? Is the "SO" meant interrogatively, as a question of what the reader will choose to do? A mocking demand: "So *what?*" Or is it a placeholder denoting this equation's distant solution: "So . . ." The title and author's name only appear on the book's spine.

As with *China Red*, the opening pages of *Hanging* reproduce a parade of rejection slips and less-than-effervescent correspondences from fellow writers. *Collier's* editor Thomas Uzzell politely describes it as "an interesting experiment," while the critic and biographer Carl Van Doren pledges that it is "original and amusing," though he doubts it will ever find an audience. *Proletarian Literature* editor Granville Hicks observes that it falls short of its aim to be "a kind of Communist Pilgrim's Progress," to which Tsiang replies in fine print at the bottom of the page, "Since I didn't attend high school in this country, I read 'Pilgrim's Progress' only after receiving G. H.'s letter."[18] This running commentary makes for a curious intrusion. Tsiang reappears two pages later, a niggling footnote to Waldo Frank's foreword. Frank describes *Hanging* as "a satiric allegory, a *potpourri* of narrative and song" that is wholly original in form. But his praise is restrained: "As a whole, I should not say that this ambitious work is a success; and it contains passages that may offend by their crudity and by the *naïveté* of their presentation." Frank nonetheless credits Tsiang for his ability to see beyond the paradigm of proletarian art:

It is a harbinger of the unguessed treasures of imagination which will be released by our proletarian writers when they are freed as Mr. Tsiang is freed, of the straightjacket of what calls itself

"Marxist realism" and of what is truly a stereotype alien to both Marx and literature, and as deadening as any other dogma.[19]

Once again, Tsiang cannot resist the temptation to reply. Down in the margin, Tsiang, unsure of what "Marxist realism" means, invents a new, nonsensical descriptor for his work: "I employed a method of 'Socialistic Realism and Revolutionary Romanticism' when I wrote the novel."

Soliciting interest in *China Red* may have been a struggle but it seems to have immunized Tsiang from the sting of rejection. This time, even more publishing houses joined in on the sport of spurning Tsiang, though he cared little. An opening page reprints notes from Little, Brown and Company, the Vanguard Press, and Harcourt, Brace and Company expressing a varied range of interest in Tsiang's experimental novel but little interest in publishing it. Only the publishers Covici-Friede offer constructive suggestions: "The idea of the book is an interesting one but we are afraid you are never going to be able to get it published as long as it remains in its present form . . . We suggest that you re-write the story in straightforward terms as a realistic novel."[20] (Again, that word: interesting.)

The negative blurbs, the academic squabbles in the footnotes, the confrontationally cryptic (albeit eye-catching) book design: why would a writer choose to undermine his own authority in such a loud fashion? There is obviously a strategy at play here, a commentary on self-promotion and publicity that is ironic but never quite spiteful. After all, Tsiang desperately wanted to be read. The 1920s and '30s were a period when the publishing industry in general sought innovative new ways to reach consumers.[21] Throughout the early 1920s, publishers began making a concerted effort to increase their advertising and marketing budgets.[22] The modest dust jacket, which had originally appeared shortly before the turn of the century in order to protect books from wear and tear, began to feature illustrations, advertising copy, and summaries designed to aid reviewers.[23] For some traditionalists, these new techniques for book selling subjected the pure pleasures of reading to an entirely different set of economic pressures. The book was no longer a catalog of ideas—it was a commodity to be bought and sold to a new, rapidly maturing reading public. During these decades, publishers and reviewers debated the necessity of blurbs, dust jackets, and even the publicity apparatus itself.

All of which helps us imagine what Tsiang hoped to dramatize with his self-aware design and layout: he was calling attention to his position outside of the traditional publishing world—and not for lack of trying. But the negative blurbs suggest a more profound kind of abjection. The most direct precedent for what Tsiang was trying to do was the fantasy writer James Branch Cabell, who included a dozen pages of bad reviews at the end of *Beyond Life*, a 1919 novel that commented on the cruel whims of the publishing industry.[24] Unlike Tsiang, Cabell was established enough to publish his books with major houses. Tsiang could not even convince his comrades at proletarian or progressive-minded presses to handle his work.

Tsiang's scorn comes into focus, then, as something deeper than the typical writer's frustrations. His categorical rejection from the traditional publishing world was one thing—it was to be expected, perhaps, given his radical politics and daring style. But the lukewarm praise and pronounced skepticism from critics, publishers, and fellow writers within the proletarian arts world: this was an altogether different type of failure. He could have been forgiven for assuming that proletarian writing was good and publishable insofar as it conformed to the ideological agenda of class revolt. But Tsiang had tried to do something more with *China Red*. He had hoped to expand the perspectives of proletarian art, to alert readers to struggles beyond the American factory or farmland, to unite them with the "four hundred million" across the Pacific. Tsiang's novels took Cowley's description of the "vast pattern" seriously, identifying struggles beyond our borders, beyond Europe, all the way across the Pacific to China and back again. He had struggled against the dictates of proletarian realism in order to develop a frenetic style more sensitive to the mad whims of the moment. But Tsiang could not find his star, even in the welcoming, inclusive world of proletarian art.

Plenty of writers fail. But few attempt to bring the entire edifice down with them. Perhaps the unwillingness of even progressive or left-leaning entities like Covici-Friede, the Vanguard Press, or Hicks to offer Tsiang a full-throated endorsement had driven him over the edge. All of these perceived slights from fellow travelers seemed to liberate Tsiang from the pressure of appeasing the proletarian arts community. He had contributed poetry and opinion pieces to the *Daily Worker* and the *New Masses*. He had attended meetings and rallies. As someone who had witnessed China's political transformations firsthand, he believed he had a global perspective on class struggle that rose to meet the movement's highest ambitions. But he could not convince this community that he possessed a perspective worth heralding. One imagines that the lukewarm letters from heroes like Hicks, Frank, Dreiser, or Upton Sinclair stung more than the rejection slips from the major publishing houses. These men were supposed to understand where Tsiang was coming from.

Tsiang displays these wounds proudly, believing that friends and enemies alike have turned their back on him. He shouts at the reader: whether any publisher considers this a proper book or not is inconsequential, for there is a weapon in your hands, one that the establishment has conspired to keep from you. The gatekeepers on the left have done so, too. Following the pages of rejections that open *Hanging*, Tsiang offers a brief note addressed directly to the reader. "The writer takes this opportunity of conveying his deep appreciation of the kindness of the various critics and publishers who had read his manuscript," he writes with a seeming sincerity. But maybe they can just agree to disagree—this is the book he wants to write, even if nobody wants to publish it. "Stubbornly or nuttily," he explains, he is compelled to advance his vision in its purest, uncut form, outside of the publishing industry that enforces our sense of the mainstream. He "is willing to be judged by the text of his book, with which he has experimented, and the writer is convinced that the reaction of the masses can't be wrong."[25] Failure may be inevitable; perhaps he even courts it. But he is unafraid. His condition cannot be helped: it is a faith in crowds as well as low-grade madness that compels him to do this his own way.

Would the masses care? Could they make sense of his unusual approach to the proletarian novel? It quickly becomes evident what the representative from Covici-Friede meant when suggesting that Tsiang pursue a more "straightforward" tack. A sense of maverick strangeness permeates *Hanging*. Tsiang's presence careens from nagging and infantile to condescending and cryptic. The story begins with an odd, tail-chasing mumble, like a child's lesson gone mad: "Money makes money; no money makes no money. Money talks; no money, no talking; talking produces no money." A manic fixation on money infects the page. "Isn't she a beautiful girl?" the narrator asks, before changing the subject: "I wish I had money. He is a nice-looking fellow. Has he any money? He marries and old maid; the old maid has money."[26] The language, repetitive and banal, grows hypnotic. "Money" is mantra, a seizure of madness, a word that seems to acquire a more mystical meaning each time it is uttered. The section ends by welcoming the reader into its internal logic: "I don't like money. You don't like money. He doesn't like money. You have money. He has money. I must have money."[27]

There is a restless, heavy-handed quality to Tsiang's writing that only appeared in trace amounts in his previous works. It is as though the impossibility of finding a mainstream audience has amplified and unleashed Tsiang's ego. A cryptic poem early on alerts the reader to the subtexts and sly allusions to come: "What is unsaid / Says, / And says more / Than what is said. / SAYS I."[28] Every now and then, these omniscient, phantom verses reappear, like an interstitial commentary on Nut's burgeoning consciousness.

Perhaps Tsiang, the prophet that the publishing establishment could not shoo away, viewed himself as the embodiment of all that America had ignored—the voices that had been relegated to the "unsaid." After all, as Tsiang's friend Rockwell Kent remarked to the publisher Richard Walsh, Tsiang's books were so obscure, it is as though they never existed.

As *Hanging* opens, Nut sits in a workers' cafeteria, listening to the sad fates of those around him, wondering to himself how he will get by without a steady job. Unlike everyone else, however, Nut has yet to surrender his by-the-bootstraps idealism. Aspiration becomes an affliction. His mind swirls with dreams of striking it rich, money-mad desires overtaking all reason or logic, like Gertrude Stein ghost-writing J. P. Morgan's autobiography. In Nut's mind, membership in the working class is but an interlude. "How could they tell that he would not, someday, by saving some money, establish a business of his own?"[29] Nut feels alienated by the workers and their pessimistic philosophies. When he innocently asks a young man tending the cafeteria how the "business" is going, the young man responds with a tirade. He accuses Nut of being an elitist cog, calling him all manner of prole slur: "a Mister," "a Boss," "a Capitalist," and "a Business Man." Nut, who aspires to become all those things, is deaf to the young man's hateful tone, thanking him for recognizing that he is indeed different: his poverty is only temporary. The young man is baffled and confused until he realizes "that Mr. Nut was not sarcastic or sneering, nor had any bad feelings; for the young man saw his face blank, his eyes sincere, his forehead perspiring."[30]

"Blank," earnest, naïve: the Nut we first encounter is a perfectly innocent foil to the cynical despair of modern life. Much like the character Chi in *China Red*, Nut is incapable of irony, engaging the world around him in a frustratingly literal manner. His outlook takes on an eccentric and slightly deranged quality, as he boomerangs through a cruel bureaucracy with a playful obliviousness, much like Tsiang himself. Nut is the one to whom things happen; he passes through life, expectant and hopeful, blind to the facts, ill-equipped to lunge for anything out of his grasp.

Like Nut, the other characters also sport heavy-handed names, signaling their relationships with the economic order that defined and divided them. The cafeteria attendant, Mrs. Stubborn, known for her obstinate, "revolutionary temperament,"[31] begins to embrace Communism after her former boss, Mr. System, guardian of the power structure, sexually assaults her. There is the cynical operator Mr. Wiseguy, who is all artifice and false surfaces: he does eye-exercises so as not to have "Chinese"-looking slanted eyes; he bleaches his hair so it is never black; he grows a beard to obscure his "weak chin"; and he wears rubber lifts inside his shoes, so as not to appear shorter than average. Mr. Ratsky embodies the decadence of the wealthy, playing every conceivable angle for maximum profit. And then there is Miss Digger, who preys on unsuspecting men to subsidize her entertainment.

The bulk of the novel tracks Nut's exploits as he wanders the grimy city, penniless and homeless yet strangely upbeat. The streets are transformative, though not in the way one might expect. They are macabre and filthy; from the surreally lavish riches of high society to the spectacular freakishness of his fellow laborers, little of Tsiang's New York indulges an us-against-them logic. The rich may be evil, but the poor are rarely any more virtuous.

Nut's semiconscious state begins to dissolve one day when a friend offers him a second-hand bed. It is an ordeal that foreshadows how his obsession with money might eventually destroy him. Despite the satisfaction he initially feels in scoring "something-for-nothing" furniture, the taxi ride home costs him more than the price of a new bed. He grows "Nut-conscious." "The more he looked at the bed the madder he became. And then, the question was not a matter of a dollar and fifty cents. It was, again, a question of principle. The question of his reputation. The bed wasn't a bed anymore. It was a symbol. It was symbolizing all the humiliation given to him and wrong done to him by others, in his whole life."[32] The bed seems to mock him, reminding him of his ultimate powerlessness, and he eventually destroys it in a fit of rage.

It would seem a fairly innocuous moment. But Nut cannot shake this pathetic feeling. His loose energies begin to find shape as a paranoid dispossession. While the nonstop proselytizing of the cafeterias and street corners leaves Nut unmoved, his experiences wandering the streets of New York do not. The more he sees, the more difficult it becomes to sleepwalk toward the American dream. Nut grows aware of his own identity when he attends a meeting to discuss the Scottsboro Boys, a group of nine young African Americans in Alabama who had been falsely accused of raping two white women. He begins to recognize how the fates of the underclass—women, African Americans, poor white laborers—are intertwined. Nut cannot shake the image of multiracial solidarity, especially as the police descend to quell the uprising. "The blood of the colored race and the blood of the white race that fell on the cement pavement were of one color." He realizes that the Communists are not the dangerous agitators; the system sustains itself through conflict, division, and violence. "Thus Mr. Nut got out—out in a no-way-out way."[33]

In other words, there is no exit from this scene, no way to forget what he has witnessed. The moment scrambles any sense that Nut's journey will lead him anywhere; he no longer aspires toward a career in "business." Perhaps there is no possible resolution in sight for the novel itself, either. An interstitial poem captures Nut's newfound awareness: "Heaven is above, / Hell below. / Nothing in pocket, / Where to go?"[34] Nut wanders the street late into the night, noticing desperate characters he had previously tried to shudder out of sight: "a half-drunk and half-awake bum,"[35] an old man rummaging through a garbage can for food, a homeless man who had come to New York from the South in hopes of finding work. Mr. Ratsky tortures Nut for sport; a poor mother offers up her body in order to buy her famished child some no doubt rotting fruit.

It is enough to drive someone nuts. Neither blind faith nor ironic detachment can preserve him. Nut tries to hang himself in Union Square—to make himself into a symbol of the common man's oppression. But Mr. Wiseguy saves him at the last moment and, inspired by Nut's hopelessness, devises a twisted scheme to both profiteer from working class misery and eliminate the unemployed. "Do you know how many persons are willing to pay big money to go to Sing Sing Prison and see an execution?" Wiseguy asks Mr. System, who hungrily affirms that he is one of these people. The nation's rising suicide rate—"20,088 in 1931 and 23,000 in 1932"—no longer represents an appalling condemnation of the state's grossly irresponsible guardianship. It is the foulest of money-making schemes. "We're going to have some poor fellow hang on Union Square and get Society to come to see him. That is a game. The rich man will get some pleasure and the poor man will get a few cents. The general situation will be bettered accordingly."[36] Using the theory of supply and demand, Mr. Wiseguy explains that they "shall make money and the country will regain prosperity." Their solution masquerades as altruism. They liken themselves to modern Gods, recalibrating the balance of the social order. "The unemployed of this country and of the world at large are day by day becoming more and more burdensome to our leading statesmen. The only way in which we can solve the problem of the unemployment is to hang all the unemployed. For otherwise they will suffer more."[37]

In the book's final pages, Nut approaches a podium that has been hastily constructed for his celebrated suicide. The eyes of the city, rich and poor alike, train upon him. Just as Wiseguy and System predicted, nothing draws a crowd like an execution.

As Nut shuffles onstage toward this spectacular end, the reader might wonder what it is Tsiang means to say. What did Tsiang, the brazen and almost obsessively self-conscious author so sensitive to this object's status as a book, hope to accomplish with this strange, sad tale? After all, the terrors of this city are unsurprising, even if Tsiang renders them in an exaggerated and garish way. The symbolism of naming characters Nut, Stubborn, or System feels brutally heavy-handed. Does *Hanging*, as the cover forewarns, actually point off the page, to truths and faiths beyond the book itself? How might Nut's ultimate fate dramatize Tsiang's own struggles as an artist who, as he proclaims in the preface, "stubbornly or nuttily" walks his own path?

When Tsiang wrote *China Red*, occasional moments of self-referential quirk seemed designed to call attention to how the book functioned as a commodity. By the time he constructed *Hanging*, this critique had grown much more pronounced. Before his awakening, Nut encounters a ten-year-old selling a Communist newspaper, who reminds him of a different, no less irritating street salesman: "Mr. Nut thought that this Russian Brat was more of a pest than a fellow who had sold him a copy of 'China Red.'"[38] A joke at his own expense, perhaps. But Tsiang's own novel never finds its readers, even in his fictional Manhattan. *China Red* enters into this imaginary marketplace of ideas, competing with all the pamphlets, newspapers, books, and slogans Nut encounters throughout *Hanging*—and it is ignored yet again.

Nut's path to the gallows is littered with clues drawing the reader's attention to the status of the writer, the literary establishment, and conventions of taste. Earlier, as Nut is wandering the street, cold and hungry, he meets a young poet who offers him a warm apartment and stiff drink. When they arrive, the man asks if Nut would appreciate the treat of a private reading. Nut declines, claiming he finds poetry incomprehensible. The poet defends his craft: "Because it is not understandable, that is why it is poetry. If you could understand it, then it wouldn't be poetry anymore. If you want to read something as plain as Autumn air, you should go to Union Square and read some of their propaganda stuff."[39] Is Tsiang ridiculing this generous if hifalutin poet or, having authored plenty of that dimwitted "propaganda stuff" in the past, is he mocking himself? The poet's opacity baffles the everyman Nut, and eventually his untrustworthiness is confirmed. The poet leaves Nut to his bread and gin, and Nut soon falls asleep, only to be roused awake by the poet's lips: not his words, but gentle kisses dotting Nut's forehead, cheeks, and lips. Nut bolts from the apartment, and the poet finally has the chance to recite a short couplet: "I wish your taste would be like mine—/ We could just be sixty-nine."[40]

Escaping the poet's grasp, Nut is taken in by an aging professor who opens his door to this luckless transient. Again, Nut's benefactor hopes this minor debt will be repaid sexually, though this time the advance is far more intimate. The two men lie spooning in the professor's cramped bed, and Nut senses "something uncomfortable touching the lower part of his back. It was not the old man's hand. Nor was it the old man's finger. Of course, Mr. Nut knew what it was."[41] Shocked by the professor's prodding, Nut leaps from the bed, provoking the old man to defend himself. "I am not prostituting you," he tells Nut gravely. "If you like, do whatever you wish with me. I review books. Now there is a depression, so there are few books and they pay me only with review copies. Tell me how I can help getting excited, when I read these sexy, hot novels. And how can I get the money to buy women and to cool myself?"[42]

The poet's lips and the critic's erection suggest Tsiang's mounting disillusionment with the literary establishment, the pillars of this world debasing the ideals of an aesthetic life: there is no art for art's sake, just art for the sake of getting laid. Was it a commentary on the transactional nature of modern life? An expression of how dehumanizing exposure to such a system could be, as these two characters ache for the touch of another person, even a random man walking the streets? Nut's obliviousness to sexual matters had been established early on, when a fellow traveler at the cafeteria had joked about the "Four F. theory regarding the technique of handling a woman." The first, second, and fourth steps were, respectively, to find, fool, and forget. "Mr. Nut asked about the third F," to which the exasperated joker lashes back, with delicious wordplay, "You understand? Nut!"[43]

Or perhaps Tsiang was mocking the popular preference for "sexy, hot novels" that left the proletarian genius in the cold, sending writers and critics down desperately perverse paths. In Hanging, literature is not transformative. It is debased, unconcerned with the world of politics and ideas, unable to feign concern. The quasi-intellectual faker Mr. Wiseguy obsesses over "publicity" and carries books as "culture-decorations."[44] When the revolutionary Stubborn begins to see the world anew, she draws a distinction between the world of literature and the world as it is: "Stubborn was not excited now. She thought it was all a story she had been reading. No. This was no fiction. Real!"[45] Readers crave the sensational and gory—a man hanging from a flagpole, for example.

In light of this, *China Red* stands no chance. *Hanging* will likely be ignored, too. What did people want to read instead? While System and Wiseguy scheme, the less empowered characters attempt to find meaning for their lives. Digger and Stubborn reunite at a hospital, where Digger is receiving treatment for an undisclosed "special souvenir" from a night spent with Mr. Wiseguy. The opportunistic Digger reveals that her lavish greed compelled her to dabble in prostitution. But after a brief relationship with Wiseguy, she had discovered that "there was something wrong with that very property by which she had made her living during the last two years." Now, she has a new scheme:

> "The only ambition I have now," remarked Miss Digger, "is to go to the Orient and do some research work there. The field there for this sort of work hasn't been touched yet."
>
> "What kind of research work?" inquired Stubborn.
>
> "I want to do some research work as a famous Missionary and woman-author did. In her book, many of her descriptions and some of her occasional remarks about what she has already described were of the same stuff as the pleasure I have given to my customers for the last two years. However, I visited a doctor every two weeks and never peddled disease. But that woman! That woman!" sighed Miss Digger, puritanically.
>
> "Who is that woman?" inquired Stubborn.
>
> "You know—the woman who made money from her Oriental novels! Here is another of her hypocrisies: She talks about 'Earth' and 'Soil' a lot, but I think what her publishers gave her as royalties was the same thing that I have received from my customers—dollars."[46]

That woman—the one who "made money from her Oriental novels" about "'Earth' and 'Soil'"—was Pearl Buck.

Tsiang had once tried writing an "Oriental novel." But in the real world as well as his fictional one, nobody had cared about *China Red*. So, while *Hanging* was on its surface a New York novel with only scant reference to China, it also functioned as an autopsy of Tsiang's own failures as a Chinese writer. He haunted his own novel like a "pest," reminding his characters and readers of what had come before.

Consider Tsiang's perspective at the time. *China Red* was published the same year as *The Good Earth*. While Buck's star was rising, Tsiang walked the streets of Manhattan, selling copies of *China Red* out of an old suitcase. He peddled this wry, knotty, and difficult tale of China's apathy and Communist awakening to anyone who crossed his path. Much like Kiang, Tsiang sought to depict a China that was young, modern, and sophisticated. This was not the version of China with which most readers were familiar, as Buck's tale of rural thrift and mellow virtue came to define how Americans imagined China. Tsiang had hoped that the long-distance romance of *China Red* would enlighten Depression-era readers in America to the worldwide struggle for justice and equality. But *The Good Earth* had comforted down-on-their-luck Americans by recounting a story of the land couched in values like patience, modesty, and perseverance. As Tsiang, speaking through his character Digger, explains, Buck's version of China did a grave disservice to the Chinese. She "gave her readers the stuff that fooled them into thinking that one should become a slave or a concubine. For instance, she would advise a girl like you to be the faithful slave of that bastard, Mr. System. The worst part, is that this woman gave advice like this, in the name of Missionary work."[47] Tsiang invokes Buck's celebrity to bemoan a publishing industry that rewards "sensation" and gimmickry[48] over skill. Buck is attacked for making "every character talk as the writer, an American woman Missionary, was accustomed to talk"[49]—an ironic complaint, given Tsiang's aggressive presence in this very scene. "What irritated me most was her repetition and repetition. It made me sick," Digger explains, to which Stubborn observes: "I guess she had to write more pages. More pages—more money." As Tsiang's fury mounts, his criticisms grow petty, erratic, and troublingly sexist. Digger accuses Buck of an overly romantic rendering of Chinese men due to her deep familiarity with the "situation as to men there," which she cryptically describes in terms of "shape and size."[50]

Digger and Stubborn's discussion of Buck suggests Tsiang's jealous and almost violent disdain for his rival author. In his later works and personal letters, Tsiang comes across as someone wholly obsessed with Buck and all that she represented. As he suggested to a writer from *The New Yorker* at the beginning of this chapter, he understood his failure in direct relation to Buck's sham success. While he embraced his position on the margins, he assigned some of the blame for his obscurity to the famous author monopolizing the spotlight. Perhaps one could not exist without the other. As Wiseguy remarks, the haves and the have-nots only make sense in relation to one another: "For instance, if there were no Third Avenue, and no Bowery, there would be no Fifth Avenue and no Park Avenue. If there were no J. P. and no J. D. there would be no Bums and no Trash."[51]

So, finally, on the closing pages of *Hanging*, as Nut approaches the gallows, the beleaguered author Tsiang himself seems to hang in the shadows. They are both—author and protagonist—self-conscious of their status as "Trash"—and they are proud of it. A novel might never find an audience. But the entire city, from "Fifth Avenue" to "Park Avenue," will turn up to gawk at an anonymous soul's execution.

Nut's manic extremes no longer shield him from an unforgiving world. He has seen the lowest depths of the city and rejected the American promise. He is "a Forgotten Man, a Little Man, an Average Man," which means he is a nobody. By the end of *Hanging*, Nut has done more than pass from right-wing politics to left. He has vaulted free of the ideological spectrum altogether. Safety nets woven in his name leave him hopeless. During his downward spiral, he began to see through the culture around him, from the empty promises of the New Deal—" . . . Try my pill—New Deal! / Hello, / Everybody: / How do you feel?"[52]—to the empty solidarity at a Communist rally: "He heard many words, many phrases. Out of it all, his mind made this: 'Masses! Masses! New Masses; Old

Masses! / 'Nothing can be said that is new. Nothing can be said that is old. Masses are Asses in all ages.'"[53] The seductive language used to spark class consciousness now left him cold. "Those fakers know what the Masses are—the Asses. The fakers use beautiful phrases with which to crown them—'average man'—'forgotten man'—names used to get something from the Masses."[54]

The flag in the sky had once inspired Nut to see "a new world. A better day."[55] But as he comes to despise all this fabric waving helplessly in the wind symbolizes, he wonders to himself: what greater expression of the system's crushing indifference than to fly oneself up the flagpole? Is he, as his name initially teases, crazy? Or is his naïveté and eagerness, which only seem troubling against a landscape in which every relation between two individuals becomes a "business transaction,"[56] actually a rejection of the world that has rationalized itself into insanity? He is struck with a vision to make a symbol of himself—to be the "Flag of Starvation Amid Plenty . . . the Flag of So-Called Civilization."[57]

The first time he decides to hang himself—the time he is saved—Nut drafts a short will divvying up the twenty-five dollars the hospital will provide him "for anatomical use" of his cadaver. He instantly feels "worriless—from care; and rested."[58] He will soon be free. The chapter ends with an observation that "Mr. Nut ended the story literarily, non-propandizingly and publishably."[59] But Wiseguy saves Nut at the last minute, coaxing him into hanging himself once more—for good, this time—as part of the Rich Men's Club's series of public suicides. Nut himself becomes a valuable commodity; he receives lucrative promotional opportunities from rope, suit, and tobacco magnates; he invents a dance called the "Hanging Technique"; "the biggest institution of learning in the world" offers him the honorary degrees of "Ph.D., L.L.B., M.M.C., Y.Y.Z." and the naming rights to "Nut Hall," where they shall teach the unemployed the trade of "How to Hang Profitably." There is even a publisher who seeks his life story.[60] When it is finally time for the hanging, the flagpole is adorned with a "Wheeling Dollar" at its apex. "Across this Dollar Symbol were two mottoes, namely: '*The Dollar is Might! The Dollar is Right!*'"[61] The mood is disturbingly light, as the crowds gather and cheer the return of "prosperity" and "happy days" as "old, pearl-necked ladies" swoon over the arrival of "Our Lord!" A parade marches by, shouting the catchy slogan of a local bank.

Nut approaches the flagpole "nuttily"—the same adverb Tsiang used to describe his own crazed endeavor in his author's preface.

Like Nut, Tsiang had undergone his own transformation, too. He had tried to work within the system, but traditional publishers and his proletarian peers alike had spurned him. Maybe nobody cared what an actual Chinese person thought about China. While Buck cultivated her authority, Tsiang nursed the chip on his shoulder. *Hanging* enacted these feelings of dispossession and frustration. It is a story about failure and the forms of madness it compels. It is a story about the invisible structures of authority that define our lives, regardless of where one sits on the ideological spectrum. It is a fantasy where the unthinkable aspects involve being able to see the power structure for what it is.

In his final moments, Nut appears to be lost in thought. Mr. System addresses the masses, which now regard Nut a hero—"We're with you! You're making money!" one smitten admirer yells. "I, Mr. System, have the greatest pleasure in doing my duty towards saving the civilization!" System exclaims, predicting that the mass execution of the unemployed will unburden society as a whole while relieving them of their unjust suffering. It is a perversion of liberty, a chilling vision of American individuality and choice: "Our philosophy is based on Individualism. And our motto is Profit for everybody. So today, a Forgotten Man, a Little Man, an Average Man, Mr. Nut, Dr. Nut, is doing his bit! Of his own free will, he is hanging himself on Union Square."[62]

Is there a more profound expression of "free will" than climbing up a flagpole to martyr oneself? This was Nut's original intention—to find a way of escaping this "no-way-out" world.[63] But the sense of oppositional abandon is lost the second time around in this authorized restaging. The notion of "free will" has been coopted, literally, by System—it is the freedom to choose between sanctioned activities. System even goes so far as to absorb the language of protest in justifying this ritual slaughter: "What is more important is, that this hanging is a symbol. For it will give inspiration to the rest of the unemployed. And this hanging is also a challenge to the barbaric and savage system whose philosophy is based on Hate. Our system is based on Love!"[64] Although, by name and deed, System is a representative of this awful system, he still tries to distance himself from its evil; it is not his fault, for he, Mr. System, is but a single man. It is a problem with society.

What obligations do we hold beyond the dignity of free will? The crowd does not recognize the horror of what they are about to see; the symbols and doublespeak go unchallenged. The eyes of this world upon him, Nut is allowed the final word:

> I am a Forgotten Man, a little Man, an Average Man, a worker, a Nut.
> "Be good and starve" is the order of the day!
> Prey on others or become a prey!
> "I *was* a Nut. But I *am* a Nut no more.
> I, a Forgotten Man, a Little Man, an Average Man, a Worker—will this time—doublecross you, Mr. System—the Exploiter, the War-maker, the Man-killer.
> Here is your neck. This is your rope.[65]

Nut takes out a pistol and turns it on System: "Nut doublecrossed Mr. System."[66]

If only it were so simple. What fantasy does this final gesture fulfill? Nut may have fooled Mr. System into providing him with a public platform for his protest. But Tsiang's portrayal of the frenzied masses suggest even this brazen an act of revenge probably failed to awaken them from their blissful slumber. In this sense, Nut's conversion into an ironic person mirrors the reader's. The proletarian critics were skeptical that the traditional novel could successfully convert the masses. Tsiang, too, had lost faith in the novel. But rather than give up trying, he tried to create something that would irk, shake, and disturb his readers awake. At a basic level, the reader was treated to a story of shifting political sympathies and the symbolisms and systems of logic that structured our sense of the world. At the same time, this was a novel that forced readers to reckon with the means of production and distribution through which books entered into our lives. The historian Michael Dening has noted proletarian art's attempts to build class-consciousness by representing "craft"; writers published stories bringing texture and sympathy to the lives of stonecutters, bricklayers, or butchers.[67] Tsiang was hoping to do something like this for the struggling writer. He was implicating the reader in this economy of exchange, harassing them into scrutinizing all that went into this object in their hands: the writing and editing, the rejection slips from the publishing house, the reliance upon friends and well-wishers, the decision to self-publish, the hand-to-hand distribution, all just to insure that another voice entered the discussion on China's fate. He forces the reader to confront the very mechanisms of publishing, the business that undergirds the arts. In a closing letter to the reader on the last page of the book, Tsiang, as the author, implores his readers to support his endeavor by purchasing extra copies of his books, as a resistance to "the realization that publishers, too, are capitalists and that proletarian literature can be produced without them."[68]

What does all this mean for the author Tsiang? His act seems no less desperate than Nut's. To kill Nut would be to cancel the position of the author—as celebrity, as inventor of meaning, and as a slave to form. Just as Nut saw suicide as his sole remaining expression of free will, Tsiang saw the negation of the novel—and the author it implied—as his. To kill System, though: this was the revenge fantasy that animated Tsiang.

As the book closes, it is unclear whether we are meant to lament Nut's act as one of clear-minded martyrdom or dismiss it as the final exclamation of a man gone insane. Perhaps both. Nut does not follow through on his suicide, just as Tsiang himself had "stubbornly or nuttily" refused to surrender his dream of publishing his work. This book floats free somewhere outside the system, launching its arrows from a distance. One of Nut's poems seems to capture his creator's plight:

> Heaven is above,
> Hell below.
> Nothing in pocket,
> Where to go?[69]

Tsiang was finding it difficult to survive as a writer. In a personal note to his readers on the last page of *Hanging*, he explained that he was already working on his fourth book, tentatively titled *Shanghai Newyork Moscow—An Odyssey of A Chinese Coolie*. He tried to rally his readers to help with publication costs. He was thankful for their support—it proved to him that proletarian literature could be produced "without being straitjacketed" by the publishers and capitalists. Maybe, in the distant future, these nutty books would be worth "hundreds or thousands of dollars" as collectors' items. He closes with a joke only a Communist would find funny, likening his own travails as a writer to Lenin's "Five Year Plan."[70]

5

Down and Out in New York City

THE CHINESE ANTHROPOLOGIST and sociologist Fei Xiaotong once wrote that America was a "world without ghosts." During World War II, Fei had received an invitation from the State Department to spend a year in the United States, collaborating with American scholars, working on translations, and studying American culture. He arrived in 1943 to find a nation united by the war effort. The patriotism, the community, the sacrifice, the sense of duty and common purpose: Fei found it all captivating.[1] But as his stint wore on, his views on the American disposition began to sour. This was a land, he believed, that was wholly uninterested in dwelling too deeply on its own past. Instead, American children believed in Superman, a symbol of resourcefulness and diligence who, in his majestic, impossible flights across the city skyline, promised a better tomorrow. He was progress incarnate, pressing ever forward, unimpeded by thoughts of how he had arrived. For Fei, this was the perfect protagonist for the American imagination. "How could ghosts gain a foothold in American cities?" Fei asked in 1944. "People move about like the tide, unable to form permanent ties with places, to say nothing of other people."[2] The nation's headlong surge into modernity had robbed it of something he could not quite describe. "In a world without ghosts, life is free and easy. American eyes can gaze straight ahead. But still I think they lack something and I do not envy their lives."[3]

Perhaps Fei overlooks the extent to which Clark Kent is indeed haunted by his extraterrestrial origins. As well, the figure of the ghost is hardly unique to Chinese tradition—there are plenty of ghosts, friendly and otherwise, floating through the American cultural imagination. But I am drawn to Fei's words because they suggest some of the unique anxieties of the Chinese migrant psyche. From his perspective, the immigrant's relationship with the immediate past could never be as untroubled as the carefree, forward-looking American's. After all, the new land's racial hierarchy would always remind them of their relative difference. So, while ghosts feature prominently throughout Chinese folklore, they came to assume a variety of new meanings once transported to America: a feeling of floating dislocation between worlds and traditions; a guilt-suppressing conscience; the nagging, ephemeral sense that something had been lost along the way. The supernatural tales from the old country became the raw materials for new immigrant mythologies, particularly the parables and tales describing the sense of forlorn attachment many felt toward the China they had left behind.

Fei, of course, was a college professor who could simply return to China; some of his countrymen were not so fortunate. The experience of the typical, working class Chinese immigrant, grappling at the phantom limb of a lost identity, was captured in Jon Lee's 1940 anthology *Chinese Tales Told in California*. In the late 1930s, Lee interviewed Chinese immigrants who had settled in San Francisco during the Exclusion era. He transcribed the stories that circulated throughout their communities. Many of these old immigrants still recalled minute details of the lives they had relinquished decades earlier when they crossed the Pacific; they clung to these folk tales as faithful reminders of a now-distant way of life. The majority of *Chinese Tales* rests on cobbled-together bits of familiar Chinese folklore, but two stories stand out as attempts to wrestle with the particularities of the immigrant experience in America. "It may perhaps seem strange for one born in America," the narrator of a story titled "The Shadow on the Wall" explains, "but in China it is a fact that everyone has heard about ghosts. Not only are ghosts a vital part of Chinese lives but they have influenced many people just as they have destroyed many people." The story describes a man who is so relentlessly pestered by a ghost that he eventually resorts to drawing a pistol on this unwanted visitor. (It does not work.)[4]

A story titled "The Sound of the Slippers" recounts a dutiful daughter's spectral visits from her late father. Each night, she is awoken by the sound of his slippers shuffling across the floor. She is unafraid and even ambivalent about this. But when she marries and moves to America, she is alarmed to discover that he has followed them across the Pacific. "She did not think it strange when she heard it in China. But in America!"[5] Does the shuffling sound of his ghostly slippers suggest the protection of an unseen guardian, or is it a reminder that she will never escape her past, despite her fresh start in a new world? For the immigrants whose stories comprise *Chinese Tales*, the presence of the ghost in American air spoke to the pressures, crazed visions, misplaced hopes, and sense of dislocation that comprised their daily lives.

Wong Wan-lee might as well have been one of the immigrants featured in Lee's *Chinese Tales*. The protagonist of H. T. Tsiang's final novel, *And China Has Hands* (1937), Wong is a lowly laundryman in New York's Chinatown who passes his days pondering the China he left behind as a child. One night, before falling asleep, Wong reads from *Strange Stories from a Chinese Studio*, a collection of Chinese ghost stories that had circulated since the mid-eighteenth century. It was a book many Chinese immigrants—like the ones who supplied Lee's *Chinese Tales*—had brought with them on their travels. The original *Stories* inverted the traditional attributes of the human and spirit world; the earthbound were portrayed as foolish and irrational while the apparitions were the arbiters of moral conscience. As Wong drifts toward sleep, a figure of an angel appears and laments Wong's displacement. "Now you are exiled in a savage land and living among uncivilized devils," she explains. "You are destined to meet many persecutions. But whenever troubles come to you, I will be with you and take you to safety."[6] Before he awakens, she assures him that they will one day reunite as humans. Her visit is both a prophecy and a promise of protection.

Over the last few chapters, we watched from afar as Tsiang desperately schemed for the type of literary celebrity he felt he deserved.

He had experienced some success in the late 1920s, publishing some of his first attempts at poetry in leftist newspapers. But his career stalled throughout the 1930s and he grew increasingly disenchanted with the publishing industry. There had never been a better time to write about China for American audiences, as demonstrated by the popularity of writers like Pearl Buck, Lin Yutang, Edgar Snow, Carl Crow, and Alice Tisdale Hobart. Ultimately it should not have been a surprise that major publishing houses showed little interest in Tsiang's work; his novels were experimental, ironic, and steeped in leftist themes. But the chilly reception from left-leaning publishers—publishers sympathetic to his politics and vision—seemed to break him. He began announcing his resentment at every turn, littering his self-published novels *China Red* and *The Hanging on Union Square* with references to his thwarted ambitions and personal failures. By the late 1930s, Tsiang had resigned himself to the realities of the business. Ideas circulated within a marketplace. He simply had to figure out how to engage that market—or expose its hypocrisy from within.

These were the stakes as Tsiang completed *And China Has Hands*, his first work to be handled by a professional publishing house. "About once in a Methuselah's lifetime there turns up a book which warrants the use of a shop-worn adjective—different," a note from the publisher, Robert Speller, enthuses. It would seem that Tsiang had finally evolved past the lukewarm praise of being "interesting." Now, he was "different." They continue: "*And China Has Hands* is different—and refreshingly so! It is quaint as its title. It is as naïve as a sub-deb, sophisticated as a chorus-girl."

One assumes that Robert Speller stopped him from excerpting his rejection slips as blurbs, as he had done with his previous two novels. But they could not prevent him from littering the dust jacket with evidence of his idiosyncratic personality. The back cover consists of a letter Tsiang wrote to his publisher explaining himself and his vision for the novel. Instead of an author photo, he provided a picture snipped from the *New York Times* depicting a Chinese woman holding a rifle. "Please print it at the back of the book jacket," he wrote on the inner flap, "and I am sure it will be more useful to show not only that China has hands, but (however limited) that China also has arms." It all feels quite whimsical and fun, up until Tsiang's jarring dedication page, in which he fantasizes of a world rid of the Japanese empire as well as all Japanese people.

Still, compared to the sarcasm and acerbic stridency that marked his previous novels, *And China Has Hands* initially comes across as a fairly earnest attempt at an immigrant tale. At first, Tsiang seems to offer himself as a translator or native informant, helpfully explaining the protagonist Wong Wan-Lee's name ("wan lee" means "ten-thousand fortunes") as well as the relative oddness of "Occidental" naming practices. Those unfamiliar with Tsiang's style could be forgiven for thinking that the novel's simple, straightforward prose and tone of cheery naivety were plays for clarity and comprehensibility. If Tsiang's literary career is remembered at all, it is usually because of *And China Has Hands*. In *The Cultural Front*, historian Michael Denning's definitive chronicle of proletarian art and literature, *And China Has Hands* appears in a survey of "ghetto pastoral" novels that pushed social realism to nightmarish ends. Set in predominantly immigrant ghettos like Little Italy, Bronzeville, the Lower East Side, or Chinatown, these proletarian "tales of terror" considered the fractures and dislocations of the 1930s as experienced in the city's bleak, often-forgotten ethnic enclaves.[7] After all, it might be argued that it was African Americans and immigrants who had first experienced the lows of the Depression; it is not as though they had shared in the nation's pre-crash prosperity. In Denning's view, these novels were valuable chronicles of everyday life in the city's obscure crevices, particularly since they were often penned by "plebeian writers" more interested in representing their lives and localities than rehashing the exaggerated, well-worn ghetto tropes demanded by the market.[8]

As Denning suggests, *And China Has Hands* scans as a fairly traditional tale of the immigrant's plight in the shadows of the harsh, corrupt metropolis. Wong's hardships certainly seem more grounded and relatable than the ambient evils and almost whimsical villains that lurked in Tsiang's previous works. That the ghetto pastoral treated city neighborhoods as quotidian rather than strange and exotic was especially significant for Tsiang, for the main reason *And China Has Hands* has survived to this day is its distinction as the first representation of Chinatown by a Chinese American writer. Tsiang's novel is mentioned in the literary critic Elaine Kim's seminal *Asian American Literature*, though her treatment is detached, bemused, and ultimately ambivalent, presumably because it was hard to describe exactly what kind of Asian American literary tradition this work anticipated.[9] In 2003, Ironweed Press republished the novel, elevating Tsiang's status as a visionary writer who foresaw the themes, ideas, and struggles that animated postwar Asian American literature.

And China Has Hands, then, has long been regarded as a valuable novel for contemporary readers because of its sociological insights. It supplies texture to literary history, whether it is a subgenre of 1930s literature or an emerging ethnic canon. But its complexities surpass this circumstance of timing. *And China Has Hands* also sits within a much stranger and intimate lineage as well—a lineage that aspired toward more abstract visions than the Cultural Front or 1960s identity politics. Perhaps Tsiang did intend to write a Chinatown tale and demystify the lives and experiences of Chinese immigrants. This was certainly one of its effects. Yet his erratic, self-published books and growing cynicism toward notions of community and belonging suggest a greater and more global ambition for *And China Has Hands*.

In the Introduction, we glimpsed a letter Tsiang had written to Theodore Dreiser in the winter of 1930, ostensibly to drum up support for his next book, *China Red*. In order to demonstrate that he was a young man of serious literary ambition, he took the opportunity to outline for Dreiser a novel "in preparation" titled *A Floating "Chinaman."* Tsiang described it as an "odyssey of a Chinese proletarian" told in four parts:

1. Life in old China's "Lower Depths".
2. Unconformity to the American Scene.
3. Inspirational regeneration from the Soviet Union.
4. Underground revolutionary work and heroic struggle of the Proletariat of the New China.[10]

Dreiser himself never wrote back. Instead, his secretary conveyed a few lines of lukewarm praise to Tsiang.

When Tsiang published *China Red* in 1931, he dutifully reprinted the secretary's words as Dreiser's own. Instead of a dedication page,

Tsiang offered his idol's supposed endorsement of this "moving and colorful" and occasionally "interesting" work. On the facing page, Tsiang listed his self-published books as well as two in preparation— *The Hanging on Union Square* and *Shanghai Newyork Moscow—An Odyssey of a Chinese Coolie*.

The most likely explanation is that *Shanghai Newyork Moscow* was just *A Floating "Chinaman"* shorn of its incendiary title. This book was never published, if it was completed at all. Its scale is awesome, mapping the flow of workers and capital across the globe. This would not have been a novel about China, the United States, or the Soviet Union but rather a remarkably ambitious consideration of all three at once. One imagines *Shanghai Newyork Moscow* as a story of how the ceaseless, global flows of ideas and things were rendering borders and discrete national identities meaningless—a tale of class, consciousness, and revolutionary struggle told from the perspective of a beleaguered worker, floating from city to city.

Although Tsiang never published this book, there are traces of its expansive vision throughout *And China Has Hands*. Perhaps we can assume that this was a scaled-down version of the "odyssey" he had been working on since the early 1930s. Like the sketch above, this was a novel about a Chinese "coolie" navigating his way through the era's ideological conflicts, including his profound "unconformity to the American Scene." While this "coolie" of *And China Has Hands* never ventures to China or the Soviet Union, his political awakening echoes that of the "floating Chinaman." The New York of *And China Has Hands* sat within a larger and impossibly capacious vision of global struggle he had described to Dreiser. For Tsiang, Chinatown was a part of town that deserved attention and dignity, which is why *And China Has Hands* could comfortably be read as a ghetto pastoral novel or a Chinatown novel. But he had larger scales in mind, as well. Chinatown, Chinese laundries, emerging communities of Chinese American immigrants: these were the local manifestations of global struggles.

When the first waves of Chinese immigrants began arriving along the West Coast in the 1840s, they were essential contributors to America's rapidly expanding economy. Their supply appeared to be endless and it was cheaper to transport these workers from across the Pacific than to recruit and retain their local, white counterparts. Upon arriving, the Chinese were quickly disabused of any dreams they had of partaking in the promise of the "gold mountain"—a grim reality Tsiang had explored in his earlier works. They took whatever work was available to them—usually physically demanding work in the mines and on the railroads.

Within a few decades, however, the Chinese laborer became the readymade scapegoat for a sputtering economy. The Chinese, who had originally been invited to these shores by American enterprise, were suddenly recast as a wily menace. In 1882, spurred by white working class discontent along the West Coast, the Chinese Exclusion Act was passed—the first immigration policy to target a specific national or ethnic group. They were portrayed as an imported scourge and the only solution was to close the nation's ranks. China—still debilitated by the uneven treaties that resulted after the Opium Wars—could do nothing on behalf of its workers.

Exclusion troubled the liberal mind, often because of its similarity to the institution of slavery. Writing in the *Annals of the American Academy of Political and Social Science* in 1909, the immigration lawyer Max Kohler questioned why the gains of the postbellum era had not extended to the Chinese and Japanese. The contradictions of a nation beholden to both slavery and the Declaration of Independence *should* have unraveled in the nineteenth century yet the Exclusion Act continued unabated. For Kohler the greatest injury resulted in casting the diverse Chinese as a single "class:"

> [T]here was instituted a constant reign of terror for all Chinese or alleged Chinese residents, laborers or non-laborers. Their liberty is constantly jeopardized by harsh and oppressive laws, and their property is accordingly also endangered under the sentiment thereby engendered that they are beyond the protection of our laws.[11]

Kohler concluded that the Chinese were "persona non grata,"[12] likening their plight to African American enslavement. Yet describing them this way—as "unwelcome"—failed to capture the textured precariousness of the Chinese presence in the United States in the early twentieth century. They were not only unwelcome; because of labor practices that kept them in perpetual debt, they could not leave, either. So long as the contradictions of Exclusion were contained within the nation, the situation of Chinese immigrants registered as little more than a nuisance.

Within a global context, however, Exclusion represented a stain upon the American creed—it made a mockery of what Kohler described as "our boasted American civilization." The 1905–1906 boycott of American goods in China temporarily highlighted China's concern with the treatment of Chinese immigrants. But China's weakened state made a return to equitable treatment impossible.[13] When the Chinese finally gained full citizenship rights in 1943, after a series of Congressional hearings reexamining the Exclusion Laws, it was largely attributed to wartime perception. Reporting from the hearings, the *Far Eastern Survey* surmised that the repeal was "intended as a final barrier against Japanese propaganda that this is a racial war."[14] While the repeal would also aid in "eliminating discrimination against the Chinese," this concern, too, owed more to the cementing of postwar relations between the nations than the conditions of the immigrants themselves.

These shifts describe the tenuous and always-contested position of the Chinese in the American imagination. During the Exclusion era, these scattered populations of Chinese found themselves trapped within a contradiction, and it was within the self-sustaining, self-incubating confines of the nation's Chinatowns that they forged new notions of community and citizenship. It was the site where their pasts—their relation to another land, government, or system of belief—could do them no harm. For some, the insularity of Chinatown provided a safe haven or a distraction from the rigors of the American experience; for others, it meant a retreat from ghosts, real and imagined.

And China Has Hands was not Tsiang's first glimpse into the lives of Chinese immigrants. In 1928, he had published "Chinaman, Laundryman," a poem written from the perspective of a lonesome laundry worker who had ventured to America in search of a better life. Predictably, he is dismissed as a "Chinaman" and "Laundryman," though even these epithets suggest a dignity that has been denied to him. "Don't call me 'man!' / I am worse than a slave,"[15] he moans, uncertain whether he will ever be reunited with his wife, who remains in China. "Only the almighty 'Dollar' knows!"[16]

The Chinatown laundry was an ideal site for thinking through the relationship between global economics and transpacific migration. Besides work in the mines and on the railroads, the early Chinese immigrants also established themselves as part of the frontier's emergent service economy, primarily as cooks and laundryman. These were formative encounters: caricatures and stereotypes of buck-toothed Chinese laundrymen or steaming piles of chop-suey persist to this day. The historian John Kuo Wei Tchen has described the laundryman as "the major occupation of Chinese in the United States," in literal, economic terms as well as within the figurative space of America's cultural imagination. The Chinese laundryman has been "a seemingly ever present fixture of the urban streetscape," the unintelligible, pig-tailed "Charlie" squawking "no tickee, no shirtee" at his bemused customers.[17] As we shall see in the next chapter, even comparatively conservative China-sympathizing writers like Pearl Buck and Lin Yutang would eventually turn their attentions to the immigrant laundryman as an embodiment of the Chinese American struggle.

In the years between "Chinaman, Laundryman" and *And China Has Hands*, the Chinese laundrymen of New York had organized themselves into a robust political community. In the early 1930s, the city had over 3,500 Chinese laundries. White competitors lobbied local politicians for protection and, in 1933, a local ordinance was passed demanding prohibitive registration fees and making citizenship a requirement to own and operate a laundry. Historians Renqiu Yu and Peter Kwong have written about the Chinese Hand Laundry Alliance (CHLA), a grassroots organization that formed to protect laundry workers. The CHLA collaborated with sympathetic American lawyers to overturn the rule and preserve their livelihoods. While the initial impetus for coming together was to oppose local ordinances, these workers soon began to understand their actions in transnational terms. The CHLA would become a prominent, left-leaning, nationalist organization, weighing in on everything from the Japanese invasion of China to the injustice of the Chinese Exclusion Act. They came to understand the relationship between China's global standing and their situation in America: their slogan, "To save China, to save ourselves," captured the broad context of their struggle.[18] Yu argues that the members of the CHLA also understood themselves as distinct from the American proletariat or working class, owing to residual memories of working class xenophobia, from the Chinese Exclusion Act to the resentful aggressions of white laundrymen.[19]

Tsiang had supported the CHLA throughout the 1930s, which might explain the more textured version of the Chinese laundryman that constitutes *And China Has Hands*. The life of the Chinese laundryman was described, in the sociologist Paul Siu's haunting mid-century ethnographic survey, as "a study of social isolation."[20] Just as the spirit who first visits his dreams exists between two worlds, so too does the laborer Wong, adrift among forces he cannot comprehend. *And China Has Hands* gently parodies the by-the-bootstraps trajectory familiar to American middlebrow readers of the 1930s, as the young and idealistic Wong lunges for the upward mobility promised to every honest laborer. In the first chapter Wong describes the complicated web of American laws the immigrant must navigate. Although he is already an American citizen—a status inherited from his father—he still faced harassment at the hands of a corrupt, overzealous immigration officer who demands a bribe. "It had cost Wong Wan-Lee ninety dollars for the passage to America, but two thousand dollars for the other expense. Why? He never talked of it and no one was supposed to ask him about it."[21] He eventually pays the officer off and cobbles together enough money to open his own laundry. But he encounters an "unwritten law among the Chinese in America"[22] prohibiting two laundries from operating on the same block. What Wong soon realizes is that legal status guarantees very little to an immigrant in his position. Perhaps these were the "persecutions" Wong's spirit-friend had described.

As Wong's spiritual guardian predicted, his laundry quickly becomes a target for both mischievous street kids and thuggish bullies. Children playing in front of his laundry yell through the window, "Where is your pigtail? Chin, Chin, Chinaman!" The chanting is incessant, and Wong tries appeasing them with chewable lychee seeds. "It's opium," one child exclaims. "The Chinaman is trying to use poison to kill us." Once they try the seeds and realize he is not, they clamor for more, their chants of "Chin, Chin, Chinaman!" now lobbed with affection.[23]

A Chinese girl speaking "smart English" shoos the kids away and introduces herself as Pearl Chang, chiding Wong for humoring his attackers: "You are not an American. When they call you names, you lose nothing."[24] But Wong hopes to win them over with kindness: "The Chinese ambassador in Washington feeds those old savages at big feasts to make friends for China: I, Ambassador Wong Wan-Lee, here in the laundry feed these little savages with Lee Chee nuts, and these little savages will become my messengers and carry messages to their old savages, and their old savages will become my customers by and by."[25] As the newly arrived immigrant unfamiliar with America's culture and informal customs—and as a proxy for Tsiang himself—Wong's optimism seems exaggerated and naïve.

While Wong quickly becomes smitten with Chang, he encounters a peculiar array of other Chinatown characters as well: con men, opportunistic academics, crooked government inspectors, leftist agitators and two cousins—Fat Wong and Skinny Wong—who kill each other over a loan.[26] There is a bumbling, overeducated traveling salesman and loan shark pursuing his PhD at Columbia University on the side.[27] (The title of his thesis: "How to Sell China More Profitably.") One Chinatown figure who actually offers Wong useful guidance is an old grocer who visits his shop. His biography is a typical one: "He said that as a young boy in China he was told that America was full of gold and one could pick as much as he liked."[28] Upon arrival he was ridiculed for his queue, which he maintained out of respect for the Manchu Dynasty. But assimilation into American culture, even its frontier outskirts, proved difficult. He worked in a goldmine and then later helped build the transcontinental railroad. "He was sorry that he had not gone back to China with Dr. Sun Yat-sen, then, and become a revolutionist." He leaves Wong with one last piece of advice: "Beware, while you are still young! America is an evil land and once you sink in you can never get out."[29] Haunted by the conditions of a homeland he will never see again, the old man's regrets echo the warning of Wong's watchful ghost.

Wong's relationship to Chinatown is initially that of an alien observer. What distinguishes Wong from his comparatively assimilated Chinatown neighbors is his bemused and at times reluctant attitude toward America. The sociologist Paul Siu's early work on the lives of Chinese laundryman described them as dislocated "sojourners" who were usually unable or unwilling to relinquish their ties to the homeland. Tsiang appears perplexed by the way this community orbits an amorphous notion of Chineseness, all the while appearing uniformly "Chinese" to an outsider. Wong, after all, comes across as a stranger to the nascent Chinese American sensibility. He does not yet recognize Chinatown's duality—it is a real place filled with laundries, restaurants, civic associations, and tenements where immigrants live and work; it is a lurid fantasy of opium dens and white slavery that informs how many Americans view and understand the Chinese. At one point he notices a crowd of white people filing out of a "so-called Chinese temple" and realizes they are there on a "slumming tour" of Chinatown. The tourists are titillated but disappointed: "No Hatchet Men! No Tong Wars! And they themselves came back alive!"[30] The laundryman Wong remains poor in part because he refuses (and is unable) to indulge this exotic curiosity in China.

Chang, on the other hand, embraces it; when Wong sees the slumming tour, he dismisses them as "all Pearl Changs," drawn to Chinatown's most superficial delights.[31] Despite Wong's obvious attraction to her, Chang comes across as banal and uncritical, spending all her time reading the tabloids and dreaming of becoming a movie star.[32] She, like the tourists in search of the Chinatown slums, abides by a misshapen vision of Chinese authenticity. When Wong cooks dinner for her, Chang is disappointed by the absence of "the Chinese national dishes" like "Chop Suey,"[33] an invention of Chinese American immigrants.[34] If Wong represents an innocent abroad, whose pursuit of the American Dream is doomed to fail, then Chang, too, stands in for a set of structures and prejudices beyond her control. The daughter of a Chinese father and a Southern "Negress," her life indexes the curious contradictions of America's racial hierarchy. "In the South, Negroes are not allowed to ride in the same street-car with white, but Chinese are. Black children are not allowed to go to school with white children, but Chinese children are."[35] The Chinese presence disrupts the prevailing understanding of race as a black or white affair, a situation that Chang herself embodies. "If a conductor sees a Chinese in a black men's section, the Chinese is put with the white men." Rather than challenging the binary, however, Chang lamented how many Chinese in the South simply clung to their comparative privilege: "Because of these things, some Chinese think they are better than black men."[36] Or, as Tsiang lamented, acceptance of this racial order merely resulted in more infighting: "When an underdog was crushed by an upperdog, the underdog dared not do anything to stop this upperdog but picked out the bottom-dog for revenge."[37]

In the South, Chang is Chinese. Once in New York, however, her identity shifts. Despite Chang's self-identification as a Chinese woman—she was "every inch a Chinese"—her boss at a Chinatown restaurant fires her because of her "curly hair" and "heavy lips." "We Chinese are dark enough and don't want to become any darker. As I am a member of the Chinese Nationalist Party, I have to respect the national race-purity. You fooled me! You have spoiled my business on account of it. You have scorned my racial theory!"[38] Chang might have been too "black" for Chinatown, but to whites, she was authentically "Chinese." At one point, she pays her bills by modeling at an art school. Wong recoils in horror at the thought that Chang allows these "foreign devils [to] look and meditate."[39] For Wong, her disgrace reflects that of their ailing nation, China:

> There were people who could be bought with money, but not Pearl Chang! Not only her own reputation but that of her race was involved. Not only her fellow-countrymen in this country, and the four hundred millions in China above the ground, but also the millions and billions under the ground, as well as the billions and billions of the future generations who are now in Heaven waiting for the opportunity to come to this earth.[40]

Of course this is Wong's perspective, as the protective and somewhat paternalistic Chinese patriot. Chang does not have the luxury for such consciousness. This is an issue of survival and, if anything, she is delighted that the school "earnestly desired a Chinese girl" and that she is recognized as such—as Chinese.[41]

Where did Chang get her ideas about Chinese identity? When she first arrives in Chinatown, she is disappointed that nothing conforms to her expectations. It turns out Chang's first name—shared with Tsiang's favorite target, Pearl Buck—is no coincidence. Chang reveals herself as an eager, gullible consumer of Buck's popular books and movies about China. "She had seen things about China in the movies and read things about China in novels. She had heard things about China from her white teachers and white schoolmates. She had a general idea of how a Chinaman looked."[42] Why, for example, had Wong cut off his queue, "so that he looked like most Americans?" "Would it not be nice if he kept his pigtail, as she saw all her countrymen with pigtails in the movies?"[43]

These popular images of China call to mind a conversation two characters had near the end of Tsiang's previous novel, *The Hanging on Union Square*, as they griped over how little the typical American—represented here by Chang—knew about China. They blamed Buck, with one of the characters even likening her work to prostitution. "You know—the woman who made money from her Oriental novels! Here is another of her hypocrisies: She talks about 'Earth' and 'Soil' a lot, but I think what her publishers gave her as royalties was the same thing that I have received from my customers—dollars."[44]

Who would disabuse Pearl Chang of her illusions? Buck was not the only author who shaped Chang's views on China. She had also encountered "a Chinese fellow who was trying to sell his own book" in the cafeteria of her school. An awful writer with but four pennies to his name, he was still exceptional to Pearl as "the first Chinese man that she had ever met"—the flesh-and-bones rejoinder to Buck's fictional, pigtailed farmer.[45]

They venture outside. As a way of testing his writerly skills, she asks him to compose a poem saying something nice about her. His reply:

> Slowly they walked through the park,
> It was not light and it was not dark.
> Slowly they walked through the dark,
> It was not light and it was a park.[46]

He continues to regale Pearl with the most banal minutiae of his career and his true identity comes into focus. This sad sack is Tsiang himself:

> My first novel, *China Red*, has been endorsed in the Soviet Union as "a valuable miniature of a great movement and the voice of a new China approaching," but the fakers here in American condemned it with " . . . we should not be attracted by its fascinating title and the seeming sympathy of the author."
>
> I kept quiet and had my second novel, *The Hanging on Union Square*, published. It was first praised as "an interesting experimental novel about the unemployed. Perhaps the first novel with a proletarian theme written in expressionistic technique."
>
> Then the fakers suddenly changed their minds and condemned the book with "he is not much of a writer and his chief literary influence is the decadent Gertrude Stein."[47]

Self-consciousness was one thing. But writing himself *into* his stories signaled a more extreme kind of desperation. His cameo appearance in his previous novel had been brief and fleeting, pestering his protagonist, Mr. Nut, into buying one of his books. As we discussed in the last chapter, these moments of self-awareness suggested Tsiang's mounting disappointments. He had tried in vain to bring his transpacific perspectives to the world of proletarian art and literature. Ignored by publishers and readers alike, he stepped into his own fictional worlds as a way of reminding himself—a way of telling anyone passing through these pages—that he indeed existed. There is a desperate quality to this encounter with Chang. It is a moment of reckoning. He will no longer be "kept quiet"; the fellow travelers whose approval he once craved are now little more than "fakers."

At this point Chang is barely present in the conversation; we all bear silent witness to Tsiang's rant. "The fellow again told her how in spite of the crookedness of those fakers he had succeeded in publishing his works and distributing sixteen thousand copies, and how he, as a proletarian writer, was proud to publish and sell his own books."[48] She is puzzled, silent, and slightly envious. While Tsiang the character revels in his accomplishment, Tsiang the author gently ridicules his proxy's rigid, self-important manner. "The fellow talked 'ism' after 'ism,' 'fight' after 'fight.' It seemed to Pearl Chang that he had not the least Chinese flavor."[49] If proletarian critics rued the self-important, condescending, bourgeois novelist for placing the individual author above the interests of the people, what better gesture of solidarity than descending into the maze of one's novel and modestly joining in their struggle? Tsiang enters into the novel as a character capable of being judged. He does not stand above the common laborer, even laborers of his own creation. At a rally near the close of the novel, Tsiang takes to the streets alongside his creations: "The author of *Poems of the Chinese Revolution*, *China Red* and *The Hanging on Union Square*, also participated, for he thought that, since he had written so much about revolution, he had better do something about it. And picketing is a revolution in a small way."[50] He relishes this moment, for the cafeteria they are picketing had once barred him from peddling his books to fellow diners.

Tsiang, after all, is probably the most luckless character we encounter. "Wherever he went, Wong Wan-Lee saw this fellow with a worn-out brief-case bulky with books."[51] Wong encounters Tsiang at a public debate about the economics of proletarian literature, where Tsiang, a self-identified proletarian artist, is trying to sell his books, *China Red* and *The Hanging on Union Square*. A "Bureaucrat" kicks Tsiang out of the lecture hall, dismissing these self-published novels as trash: "You know nothing about big words, you know nothing about long sentences!"[52] He bullies Tsiang with a string of questions that cut to the heart of his professional insecurities: "Why can you not get a respectable publisher? Why can you not get a Guggenheim scholarship? Have you ever been to Hollywood?"[53] The criticisms of his work that had previously appeared as blurbs and reprinted rejection slips have now been integrated into the novel itself.

Wong witnesses this moment "humiliation" and invites Tsiang to his laundry. Tsiang is still indignant: "In Soviet Russia, they give new writers encouragement. Here they only look for big names." After Wong feeds him, the struggling writer offers to repay his goodwill by working in his laundry. "Since in this fellow's book the word 'workers' was repeated so often, Wong Wan-Lee let the fellow work," pointing him toward a pile of dirty socks. The writer makes good on his promise, grimacing at the odor.[54]

Of course there is an element of self-pity here, as Tsiang seems incapable of awakening even his own characters. Chang remains unmoved by his screeds. Instead, it is Wong who shows her what it actually means to claim Chinese identity. He teaches her about foot-binding[55] and the proper way to drink tea.[56] At one point, Wong censures her for putting their budding relationship on hold, unfurling an entire history of Chinese dynastic infighting to emphasize his point. They must stick together: "Then another kind of savage came . . . Their eyes were blue like the eyes of the fisherbirds . . . Their hair was yellow or even red and they looked like the devils one sees in Hell in a Buddhist temple."[57] From here Wong pins the bulk of Chinese suffering on these outside intruders. Frustrated by their inability to outsmart the Chinese, these outsiders conspired to destroy the fabric of their society. They "sold Chinese fancy goods . . . and opium. They sucked Chinese blood. They ate Chinese flesh."[58]

Wong's rant inspires something in Chang. She begins to embrace her heritage, discarding "a small picture of a white movie actress" she kept in a locket.[59] She begins to blame the Chinese for allowing themselves to be victimized by the Japanese, and she encourages Wong to eat more meat, for "meats make a man brutal and able to kill!"[60]

The unacknowledged backdrop of *And China Has Hands* is the formation of the CHLA and the radicalization of Chinatown. When Wong's laundry business fails, the couple ends up working at a cafeteria together, and in the book's final scene, they unite to protest against their employer. The boss fashions himself an "Internationalist," although within the logic of capitalism, this merely means that he plays his Chinese and white employees against each other to stoke the collective work ethic. By creating artificial competition between them, he energizes the workplace. Eventually the workers begin to recognize their boss' contradictions—"He advertised in a radical paper that he was a radical and he advertised in Hearst papers that he was a true American and a friend of Hitler"[61]—and they organize in front of the cafeteria.

All the workers in this cafeteria paraded.
The workers in the other cafeterias joined:
The white, the yellow and the black,
The ones between yellow and black,
The ones between yellow and white,
And the ones between white and black.
They were marching on, singing their song:
The song of the white,
The song of the yellow,
The song of the black,
The song of the ones who were neither yellow nor white,
The song of the ones who were neither yellow nor black,
The song of the ones who were neither black nor white,
And the song that knows nothing of white, yellow or black.[62]

As a proletarian writer challenging the strict binary of black and white, Tsiang dreams of a new class consciousness, where the Chinese won't merely function as middlemen. By creating a half-Chinese, half-black character in Chang—perhaps the first time this specific expression of interracialism had been explored in American literature, and certainly the first by an Asian American author—he drew attention to this condition of being in-between.[63]

At the rally—and seemingly apropos of nothing—a Japanese assassin shoots Wong. As he bleeds to death on the street, Wong searches for a reason why he has been targeted. Was the assassin an agent of a Chinatown gang seeking revenge for Wong's refusal to submit to their extortionist codes? Or perhaps the gunman acted in the interest of the boss and in the preservation of capitalistic order? As Wong passes, he takes one last parting shot: "My dear angel, the Chinese now have one-fifth of the whole Chinese population and one-sixth of the whole Chinese territory. In the years to come they shall have more, more and endlessly more and as I'm the one who works for my rice and I'm a Chinese, so I'm the boss and I'm the owner!"[64] He closes with a poem imploring China to unite, either around Communism or not, in order to vanquish his death and turn back the Japanese aggressors: China's four hundred million customers, workers, and heathens have now become a force of "eight hundred million hands."[65]

The explanation for Wong's assassination is notably peculiar. It turns out that the shooting is retaliation for something that occurred entirely outside of the text. As the book ends, Tsiang matter-of-factly explains, "Wong Wan-Lee had picketed the Japanese Consulate on 5th Ave. a few days ago with thousands and thousands of New York Chinese and Americans against the Japanese invasion in China."[66] There is no prior mention of this event, nor was there any hint as to the intensity of Wong's anti-Japanese sentiments. By withholding this key narrative driver, it is as if Tsiang is dismissing his own novel—as if the point of it all was never the drama contained inside these pages so much as the real-life struggles just beyond the frame. Just pages earlier, in his final appearance in *And China Has Hands*, Tsiang had confronted the audience as well as his publisher, breaking down not only the illusion of authorship but calling attention to the entire market of commodities as well: "By now, our author had secured a publisher for his fourth book, and the publisher was taking a deep interest in observing the moves of his writer—hoping the author would get his head clubbed so his picture would appear in the papers and, by-productingly, his books be mentioned."[67]

This—*And China Has Hands*—is his fourth book and he must do whatever he can to sell it, even if it means getting clubbed in the head. His frustration is palpable: after writing so much about revolution and seeing little impact, his prolonged appearance here feels like harassment, a literal kind of intervention. Still, none of the other characters relate to him, or treat him with any real dignity. He is marginal and broken, floating on the fringes of his own book. But he sees something just out of his characters' focus:

> Poor Wong Wan-Lee, who had made no ten thousand fortunes, was a failure; but his cousin Wong Lung had made a million and had become the hero of The Good Earth—Horatio Alger!
> Poor Pearl C, who had become no star, was a failure; but her cousin Pearl B, had married her boss, a publisher.[68]

His characters are ultimately doomed, for Tsiang has created them this way, as the far less successful cousins of Buck and her far more relatable characters. He would never surpass Buck, her publisher-husband Richard Walsh, and their cohort—the realization of this had pushed his work toward strange, new extremes and moments of self-reckoning.

Earlier in this chapter, we revisited the letter Tsiang had written Dreiser prior to the publication of *China Red* detailing a never-to-be-completed version of his fourth novel. At the time, we speculated that *And China Has Hands* was all that remained of this gargantuan project. But the novel's final pages, so strange and unpredictable, chart other possibilities. It is as though Tsiang, as much a presence here as his fictional lovers, wanted his own life to be read as a text. Maybe Tsiang himself was the "floating Chinaman." The novel's different sections corresponded to chapters of his own life: he had started out in "old China's 'Lower Depths.'" He had come to America and found himself unable to "conform." He had drawn inspiration from the Soviet Union. Now, all that remained: a return to "New China," where the dangerous work of revolution awaited.

What did it mean for Tsiang to fail? In some ways, his unflattering representation of himself in *And China Has Hands* might have seemed inevitable, given the negative blurbs and moments of playful self-mockery in *China Red* and *The Hanging on Union Square*. But there was a more desperate feeling of abjection here. This was not a fleeting appearance to remind the reader of the toiling, penniless author somewhere out there. He remained on the edges of *And China Has Hands* until its final pages, when we learn of the doom that awaits his hero and heroine. Poor Wong and Chang, Tsiang writes, have fallen short.

It is a strange and affecting moment. Tsiang's previous poems and novels had been filled with martyrs, revolutionaries, and utopian schemers, all of them rendered with a touch of sympathy. On what grounds was Tsiang judging Wong and Chang—his own creations—"failures?" How did their failures stand in for Tsiang's evaporating sense of self?

The historian Scott Sandage has argued that the principle drivers behind American attitudes toward failure have been economic: the growth of capitalism and the emancipation of slaves. While broad categories of success and failure had always existed, Sandage argues that the distinction between these two markers became inflected

with a new, zero-sum vitality after the Civil War. Markets, meritocracy, the American Dream: all of these contests presumed winners
and losers, arranged along a continuum from the morally fit to the
fatally flawed.[69] Tsiang certainly diagnosed his situation in economic
terms. At a basic level, he was a frustrated writer like all the other
frustrated writers, his folder of rejection slips fattening by the year.
But Tsiang was also different. He seemed convinced that his status
and perspective as Chinese should help rather than hurt him. He
internalized the disinterest of major publishers and fellow travelers
alike, reading their rejection as outright scorn. At first, his brush with
failure compelled him to scrutinize the rules of polite fiction and tear
them apart. His self-aware poetry and *China Red* suggested an ambitious writer who sought to push the accepted limits of artistic form.
But by the time of *The Hanging on Union Square* and *And China Has
Hands*, failure had driven him to revenge. Recall his desire to write
a book like *The Good Earth* "but much better."[70] In fact, he barely
made it onto the playing field long enough to properly lose. These
later works feel hypersensitive to his status as Kohler's proverbial
"persona non grata." He is conscious of his exclusion from the games
people played. He luxuriates in being outside.

All of this gives his final failure a very modern feel. The theorist
Judith Halberstam has built on Sandage's work by exploring the contemporary aesthetics of failure, particularly as it relates to capitalism and its stock characters: "winners and losers, gamblers and risk
takers, con men and dupes."[71] For Halberstam, there is a virtue in
choosing the lost cause: choosing to fail might illuminate the playing
field, its rules and values. Who knows what other designs for life begin to seem possible once we lose ourselves in "art without markets,
drama without a script, narrative without progress."[72]

These visions of artistic relativism—art that refused and rebuked
and commented on its own reception—were unavailable to Tsiang.
Even if he was drawn to avant-garde experimentation, he would
never, as an overeager, Gertrude Stein-aping "Chinaman," be invited
to stand among them. Even if his idols in the world of proletarian
art had set out to expose the ways in which the cultural elites reproduced their own bourgeois values, they were still, ultimately, beholden to a programmatic vision. When Tsiang took the proletarians

themselves to task for their scaled-down markets and faddishness, he was choosing a spectacular, showy kind of failure. Tsiang was writing in the 1930s at a time when America itself—the dreamy, triumphalist America that Sandage describes above—appeared to be wounded and imperiled. How could his writings not lunge for different standards of hope and success?

When Tsiang described Wong and Chang as failures, it was because they fell far short of their "cousins," who had become America's darlings. Wong was no "millionaire," unlike his cousin Wang Lung, the rags-to-riches hero of *The Good Earth*. Chang never became a "star," unlike her cousin Buck. In Halberstam's view, the embrace of failure relieves the artist from the oppressive obligations of everyday life: it is the power of negative thinking unleashed.[73] By positioning his characters in relation to *The Good Earth*, Tsiang was conceding defeat. But he was also calling attention to the ways in which Buck's immovable work—a masterpiece of by-the-bootstraps optimism—flattered a rotten value system.

A history of failure is an index of what once seemed impossible. As the sculptor Joel Fisher writes: "Failure itself draws a distinction. Where failure occurs, there is the frontier. It marks the edge of the acceptable or possible, a boundary fraught with possibilities."[74] But this perspective usually lies far beyond what we are capable of seeing. In the moment, there is little more than the sting of refusal. He continues: "There are times when pain blocks a conscious recognition, when our failure taints our own abilities and what we and others expect of ourselves. It is generally felt that we 'own' our failures in a different sense than our successes. We share success; failure, no matter what, is more private."[75] The hopeful version of this is that Tsiang courted this failure and that his novels were grand, public acts of martyrdom. Still, there are limits to reading Tsiang's forlorn, lonely and "floating" life as one of resistance.

Tsiang himself never achieved any success comparable to Buck and her coterie of China-watchers. Throughout the twentieth century, the term for these China experts was "China hands." Maybe this explains his final novel's peculiar title. The 1930s was a peak era for American commentary on China. China had hands—too many, perhaps—and he was not allowed to stand among them.

Tsiang would not make it back to China. In fact, he would fight tooth and nail to stay in the United States.

In the next chapter, we will consider some of the debates that took place within the Chinese American community in the 1930s and 1940s around returning to China. While few of these young students and strivers shared Tsiang's radical politics, many were drawn to the possibility of bringing their American educations to bear on Chinese problems. As we shall see, even Buck and her collaborators would begin writing sympathetic tales about Chinatowns, Chinese laundrymen, and Chinese Americans, as a way of imagining a more perfect union between China and the United States.

Given the career arc that resulted in *And China Has Hands*, Tsiang's final published work might just be his strangest, which is saying a lot. In August 1938 Tsiang self-published a play titled *China Marches On*, a propagandistic attempt to generate interest in the Chinese resistance effort and forge a spiritual bond between the people of China, Japan, and the United States. The play begins in 1915 with Papa and Mama Chung and their two-year-old baby bracing themselves for an invasion by the Japanese. They hastily christen the child Mu-Lan, after the Chinese folk hero, and agree to split up. Mama stays behind, essentially sacrificing herself to the brutal sexual advances of the Japanese soldiers so that Papa can escape and deposit Mu-Lan at the "foreign mission house."[76] As he and Mu-Lan flee and the lustful soldiers arrive, Mama comforts herself: "My dear daughter, Mu-Lan Chung, Live! Revenge!"[77]

Each subsequent scene reveals the fate of one of these three characters some twenty years later. We pick up Mu-Lan's story in 1927, when she is sixteen. Miss Drinkwater, a well-meaning American missionary who embraces the principles of moderation to a comical extreme, has adopted her. ("My family name, Drinkwater, gives me a good motto:—If one drinks too much milk, one might become too fat. If one drinks too much liquor, one might go crazy. Drink water!"[78]) Her philosophy of consenting to "God's will" is lost on the fiery Mu-Lan, whose young lover has been killed by Chinese collaborators with the Japanese regime. Eventually, her will grows too strong and she abandons the polite domesticity of Drinkwater's home to join the Chinese resistance.

When Tsiang reintroduces Papa, he has relocated to a modest but happy life in America, where he runs a laundry with his adopted son, Johnnie. Another example of Tsiang's attempt to confound the color line, Johnnie is white yet speaks fluent Chinese. "Do you remember the reporter who was here a week ago?" he jokes with Papa. "You, a Chinese; and I, a white man. That's a novelty."[79] Soon, Johnnie leaves to fight in China as part of the United States military. Meanwhile, Mama lives in Japan with her adopted Japanese son, Nikochi. The son's father, the Japanese soldier who brought her back to Japan "as his prize" has since passed away. But she continues to suffer this man's cruelty—he blinded her years before in a fit of rage.

Before her son departs for the Japanese army, they talk of this war's enormous stakes. "If the Mikado will not take China, the white men will," Mama remarks. "Yellow space should belong to the yellow race." Nikochi protests that such pan-Asian essentialism is overrated; instead, he vows to seek revenge on his mother's behalf by joining the Japanese army and sabotaging their efforts. "Go, join the army!" Mama pleads. "Be a spy! Destroy from within!"[80]

Inevitably, Johnnie, Mu-Lan, and Nikochi—each fighting for a different nation's military—meet one another in China. Each of them dies at the hands of the Japanese. Nikochi races to the Chinese camp to alert them of a Japanese attack, and as he and Mu-Lan discover that they share the same mother, a bomb detonates and wounds him. As they lay dying, Johnnie arrives on the scene to join the Chinese resistance. Mu-Lan orders him to shoot her, to save her from the same brutal Japanese troops who raped her mother, but he is shot dead before he can help her. As the play closes, all three children rise from the grave to rouse the crowd in unison: "March On! March On! China Marches On!" In that moment, these three nations of the transpacific unite.[81]

China Marches On is a confounding work, bereft of the bewitching humor and self-awareness of his novels. Where the deaths of Nut and Wong could be read as acts of martyrdom or sacrifice, the final massacre of *China Marches On* only portends an ambivalent doom. Strangest of all: there is a line of actual *praise* from C. T. Wang of the Chinese Embassy, printed on the cover. (Some things never change, however. The praise—"Interesting and instructive!"—is tepid at best.)

Did *China Marches On* signal a shift in Tsiang's sensibilities, or was something else behind it?

In 1940 Tsiang was nearly deported back to China, where he was sure to face government persecution. The United States government claimed that the terms of his visa had lapsed when he failed to enroll in any classes from 1938 to 1939. Tsiang explained that a series of illnesses had kept him away from school, but that he was technically still a student. He suspected that he was being targeted for his revolutionary poetry. While his case snaked its way through the American courts, he was detained on Ellis Island in New York.

The possibility of repatriation did not slow his zeal for writing: he could often be found in one of the facility's large halls with a typewriter balanced on a tiny desk. During his detention, which appears to have been for about a year and a half, he returned to the lively, bizarre poetic style of his early work. In December 1940, Tsiang began writing Rockwell Kent, a progressive writer and artist who had taken an interest in his case. Kent even liked Tsiang's style, assuring him that his books "are much finer than any of your endorsers have stated."[82]

Tsiang often went to great pains to amuse Kent with lewd double-entendres, rambling marginalia and doodles, strange poems, and a recipe for chop suey.[83] He mailed him a thirty-page poem called "The Pear," its cover page adorned with fragmentary scribbles, including a request to make sure that the letters Kent wrote on his behalf were "Diplomatic + Humorous."[84] Many of Tsiang's Ellis Island poems explored the experience of detention, like the desperately grim "He is Not Worried," wherein a hopeless migrant smashes his head against the wall. One of the early letters included a short poem titled "Top-Side," which mocked the intrusive entry interview awaiting new immigrants. The interviewee is Wong Wan-lee—the protagonist of *And China Has Hands*—as a six-year-old boy. The interviewer asks young Wong a series of questions about his parents in order to verify that he is indeed their son and therefore eligible for American citizenship. When quizzed about his parents' sleeping habits, he explains that his father slept "sometimes left side, sometimes right side." The correct answer, according to the father: he preferred his wife's "top-side."[85]

Despite his irrepressible sense of humor, Tsiang's early correspondences with Kent suggest a man deeply fearful of deportation. And they allow for the possibility that *China Marches On* was merely a hyperpatriotic gesture designed to appease the American government. In January 1941 Tsiang wrote Kent a paranoid letter detailing the progress of his case. He feared that the immigration officials would use his old work against him.

> I hope and still hoping. But I doubt. For They must have gone to Library of Congress to look over all my books and what conclusion they would have made can be imagined.
>
> My latest work, "China Marches On" . . . is a Common cause. Otherwise I would not have taken the trouble to get endosement (sic) from Mrs. Roosevelt. These can be explained in an American saying "I laid all the cards on the table." Well, they can be cruel but not always be intellegent [*sic*].[86]

Did Tsiang write the play merely to flatter his American readers? This would explain the play's overly simplistic message as well as Tsiang's solicitation of praise from the Chinese Embassy. As he notes in the letter, *China Marches On* did indeed find its way into the hands of Eleanor Roosevelt, who offered her own, predictably unenthusiastic note of encouragement: "I have read your play, 'China Marches On', with a great deal of interest. I cannot tell, of course, how well it will go on Broadway, but it certainly as much that is of interest."[87]

The letters and never-to-be published poems and short stories Tsiang mailed Kent rarely echo the play's somewhat conservative political sentiments. They rival the boldest moments in his published works.[88] He refers to his detention as an extended stay at "Ellis Island Hotel."[89] One message to Kent is inscribed on a yard-long strip of toilet paper,[90] while another praises, "Long Live Rockwell Kent! My Savior, Our Lord, Jesus Christ, Amen!"[91] He refers to himself as "Charlie Chang on Ellis Island,"[92] a reference to the pulp detective Charlie Chan, and as "a sinner, Napoleon-Shakespeare, Shakespeare-Napoleon, A Chinaman, Father of William Soloyan," over-enunciating the writer William Saroyan's name in a stereotypical Chinese accent.[93] His communications with Kent's secretary, Shirley

Johnstone, are clumsily flirtatious. "[Y]ou have more brain than all the brains in the Brain Trust put together," he tells her.[94] For his part, Kent referred to each new letter as the latest installment in an ongoing drama titled "The Life and Laughs of H. T. Tsiang," calling him the hero of his own Odyssey.[95]

Kent was not the only name in Tsiang's address book. He wrote a letter to the White House containing veiled references to his own books: "Not all Chinamen in America are the Laundrymen and the one, who thinks that I may [sic] worth no more than a Nut, to the Chinese people, is a jackass, A Nut can't and dare not write you this letter . . . Well, well, that's Nut talking Nuts to you."[96] He sent Vito Marcantonio, a famed New York labor lawyer and East Harlem congressman, an ecstatic poem about the virtues of the letter "o."[97] (In subsequent letters to Kent, he referred to Marcantonio as "Representative O! O! O!")

Tsiang's intense letter-writing campaign earned him the support of New York's liberal intelligentsia. Kent, Dewey, Bruce Bliven, Archibald MacLeish, John Haynes Holmes, Lewis Gannett, and Waldo Frank each wrote appeals on his behalf. Gannett wrote Eleanor Roosevelt directly, confessing that he had "never been much impressed with the quality of Mr. Tsiang's literary work" but he nonetheless deserved justice.[98] In April 1941, Frank published "The Case of H. T. Tsiang" in the *New Republic*, soliciting sympathizers to write the Department of Justice on Tsiang's behalf: "No one, so far as I know (except perhaps his enemies, the Japanese army), thinks the man should be sent back to China, where possibly death awaits him."[99] Holmes wrote a letter to *The Nation* about Tsiang's case, praising his passion, intellect, and infectious positivity. "Extraordinary is his sense of humor as revealed in his correspondence—a sense of humor hard to achieve by Americans who contemplate the spectacle of what a so-called free country can do to a single helpless individual."[100]

Badgering his correspondents with letters and poems kept Tsiang busy. But by mid-1941 his spirits began to waver. "I have almost finished all jokes," he told Kent.[101] "The chief reason I want to stay in the United States," he wrote a few days later, "besides studying to improve myself, is that I want to be a writer. United States is my jail. I want to stay in jail as long as possible!"[102] Tsiang pressed other potential allies, writing Hu Shih, the Chinese ambassador to the United States he had disparagingly referenced in *China Red*. He sent him a letter describing the threats to his life should he be forced to repatriate to China; Hu never wrote back.[103] He was at his wit's end. His friends were powerful but not powerful enough. As he wrote to Kent: "Lin yu-tang can stay here why should not I. He only a Translator, with Pearl Buck's backing."[104]

In the late summer of 1941, Tsiang's deportation order was annulled, thanks largely to Kent's efforts. He was able to return to the hard work of accumulating rejection slips. That August, Kent mailed a package containing Tsiang's works to two publishers, hoping to net him a publishing contract. He acknowledged that quite a few houses had already rejected these works. "Times, as I have said, have changed. And I send you Tsiang with his books in the belief that he has got something tremendously important for the American public today." (He also compared Tsiang's style to "the flavor of Indian curry tamed down to suite the palate of Americans.")[105]

After Random House rejected Tsiang's works, Kent tried the John Day Company—Pearl Buck's publisher. Kent addressed the fawning cover letter to his good friend Richard Walsh—Buck's editor and husband.

Walsh received Kent's letter—but the books were somehow lost in transit. Walsh dashed off a quick reply expressing his excitement to delve into Tsiang's works, once they arrived.[106] "We publish a good many books about China and some by Chinese authors, including Lin Yutang," Walsh wrote, unaware that Tsiang despised both Lin and his wife. "Therefore I should be particularly interested in looking at Mr. Tsiang's books."[107]

Tsiang was petrified by the thought of Buck and Walsh reading his literary character assassinations of them in *The Hanging on Union Square* and *And China Has Hands*. He sent a hasty, mistake-filled letter to Kent, hoping to lessen the potential damage. "Do you know who is MRs. Richard J Walsh?—Perl Burk [*sic*]!"[108] The following day he wrote Walsh, begging him to leave Kent out of it. "I am used to the rejection slips, and he isn't," Tsiang explained.[109] Tsiang copied this letter to Kent and explained in a handwritten margin note that he had a plan for getting out of this mess. He would mail Walsh copies of *The*

Hanging on Union Square and *And China Has Hands* with a few pages
cut out—presumably the pages slandering Walsh and his wife. Along
with these abridged versions of his novels, he would send some articles
about Chinese politics he wrote while in graduate school, as a way of
proving his worth to the growing China lobby.

> The whole thing has to go through his <u>Mrs</u>—<u>Perl Burk.</u> That's
> the reason why I must send him <u>the Chinese matterial</u> [*sic*]. She
> can read Chinese. She won't like the opinion of the Chinese
> matterial, but would be impressed with the fact that, since I
> know all the top-men of Chungking government and yet I am
> willing to be a bum here in America.[110]

While Walsh awaited the arrival of these doctored books, Tsiang
wrote Kent: "You know we writers are very jealus [*sic*] person," he
admitted, "and one wants to eat up the other."[111] Hopefully Buck and
Walsh would magnanimously overlook his previous foibles.

A week later, Tsiang was back to desperately harassing Walsh. He
begged him not to reject his books immediately. "You are a very a
nice person," he wrote. "[N]o wonder, Author of The Good Earth,
married you." He pleaded with Walsh to be professional and keep
his work in consideration—"patience is always the best virtue. . . .
sounds like Lin Yutang?" He closed by giving his warmest regards
to Buck.[112]

The very next day, Tsiang wrote Walsh again: "So please don't
send your rejection slip to Mr. Rockwell Kent right way [*sic*]. Take
your time live longer. Please wait! By all means. I thank you and
Mrs."[113] The following week, a friend of Walsh contacted Tsiang and
asked him to stop writing.

Tsiang responded by firing off a frenzied, five-page letter to Walsh
pleading him to reconsider. "Let everybody have the HOPE." By this
point Tsiang had all but jettisoned his political ideals; he just wanted
to have his books published. "You Richard J Walsh, the President of
The John Day Company—The Makers of THE GOOD EARTH,
and THE SONS and My Country and My People, The Importance
of LIVING can make a best seller of my books!"[114] As a way of un-
derscoring the excitement of following in the footsteps of Buck and

Lin—the authors of the aforementioned works—he inked the exclamation mark in by hand. He then requested that Walsh never show this letter to Buck before claiming that his "English is Chinese more Chinese than Lin Yutan [*sic*]."

The idea of Tsiang prostrating himself at the foot of Walsh, the publisher responsible for the success of both Buck and Lin, is unbearable. If Tsiang's novelistic attacks on Buck had not already doomed his relationship to John Day, his desperately dogged pursuit of Walsh certainly clinched it. In late October, Walsh finally wrote Kent:

> But I will tell you frankly that, while I do not think his new poems are any good, my chief fear is that he will be a personality problem for any publisher. He is gifted and he has interesting things to say. But he is, to put it mildly, eccentric. One can hardly blame him, considering all that he has gone through. Yet it is alarming for anyone who might have to do business with him, to trace in what he writes an increasing wildness and confusion. I went back over everything of his, beginning in 1929, and I should say that there was a steady trend there which would make him a less and less promising author, and more and more likely to be troublesome in personal relations.[115]

Despite having "interesting things to say," Tsiang's last-ditch effort had failed. Like a character in one of his own novels, systems beyond his control were closing on him. First it was the United States government, detaining him unnecessarily and using his collected works—which few people ever bought anyway—against him. Now it was a publishing industry that was as insular as he suspected, politely showing him yet another door. It was enough to drive him nuts, once and for all.

Perhaps these letters to Walsh revealed Tsiang to be craven and opportunistic. But I read them as the outsider's glimpse of a different life-possibility: one, to paraphrase the doomed hero of *Oil for the Lamps of China*, "inside." Having pushed his complaints to the edge of reason, someone paid notice. It was not to be. In one of his last letters to Kent, he lamented Buck and Lin's prominence in the wartime China relief effort. "How they get their names? Because they wrote books. Because they wrote best sellers. That's all. So the best is to write and write better and pray to God to have a Publisher and put the writings over."[116]

Tsiang had arrived in the United States without any real sense of purpose or direction. He had witnessed the founding of a new republic, but the conservative mobs and China's uncertain future sent him fleeing. He thought he had found his second calling when he discovered the proletarian arts movement, but this world, too, failed him. All he wanted, as he told Kent, was to be a "writer." While Tsiang was certainly given to moments of narcissism and self-absorption, it was his unwavering faith in his own social and political vision that pushed his artistic style to such radical extremes. He still called his literature "proletarian," only his version expressed a sense of terminal alienation, the collateral damage of his rootless, transpacific existence. He drew on these feelings to dismantle our accepted notions of how we saw China, how novels and poems worked, and how the nations of the Pacific might consider relating to each other.

The disappointment of near-deportation and his failed writing career sent him in search of new adventures. Tsiang gave up writing and turned his attention to theater, staging *China Marches On* and his theatrical adaptation of *The Hanging on Union Square* around Manhattan. But he needed a change.

In *And China Has Hands*, as Tsiang walked within the pages of his own novel, trying to sell his self-published epics, a fellow traveler had mocked him, badgering him with questions about his stalled career. Why had all the respectable publishers rejected him? How come he had never earned a Guggenheim scholarship? In both cases, it was not for lack of trying.

He needed a fresh start.

And so, the man asked Tsiang a third question: "Have you ever been in Hollywood?"[117]

6

Pacific Crossings

It is 1941: H. T. Tsiang schemes in his Harlem apartment, firing off letters to Rockwell Kent and anyone else who has ever shown him even a touch of sympathy, pondering his next move.

A couple miles away in Morningside Heights, Chi-chen Wang puts the finishing touches on a new translation of Lu Xun's stories and essays to be published by Columbia University Press. Though Lu was one of the most important Chinese intellectuals of the 1910s and 1920s, he was largely unknown to American readers until 1937, when one of his short stories was included in a collection of tales from "modern China" edited by Edgar Snow and published by the John Day Company. As Wang, a professor of Chinese literature and language at Columbia, wrote his introductory remarks to Lu's volume, he wondered how these works would be received. There seemed to be an ambient interest in all things Chinese, especially as America's entry into World War II began to feel inevitable. But what did the average American really know about China? Where did these feelings of sympathy for the Chinese people come from? And would Lu challenge the easy sentimentalism that prevailed?

This has been a story about how one acquires authority—how, for example, the imprimatur of a recognizable press might distinguish an expert from a madman. The tumultuous curves of Tsiang's career dramatized the frustrations of someone hoping to publish work far beyond the acceptable orbits of China discourse. Wang's ambitions

166

were modest by comparison. He simply hoped to offer a gentle pushback against these readymade narratives. How could he restore the texture and complexity to the mythic, windswept China that sat in the imagination of the average American? Wang found himself painted into a corner, and not by his own hand. His introduction to Lu's translations began with a survey of the typical Chinese people and things available stateside:

> To the average American who gets his ideas about China from the movies and detective stories, China means Charlie Chan, Fu Manchu, and other nameless but equally familiar figures, it means chop suey, and Chinatown shop fronts covered with picturesque but meaningless hieroglyphs. Upon this fantastic hodgepodge of inventions and half-truths, sympathetic writers have in recent years superimposed a sentimental montage of a land where peace and tradition reign, where every earth-turning peasant is unobtrusively a philosopher. Now, sympathetic and flattering as this picture is, it has brought China no nearer to the American people and made China no more real. The fact is that there is no short cut to mutual respect and understanding between peoples any more than there is between individuals, the claims of the experts in how to perpetuate the honeymoon and how to win friends to the contrary notwithstanding.[1]

In the space of a paragraph, Wang neatly summarized the varied, often competing Chinese archetypes that had cluttered the American imagination over the preceding fifty years. Everything he named had helped bring China into ever-clearer focus for the average American, a story that would later be picked up by Harold Isaacs's *Scratches on Our Minds*. First came the ugly caricatures and demeaning stereotypes: movies, pulp novels, whatever grim misperceptions guided an outsider's stroll through Chinatown. Then came the "sympathetic and flattering" correctives, from the mellow Chinese philosopher-peasant to the clever and perpetually underestimated Chinese American detective. But despite the kind intentions that animated some of these works, Wang felt that these overly sentimental gestures had failed to render the Chinese experience with any true complexity.

There was a more immediate concern in all of this: if Americans freely projected their desires onto the ancient, wise China and the earnest, poignant, pitiable Chinese, then what of the actual Chinese American people living in their midst? His introduction captured the peculiar situation of the Chinese émigré living in the United States at a moment when the country's feelings about his native land had begun to turn. Wang had come to the United States on a study grant in the 1920s and stayed at Columbia University to teach. Around the time when he was preparing his translation of Lu Xun, there were small pockets of expatriate writers and scholars like him living in American cities and traveling across the country. But the vast majority of Chinese Americans claimed much deeper (and far less privileged) roots. These were the descendants of the early waves of Chinese immigration, living modestly in working class enclaves. To the typical American, this was too fine a distinction: the Chinese in China and the Chinese in American Chinatowns were one and the same. While Wang's chief concern was with how writers and scholars represented his former home, he could not help but notice the shadows these representations cast upon the Chinese in America. From characters in books and movies to his privileged seat at Columbia University to Manhattan's Chinatown a hundred blocks to the south: they all comprised an undifferentiated mass of Chinese.

One representation in particular disturbed him. The deeply philosophical, "earth-turning" peasants, written into the American consciousness with a sympathetic hand: this was clearly a reference to Pearl Buck's *The Good Earth*, which had become ubiquitous in the decade since its publication. While haughty American critics eagerly debated whether or not *The Good Earth* even qualified as passable literature, few took aim at its portrayals of the Chinese. As the daughter of missionaries who had spent her youth in China, Buck possessed an authority in the American literary marketplace that was rarely challenged. But she had intended *The Good Earth* as a work of realism about a very specific Chinese experience. She never anticipated that it would be read as a definitive account of Chinese society let alone that it would affect the lives of Chinese living in America. As a response to the lurid pulp fictions about the mythical, exotic Orient, Buck did not imagine that her spare tale of rags-to-riches would simply produce a new set of stereotypes. She could not have foreseen the strange plight of someone like Kiang Kang-Hu, the Chinese traveler we encountered in Chapter 1 who was peppered throughout his American travels with questions about *The Good Earth*'s accuracy.

What's more, Lu Xun himself is alleged to have bristled at *The Good Earth*'s "superficial" representation of China: "It is always better for the Chinese to write about Chinese subject matter, as that is the only way to get near the truth. Even with Mrs. Buck . . . what her books reveal is no more than her stand as an American missionary woman who happens to have grown up in China."[2] Not that these distinctions were apparent to American readers. *The Good Earth* had profoundly colored the typical American's understanding of both China and Chinatown, flattening the distance between the nearby and the faraway. In 1932, for example, Irving Thalberg had adapted *The Good Earth* for the screen, filming parts of the movie around Los Angeles. In 1938, a local businesswoman named Christine Sterling repurposed the sets from Thalberg's production for China City, a tourist attraction enclosed within a faux-Great Wall. Inside were curio shops, restaurants, rickshaws, dance pavilions, gongs everywhere.[3] It was a Chinatown reimagined in the spirit of what the historian Charlotte Brooks has termed "*Good Earth* Chineseness." The following year, in preparation for San Francisco's 1939 World's Fair, a Chinese American group hoping to play up the city's distinctive heritage built a Chinese village at the Exposition grounds and called it the Good Earth Settlement.[4] The village featured a farmer manning an old wooden plow, a temple, even topsoil that had been imported from China.[5] Never mind that most of the setting was outdated. The only real ambition was to humanize the Chinese and depict them in scenes of nonthreatening diligence. For Chinese Americans eager to shed the "sordid" impressions associated with Chinatown, this was a welcome conflation.[6]

For Wang, the American understanding of China had grown out of a "fantastic hodgepodge of inventions and half-truths" that confused fantasy with history, a set of ideals for an outline on a map and the mythic, far-away Chinese in books and movies for the immigrants down the street. It was the fault of the "experts." Whatever intentions guided these various works, they produced a common effect.

Distinctions were forgotten and the fluid mystery of China was transposed onto the Chinese Americans. Charlie Chan paperbacks, Chinatown restaurants, local businesses—all pieces of a distinctly American experience—were subsumed by China, which became the sole context for understanding them. Whether Wang was arguing for a more nuanced understanding of these longstanding immigrant communities or merely irked to be associated with them—after all, he shared little in common with their day-to-day struggles—he at least recognized a shared, if imposed, fate.

It probably never would have occurred to Buck that the great Chinese writer and critic Lu Xun would have to be introduced to American readers in relation to Chinatown—let alone that his China would be offered in contrast to hers. But it was why Wang championed Lu Xun as the anti-Buck, a complicated, unsentimental figure skeptical toward both Western and Chinese idealisms. Lu found fault with both the old gentry—"men who had seen better times and would preserve the 'national essence'"—and the new elites eager to implement the "gentlemanly" ideas they had learned at school in England and the United States.[7] While Buck had offered the simple, yeoman peasants of The Good Earth as authentic representatives of a dwindling Chinese spirit, Wang pointed to Lu's thorny essays and parables as a radical break from the agrarian humility and genteel "traditionalism" prized by overly romantic American readers.[8] The pages that follow, he explained, might "shock and displease those Occidental and Chinese who make it their profession to tell the Western world what a wonderful country China is (or was, if they happen to be those who pine for the olden times) and what a happy people the Chinese are in spite of their squalor and disease."[9] Nobody is happy in the face of squalor and disease.

This was one of the unintended consequences of The Good Earth's astonishing success. Buck introduced a version of China for the American middlebrow; in her wake, a new market for similarly breathless, China-loving books and articles emerged. But deep inside the sympathetic treatment of the Chinese, Wang contended, there lurked a condescending desire to preserve China in amber. Meanwhile, works that failed to echo these themes—from Wang's translations to Tsiang's self-published screeds—had to at least *reckon with* Buck. An internal Columbia University Press memo from 1940 illustrated this need to consider the positioning of any book on China. The memo—presumably drafted by an acquisitions editor—is addressed to the Press's director. It reports on a lunch meeting with Wang, who had proposed the idea of a Lu Xun translation. For the Press, the issue was market saturation. "I told him that any such book presented to a general public would have to compete and would be compared with Pearl Buck, Lin Yutang, and Karl Krow [*sic*]. This had not occurred to him previously, or if it had, had not seemed important, though he was inclined to agree with me after we had talked about it."[10]

Wang eventually acted on the editor's advice. His introduction acknowledges these inevitable comparisons and addresses them directly, arguing that Lu Xun's writings offer a far more sophisticated vision of modern China than his sentimental competitors in the marketplace. As we saw in the last chapter, Tsiang had made a similar gesture to Buck's looming influence in his later novels, albeit in a desperate, largely self-destructive manner. But Wang and Tsiang's own positions as outsiders dramatized a more immediate consequence of the *Good Earth* effect. What about the people whose identities were constructed within this field? How did these impressions of China shape racial attitudes toward Chinatown and Chinese Americans?

Put another way: the excitement about all things Chinese dramatized just how little Americans had cared about the Chinatowns and Chinese Americans just a few blocks away. What would it take for this circle of China-watchers to shift their gaze downtown?

This has been a story about the cultivation of authority: its acquisition but also its maintenance. There was nothing particularly new about this dynamic, as the prerequisites for being qualified to speak on behalf of China had always been quite minimal. The historian James Hevia, for example, has pointed out the degree to which turn-of-the-century missionary accounts took an undue certitude at a time when there were few dispatches from China. They both represented and shaped reality for readers back in the United States.[11] This dynamic intensified in the 1920s and 1930s, as America rediscovered

China. The American prophets of China's future had consisted of a close-knit circle of writers, journalists, and scholars. They had been the chief explainers of the transpacific possibility, whether through the fictional characters they created or the real-life positions of influence they had carved out for themselves. The Columbia University Press editor who warned that Wang's translations would have to contend with Crow, Buck, and the witty, lighthearted Lin Yutang was probably more right than he knew.

The trajectories of these three dominant figures captured the rough parameters of this limited field of conversation. While many early twentieth century scholars and missionaries had found success authoring dispatches from China, Crow represented a new possibility: he was a businessman, a well-connected go-between offering the elite classes in both China and the United States visions of a new, transpacific market. As an advertiser, he had studied Chinese attitudes toward commerce and status and sold them visions of what it meant to be modern. As a journalist and best-selling author, he regaled American readers with tales from a new frontier and the ever-renewable promise of China's untapped "400 million customers."

Buck's popular novels and reportage had helped cultivate an American middlebrow interest in all things Chinese. Where Crow's work portended a collective future predicated on trade and barter, Buck strove to establish a transpacific bond borne of empathy and shared struggle. Beyond the sentimental immediacy of her own works, Buck's celebrity had allowed her to become a de facto gatekeeper. It had been Buck's encouragement, support, and cosign that had paved the way for Lin's move to the United States in the early 1930s, where he became known for a string of popular books about Chinese manners.

The interwar interest in China always assumed a kind of oceanic distance. This is not to say that their general disinterest in Chinese American immigrants bespoke a willful ignorance or nefarious ends. But as evidenced by the frustrations of Tsiang and Wang—not to mention the effect of *The Good Earth* on Chinatown storefront design—popular works about far-away China had unintended consequences on those living in America.

What makes the general invisibility of Chinese American immigrants so intriguing, then, was the emergence of a domestic angle to this longstanding China obsession. In 1946, the John Day Company published a book titled *Chinatown USA* as part of a joint venture with the Asia Press. The figure behind this publishing alliance was Richard Walsh, the head of John Day who was famous for handling *The Good Earth* and marketing Buck as America's foremost voice on all things Chinese.[12] The triumph of *The Good Earth* and Walsh's budding relationship with Buck had gotten him interested in the politics and culture of Asia. In 1934, Walsh assumed control of *Asia* magazine and turned an up-market publication advertising package tours and exotic luxury goods into a serious journal of Pacific affairs.[13] In the 1940s, Walsh started the Asia Press imprint at John Day in order to introduce the works of liberal thinkers like Lin and Jawaharlal Nehru to American readers.[14]

Chinatown, USA was an unusual entry into this field—it was neither by an Asian author nor strictly about Asia. Rather, it was a book aimed at Walsh and Buck's fellow Asia-watchers, about the Asians in their very midst. It featured the photography and prose of Elizabeth Colman. An introductory section guides the reader through the finer points of the Chinese experience in America, wearily accenting moments when the nation had failed its creed in its treatment of Chinese Americans, and offering a thin ethnography of urban Chinatowns and their present-day inhabitants. This is followed by eighty pages of photographs, consisting mostly of staged images of daily life in Chinatown, or pictures of buildings and facades.

"In the center of some of our biggest cities," Colman writes, "often confined within a few blocks, a quiet people lead their lives, side by side with us. We have come to meet them very superficially only. We are only dimly aware of their sorrows, their struggles, their hopes and joyful celebrations."[15] The self-congratulatory discovery of the Chinese American by Colman and her cohort was somewhat ironic, given their broad, abiding interest in China and its people. While there had already been communities of Chinese in America for at least a hundred years, the China watchers in the interwar period had never extended their pet interest to include the Chinese living nearby. Throughout the 1910s, '20s and '30s, they had set across the Pacific, literally and figuratively, to ponder the fate of an abstracted mass. They had produced thousands of pages of novels, reportage, and opinion journalism on the twinned fates of China and the United States. There was a circle of liberal China sympathizers for whom John Day, the Asia Press and *Asia* magazine, and organizations like the China Emergency Relief Committee, United China Relief, and East and West were essentially synonymous. As Buck explained, these were organizations that had been founded "to help ordinary people on one side of the world to know and understand ordinary people on the other side."[16] But what of the "ordinary people" down the road? It was not until the 1940s that this group of China watchers became fascinated with the Chinese American, realizing that these—in Colman's words—heirs to a "rich cultural heritage" that predated that of the West, had been hidden in plain sight.[17]

What prompted this sudden reappraisal of the Chinese American subject, and what were its consequences? Wartime allegiances had resulted in the push to revoke the Chinese Exclusion Act—the 1882 provision that severely restricted immigration from China, and the first policy of its kind. In 1942, *Asia* published Charles Nelson Spinks's influential editorial "Repeal Chinese Exclusion!"[18] Momentum gathered around Spinks's call, primarily in the form of a spirited media campaign.[19] Buck contributed a series of articles about exclusion as well as a sympathetic children's book titled *The Chinese Children Next Door*, which was meant to underscore the common humanity of young people in China and the United States.[20] By 1943, Walsh and Buck had become leaders within this growing movement, establishing the Citizens Committee to Repeal Chinese Exclusion (CCRCE) out of the John Day offices. In May, Buck testified before the House Committee on Immigration and Naturalization, arguing that exclusion undermined America's democratic principles, as well as America's wartime relationship with China. The act was finally repealed that December with the passage of the Magnuson Act. Buck celebrated with dinner in New York's Chinatown.[21]

The end of the Exclusion era coincided with a growing, postwar fear of losing China to Communism. In the words of historian Ellen Wu, so began an era of "Chinese inclusion," as Chinese immigrants were recast as faithful contributors to America's diverse, liberal postwar society.[22] This was how the Chinese American, Wu convincingly argues, was elevated to the status of a model minority—as evidence that America's institutions still worked. But there were also global consequences to "inclusion." Buck, Walsh, and the CCRCE lobby, for example, had been drawn to the issue primarily out of an interest in China rather than the specific plight of the Chinese Americans. After the repeal of exclusion, China watchers began to appreciate the unique situation of the Chinese American and ponder the possibilities of accessing this liminal space. In books like Colman's *Chinatown USA*, Buck's *Kinfolk*, and Lin Yutang's *Chinatown Family*, there emerged a new Chinese American possibility. The Chinese Americans dreamed up in these texts ran counter to the dominant paradigms of the time. Rather than the anxiety about purity or hybridization that had marked many representations of this immigrant community, China watchers like Colman and Buck perceived the Chinese Americans' hybrid nature as their primary asset—the asset that made them good citizens, not just as a model minority but as transpacific go-betweens. The unwillingness to fully assimilate, for example, was an advantage. Perhaps the Chinese American represented the perfect interlocutor of China to America, and vice versa.

Colman's *Chinatown USA* models this perspective. Her text traffics in a sheepish, vaguely guilty tone, and it seems to presume that her audience shares such feelings—that they were similarly unaware of the modest Chinese Americans. While everyone depicted in the book is presumably an American citizen, she notes that few enjoy the benefits of cultural citizenship. "We created almost unsurmountable obstacles against their Americanization. Segregating them from our lives, we accused them of not wanting to participate."[23] In moments like these, the prompting for *Chinatown USA*—its possibility as yet another corrective—becomes clearer. While the struggle of the Chinese in America, the embodiment of a history of legal, political, and capitalistic contradiction, had been of little concern to most Americans of the early twentieth century, their situation had changed. Colman continues: "A gesture has been made. The Exclusion Acts were revoked and in 1944 Chinese became again admissible for immigration and eligible for naturalization . . . At least one manifestation of discrimination has been abolished and this is highly important for us and for a people with as keenly developed a feeling for personal and national dignity as the Chinese."[24] This summary of Chinese immigration history closes with a light call for removal of the national quota limiting entry to 105 Chinese per year.

The photographs of *Chinatown USA* illustrate Colman's claim that the Chinese Americans lead ordinary, mundane, vaguely dignified lives. The book situates them within a liberal and "inclusive" political agenda. As she asks near the end of her introduction: "What will be the future of these young Americans?"[25] Colman's images are sequenced to suggest a narrative of progress. A two-page spread introduces us to the setting: on the sill of a window sit porcelain figurines and vases, and beyond them one spies a neighboring apartment building, presumably full of more Chinese people and things. We are introduced to the people of Chinatown on the following pages: "Mother and Child" and "Father." The fate of the child—the representative of the new generation and a seed of pure progress— is central to Colman's project, and so we are introduced to various Chinatown children as they take their "First Steps," build airplanes in nursery school, and befriend chums from "other backgrounds." There are scenes of schooling and then youthful horseplay in a variety of patriotic contexts: Chinese American servicemen enjoying their "week-end pass," a young boy lured in by a "peep show," members of an Aviation club, and young men practicing "Eastern Instruments" and "Western Music." As well, there are various sites that together describe a robust civil society: barbershop, newsstand, public parks, herb stores, restaurants, and theaters.

Nobody is ever named in Colman's book. Her captions are sparse, and although this is a project advancing the dignity of the Chinese American, the book conveys them as an undifferentiated mass. But individual faces recur, in a way that is suggestive of narrative. Two young lads playing football are shown lining up for a play; some thirty pages later, we rejoin them, mid-stride. Sailors embarking on furlough are joined pages later at a social dance. The attempt to illustrate how Chinatown kids get along with kids from other backgrounds is complicated by the fact that the Chinese boys all seem to share the same white friend. As the book ends, we return to the children. A young girl does her homework underneath a Red Cross poster imploring personal sacrifice. A newborn baby is shown in the

arms of a nurse, with the caption, "A new citizen." The last three
pages show three children with the captions: "What will . . . their
future be . . . and his?" Colman lingers on one such "young representative of a new East, of a China in the making," a Chinese-born
and American-educated young man employed by the China Aircraft
Corporation. In his spare time, he is the caretaker at an old temple
in San Francisco's Chinatown. She writes:

> His situation impressed me as being strangely symbolic of the
> present stage of the country of his birth, where the very new is
> now being grafted onto very ancient forms of life. His outlook is
> perhaps symptomatic of current trends of development among
> Chinese young people. He is devoted to his work and extreme-
> ly well informed on the international political and economic
> problems of these days, and passionately conscious of all their
> implications. He is eager to go to China to help in its industri-
> alization and willing to put up with any material sacrifices that
> may be necessary.[26]

It is the gentlest of nudges back across the Pacific. The collective
fates of these young immigrants fanned out to larger questions about
the global future. Soon, the transpacific circulations of ideas, bodies,
capital, and things between America and China would only intensify.
Could the unique perspective of the Chinese American help us mediate this emerging space? As Colman concluded, Chinese American
youth were "the natural human link between the East and the West
and with their Chinese and American training they will be an asset
to both America and China. They should have an important role to
play, which no one could do better, in the future of co-operation between the two countries for the coming industrialization of China."[27]

Could the long-ignored Chinese Americans be the ideal citizens of
this new age? What role did they play in the era's transpacific dream?
Were they, as Colman suggested, truly "eager to go to China?"

Buck and her cohort had spent the preceding decades with their
sights firmly on China, seemingly unaware that similar conversations about the fate of the transpacific were being staged in nearby

Chinatowns. In the early 1900s, before the category of the Chinese American had been named and defined, the people of Chinatown ferociously debated the politics of a China to which many would never return. H. T. Tsiang had experienced this firsthand, when he was chased out of the Bay Area for his incendiary writings opposing the Kuomintang. As a Chinese American ethnos emerged, the discussions and points of reference grew more varied. The 1930s were a particularly rich time for this new cultural formation. An important example of this was the *Chinese Digest*, the first English-language Chinese American newspaper. The *Digest* began publishing in San Francisco in 1935, responding to the absence of a hub for and about "young Chinatown." In its first issue, the editorial board explained that Chinese Americans were working hard to correct racist misapprehensions of China and advance a notion of a unified Chinese diaspora. This was a newspaper for "Young Chinatown," a new generation that thought in English and recognized the significance of China's stature to their lives in America.[28]

One of the most frequently praised representations of China and the Chinese was *The Good Earth*. In the *Digest*'s very first issue is a brief news item hailing the adaptation of Buck's novel for the screen. A couple years later, they commemorated the film's release, with an entire issue devoted to *The Good Earth*, from features praising it as "one of the great novels of our time" to cooking columns detailing how Chinese commoners like Wang Lung prepared their rice.[29] Local advertisements all capitalized on the film's release. One tailor recommended their wool suits "for perfect poise and relaxation when viewing the GOOD EARTH epic"[30] while the Twin Dragon bar proclaimed itself the ideal spot for a post-movie drink: "AFTER THE GOOD EARTH COMES GOOD LIQUOR."[31]

As the *Digest* and the communities the paper served continued to mature, debates around the meaning of Chinese American identity intensified. In 1936, the Ging Hawk Club, a Chinese organization in New York, sponsored an essay contest around the prompt, "Does My Future Lie in China or America?"[32] There was a significant movement among Chinese to return home to China in the 1910s and '20s. By some estimates, nearly 10,000 more Chinese people left than arrived between the years 1909 and 1932.[33] The number of arrivals held steady, since this was the Exclusion era. As the historian Gloria Heyung Chun has noted, a host of factors drew the Chinese back to China: frustration with racial politics, a desire to return to newly republican China, an ambiguous feeling of moral imperative.[34] The Ging Hawk essay contest might have originated as a standard exercise in civic pride. But as the *Digest*'s staff discovered after they reprinted the two top essays, the contest captured a community at odds over its future.

A Harvard University student named Robert Dunn won the contest with a heartfelt plea for staying put. "In determining whether my future is to be in China or America, I have naturally come to ponder the question: To which of these two countries do I owe allegiance? Which country am I obliged to serve?" Throughout his entire life, he had been raised to admire China for its "four thousand years of glorious and continuous history" and "four hundred million population." Yet this sense of innate allegiance left him cold. Dunn openly admitted that the Chinese in America were frequently mocked, "trodden upon, disrespected, and even spit upon."[35] But what kind of life awaited him in China, where the youth are beholden to "utilitarian ideals, conservative attitudes, and a fatalistic outlook upon life?" By staying and flourishing in America, Dunn believed he could help improve the image of China and the Chinese. Rather than pursuing a life of "discontent and despondency" in a foreign land, he could become a model of success.[36]

There is an intense earnestness to Dunn's essay, a belief in the promise of assimilation, meritocracy, and the American dream that feels almost charmingly naïve. As might be expected, the *Digest* received quite a few heated responses to Dunn's call for Chinese Americans to put down roots in the United States, native racism notwithstanding. The Stanford University Chinese Students' Club sent the *Digest* a series of letters accusing Dunn of being "unwise" and even "unpatriotic."[37] Perhaps the most eloquent statement in favor of returning to China was the second-place essay by a University of Washington student named Kaye Hong. Hong focused on the paradoxical situation of the Chinese Americans, who had lived under the Exclusion Act for over fifty years. "When the conquest of new territory in the United States had stretched to the limits of the

Pacific, the old adage of 'Go West, Young Man' no longer became applicable to the American youth." A changing economy and growing population throughout the mid 1800s resulted in stiff competition for work. All the same, the Chinese were the easiest scapegoats, resulting in "distaste for Oriental rivalry in every type of work"—the preconditions for passage of the Exclusion Act. As a result, Hong powerfully argued, "the present generation of American-born Chinese absorbed a bitter diet of racial prejudice." Calls to pledge allegiance to America had left him "coldly unresponsive."

> My patriotism is of a different hue and texture. It was built on the mound of shame. The ridicule heaped upon the Chinese race has long fermented within my soul. I have concluded that we, the younger generation, have nothing to be proud of except the timeworn accomplishments of our ancient ancestors, that we have been living in the shadow of these glories, hoping that these arts and literature of the past will justify our present. Sad but true, they no [sic] not. To live under such illusions is to lead the life of a parasite.[38]

Where Dunn argued for Chinese Americans to claim a place in American society, Hong seethed with indignation. While Hong acknowledged that pursuing a livelihood stateside guaranteed a much better quality of life, his romanticized homeland offered the far richer reward of a common struggle. He held tight to his own twist on the pioneer's slogan: "'Go Further West, Young Man.' Yes, across the Pacific and to China."[39] In the informal arena of the *Digest* letters page, Hong's vision triumphed. A letter from George Grace echoed Hong's call for individual sacrifice. There would never be true equality for the Chinese in America, Grace wrote, so why not go where we were wanted? "So let us not be fooled by a mirage, but set our faces toward our home land, which is rich in untold opportunities for all. We cannot all be leaders, some must be oil for the smooth running of the machine."[40]

It was one thing for idealistic young students, deeply skeptical of the American promise, to seek an escape. But what political possibilities did Colman, Buck, and others see in this moment of reverse migration? Pearl Buck had first explored these circuits of transpacific knowledge in *A House Divided* (1935), a completion of the multigenerational trilogy that had begun with *The Good Earth*. Yuan, one of the grandsons of *The Good Earth*'s heroic farmer, Wang Lung, travels to the United States as a student. It is a disillusioning stint. At one point, he ends up in a very public argument with a white missionary who has just returned from China. As the missionary peddles "gruesome, filthy tales" of this distant land, Yuan rises to defend his home: "I—I speak for my country!"[41] The missionary accuses him of being privileged and out of touch; *he*, the selfless man in touch with the suffering masses, speaks for China. Later, two witnesses to this exchange pass by, bemused by what they have heard: "Queer thing, that Chinese fellow getting up like that, wasn't it?—Wonder which of 'em was right?"[42]

Buck returned to this examination of a traveling Chinese sensibility in two works of short fiction written prior to the 1943 repeal of the Exclusion Act, only this time she sent her Chinese characters in the other direction. The campaign for repeal had exacerbated divisions between Buck and Chiang Kai-shek, leader of China's nationalists, and his wife, Soong May-ling.[43] Buck's hostility toward the American-educated Soong deepened during the latter's 1943 tour of the United States, when she refused to speak out on behalf of her overseas countrymen against Exclusion. Buck's fiction had always expressed distrust toward China's pampered, overly Westernized elites. Books like *The Good Earth* had entrusted China's future to the common folk, instead. In her Exclusion era fiction, she tried to locate representatives of that spare, admirably humble sensibility in the obscure corners of America's own cities.

As with Colman's glimpse into Chinatown, Buck's short stories are relatively transparent attempts to offer Chinese Americans as model citizens. "John-John Chinaman" was published in 1942 in *American* magazine. It details the various forms of abuse weathered by John Lim, a young Chinese American living in a small, idyllic town in the Midwest. The racism to which he is subjected charts a range of motivations, from the nasty and truly hateful to the negligent and condescending. "According to the laws of this country," his father explains, "you are American. But the hearts of people decide these things, not laws."[44] Unable to rationalize the behavior of bullies and contemptible city officials, Lim grows weary of the American promise, concluding, "I have no country."[45]

At a lavish town ceremony, the young man, by now cynically disillusioned, becomes the first citizen drafted for military service. He imagines using this moment of public visibility to renounce his neighbors and their sham liberalism. But his father happily accepts this honor on behalf of the family, instantly recasting his son as a local hero. While his inner discontent only deepens at the town's situational embrace of him, Lim's quiet dignity suggests that he better embodies the values of American citizenship than any of the locals.

If "John-John Chinaman" aspired to alert Americans to their hypocrisies, then "His Own Country" was an attempt to explore what these hybrid Americans were capable of. The story was written in 1939 and published two years later in *Today and Forever: Stories of China*. It focuses on a Chinatown outcast named John Dewey Chang—a reference to the philosopher John Dewey, who wrote a series of influential articles about Asia in the late 1910s. Like Buck's other John, Chang is a quiet, observant Chinese American with reservations about his place in America. Instead, he aspires to move to China, even though he has never been there. He leaves New York as soon as he finishes college, arriving in a China that is far from the idealized lodestar of his dreams.

Buck's reference to Dewey seems to be a sign of reverence—his father names him John Dewey because of "an American who had helped to start good new schools in China. He had read about it in the papers from his home town there."[46] Yet there is something uncomfortable about this nod to Dewey, whose writing about China is notable for its rhapsodic and overly idealistic tone. The family runs a curio shop on Mott Street in New York's Chinatown dealing in Chinese ephemera like miniature Buddha statues or mandarin coats—signifiers of a nation that the younger Chang has never seen. Perhaps it was the kind of place the Columbia University scholar Wang might have seen when he ventured downtown from Columbia, a store that recognized America's taste for the exotic but made China no more real to the average passerby.

This simply made Chang, with his romantic vision of a rising China, truly American. Once he actually sets foot in China, however, his quest to discover "his own country" evolves into a haunting question: "Where, where was his country?"[47] The streets are anarchic, the citizens far from the spiritual brothers and sisters he had imagined. He continues to imagine that China must be somewhere else, past the modernizing city. He decides to go further inland, though his travels only exacerbate his feelings of disenchantment. He is constantly disturbed by the nation's filth. Chang eventually acquires the nickname "Foreign Devil."[48]

Eventually, Chang's childhood sweetheart experiences her own awakening. Ruth Kin begins the story as "slangy," modern, and comfortably assimilated, the type of Chinese American who idolizes actress Anna May Wong but cares little for the fate of the nation. But Kin, too, grows weary of America and decides to join Chang in China. This terrifies him: he does not want her to see China as it is, to experience this "sudden death of dreams" that has struck him down.[49] Rather, he tries to recreate New York in China, preserving an ideal, sanitized image of China that shields her from the squalor and disarray. As Japanese gunboats approach and the streets fill with hungry Chinese, she realizes John's deception and ridicules him for projecting this illusion for her benefit. Instead of disappointment, she comes alive, opening their home to the impoverished Chinese outside and feeding them all. As the story ends, Kin resists Chang's suggestion that they leave the country, proclaiming, "My baby is going to go be born in his own country where he belongs."[50]

What versions of American citizenship emerge from this story? "John-John Chinaman" had fixed on the disparity between legal citizenship and a less formal sense of belonging—even though Lim could die for America in armed conflict, it remained doubtful that he would ever feel a part of his modest community.

Belonging means something different in "His Own Country." The antagonizing force is not the provincial racism of small-minded, small-town America. Instead, it is the immigrant's ambient sense of dislocation. Unattached to New York, he imagines a China to which he can return—a land deserving of his dreams. For Chang, this is a story about trading one set of myths for another. As the actual John Dewey once remarked, "China tends to become an angel of light to show up the darkness of Western civilization. Chinese virtues are made a whip of scorpions with which to lash the backs of complacent Westerners."[51] Chang's indifference to America pushed him toward this fantasy. Instead, it was Kin's gradual and more thoroughgoing self-discovery that allowed her to recognize a different reason for returning.

What both Buck (and, to some extent, the actual Dewey) sought was a new sensibility that idealized neither civilization of the Pacific but remained sensitive to the strengths and weaknesses of both. And it was this figure of the transnational, proto-Chinese American couple of Ruth and John and the symbol of their child that best embodied this promise of a new global democracy. Despite the absence of these Chinese Americans in so much of the era's writings on China-United States relations, Buck here elevates them as heirs to this transpacific promise. As a story about Chinese Americans, Buck's story achieves surprisingly prescient insights into the pressures, hopes, and existential quandaries of immigrant settlement. But as a story of international politics carried by prophetic desire, the dilemmas faced by John and Ruth stood in for an array of global tensions and misunderstandings. The crude, almost primal idealism of John only leads to disappointment and delusion. It is Ruth's patience, pragmatism, and more generalized sense of compassion that builds a solid bridge between them and the teeming Chinese agitating in the streets.

The question of authority took on a new dimension in the 1940s. Over the preceding decade, Buck and her circle of China-watchers had been held aloft as the ideal intermediaries of the Pacific world. This would be a space pioneered by authors, advertisers, American businessmen who could speak fluent Chinese. But whether this clout extended to the political conditions in China was another question, particularly as Buck's idealism seemed increasingly untenable in the wake of World War II. How, then, could Buck and her cohort accommodate the shifting winds? How could their authority be shared or extended to new voices? What did it mean that Buck was now sending her Chinese American characters back to China in her stead?

In 1949, as the Communist Party verged toward control of the Chinese mainland, Buck published *Kinfolk*. Of the thirty-eight or so novels about Asia she published during her career, *Kinfolk* is one of the few set in the United States, and the only populated entirely by Chinese Americans. Set in New York, China, and London, the story follows the Liangs, a middle-class family living in upper Manhattan, far from Chinatown. The symbolic distance between Dr. Liang Wen Hua—the intellectual who translates Confucian ideas and Chinese culture to the city's uptown elite—and the actual participants in that culture downtown serves as the novel's engine. This distance animates Liang's children, who perceive something *inauthentic* about their upbringing and choose a future among the real Chinese of their ancestral countryside. Slowly, each of them moves back to China, and each becomes a symbol of the transpacific future. The eldest son becomes a doctor who grafts Western and Chinese medicinal practices—a literal bridging of traditions. Another becomes an insurrectionist and tries to remake China according to his own revolutionary romance. One daughter grows to love the rural backwardness of China, while the other refuses to forfeit her American ways and returns to New York with her serviceman husband. Over the course of the novel, the siblings meet predictable ends: the doctor grows in heroic stature while the revolutionary is murdered. The book closes on a purposefully vague note, with the surviving siblings setting into their respective destinies, united in the hope of rebuilding China.

While Buck's novel—as with nearly all her novels—rewards the thrift, diligence, and faith of its characters, it also functions as a commentary on the public narratives about China that she herself had helped produce. As the novel opens, we join Liang Wen Hua— which translates, homophonically, as "two cultures"—in a crowded theater in Chinatown for a performance of the play *Mu Lan*. Buck idealizes this space as one where the authentic masses are free to indulge their nostalgia. It is a reminder of who they once were. "The theater was a bulwark of home. Their children went to American schools, spoke the American language, acted like American children. [. . .] But in the theater the children could see for themselves what China was."[52] That the theater, a space predicated on performance, stands in for an ideal homeland is an irony Liang readily enjoys. A professor who lives and works uptown, Liang rarely ventures to Chinatown. But he has come to this theater downtown in order to see whether his American students "might understand this play, as presented by Chinese actors." He guesses that they probably won't be in any position to pass judgment one way or another. "I suppose American students will not be critical," he thinks to himself.[53] Liang treats his position as a cultural go-between with a lazy cynicism. He is certain that neither his American students nor the Upper West Side women's clubs he lectures on Confucianism would ever dare challenge his authority.

As the play continues onstage, Liang's mind wanders: he finds the "gaudy scene" deeply unsophisticated compared to the delights of Radio City and Broadway; he grows annoyed at the children pattering back and forth. "It was most unfortunate, he thought, his handsome lips set and his head high, that Chinese like himself were not the sole representatives of his country. It was a great pity that Chinatown had ever been allowed."[54]

Liang's condescension points to the true diversity and at times irreconcilable social divisions within the Chinese American community. But even as he privately mocks the uncultured Chinese of the theater, he addresses them as sharers of a common secret. He is recognized by the theater's owner and accepts an invitation to take the stage himself and share his thoughts on *Mu Lan* and Chineseness with the crowd. Liang "took the opportunity to remark that it was the duty of every Chinese to represent his country in the most favorable light to Americans who were, after all, only foreigners."[55]

Buck seems to question the capacity of an audience—the audience in the theater, the American audiences of Liang's lectures, maybe even her own readers—to discern projection from something resembling truth. As Liang heads home from the theater, he looks out the window of his cab and remarks there is no true "evil" or "mystery" to Chinatown, as the "Americans liked to believe."[56] But more to the point: Liang's willingness to abuse his position as interlocutor and the public's willingness to leave his claims unchallenged seems to restage the previous decades' debates around the representational politics of China advocacy and China writing. Buck is critical of how Liang's Chineseness underwrites his authority as a cultural translator. Liang begins to resemble the "modern Chinese writers" who Buck attacked in her 1938 Nobel address for having "been too strongly under foreign influence while they were yet ignorant of the riches of their own country."[57]

Liang occasionally sounds like one of Buck's real-life foes: Kiang Kang-Hu, the Chinese politician and scholar who had railed against her representation of the Chinese back in the 1930s. Both Liang and Kiang saw themselves as representatives of what China was becoming: educated, modern, urbane. The impoverished laborers of Chinatown or the Chinese countryside prized by figures like Buck actually represented the China being left behind.

Whether or not this resemblance to Kiang was intentional, Buck briefly indulged the latter's anti-Buck perspective. After all, both Liang and Kiang viewed their work as fundamentally corrective—they sought to normalize a modern alternative to the simple, downtrodden Chinese archetypes produced by Buck and others. While eating dinner with his family, Liang's thoughts drift to the miscellaneous sites where this work of correcting American misperceptions takes place:

> When guests were present he used a small bowl, a gentleman's bowl, he laughingly explained. Only peasants used large bowls.
>
> "But I thought most of the people of China were peasants," the guest would reply. Dr. Liang deprecated this with a graceful left hand.
>
> "An unfortunate impression," he always said gently. "Due, I am afraid, to best sellers about China—written by Americans. A very limited point of view, naturally. It is quality that is meaningful in any nation, the articulate view, the scholars. Surely men like myself represent more perfectly than peasants can the spirit of Chinese civilization. Our nation has always been ruled by our intellectuals. Our emperors depended upon wise men."[58]

Buck is, of course, talking about her own "best sellers about China," peasant-dominated fare like *The Good Earth*, *Sons*, and *A House Divided*. Liang's dismissive tone is supposed to signal his own elitism. But this chasm between representation and reality was a widely held concern. Buck's "best sellers about China" had inspired Tsiang's most radically acerbic works. They had also nagged at Wang, the afore-mentioned Columbia professor, as he prepared to introduce Ameri-can readers to the works of Lu Xun. Wang's relative privilege could not insulate him from the demands of the publishing marketplace.

Despite Buck's ultimate ambivalence toward Liang—he starts feel-ing ulcer pains further down the page—this imagined conversation offers a fascinating moment of self-censure. Even though Liang's ar-rogance alienates the reader, his criticism of how the average Ameri-can "dinner guest" regards China has its merits—and it is a criticism aimed squarely back at herself. Her characters repeat the various ideas about China in circulation at the time: they are "poor, dirty ignorant people"[59] and "as medieval as Europe in the sixteenth century" to some, a "great civilization" ready to "shine forth" to others.[60]

If *Kinfolk* expressed skepticism that neither she nor an out-of-touch Chinese intellectual like Liang could properly grasp the com-plexity of China, then who could?

One needed to find the right go-between. It would be Liang's chil-dren—the literal offspring of "two cultures." Like the student essay-ists we met earlier in this chapter who debated whether their futures lie in China or America, the younger Liangs sought to "go west . . . to China."[61] The eldest, James, is the first to return to China, against his parents' wishes. Born in China but raised and acculturated in the United States, James represents the perfect embodiment of "East and West." His parting words for the girlfriend he leaves behind in New York best sums up his inherited idealism. "Our people are good—our people are wonderful. China is great. She is not really weak. She is only in distress. All the great strength is simply waiting until we come to her help. She has lived in an old, old world and she needs to be born into the new one."[62] He aspires to bring the medical knowledge he has acquired in the United States back to China.

James's journey across the Pacific Ocean captures Buck's hopes for his future. His fellow passengers on this ship include "two solitary old Chinese who he suspected were Cantonese going home to die, a hard-bitten American businessman, a Standard Oil executive, a jour-nalist, two or three missionaries and their wives."[63] The scene index-es the early twentieth century expatriate community: businessmen,

journalists, and missionaries were all central to the history of transpacific encounter. There is the "hard-bitten" businessman of a previous era, reminiscent of Carl Crow's widely read 1937 *Four Million
Customers*. There is a representative from Standard Oil, the path-
breaking corporation whose successful breach of China had been
satirized by Alice Tisdale Hobart in 1933's *Oil for the Lamps of China*.
The journalist stands in for any number of Buck associates and rivals:
Edgar Snow, Agnes Smedley, John Hersey, Henry Luce, *Asia* magazine. And then there is the missionary and his wife—a reference to
Buck's own parents and her first husband, John Lossing Buck. It was
while accompanying her husband on his agro-missionary campaigns
through rural China that she began to conceive of the *Good Earth*.

There is a powerful symbolism to Buck's placement of James
within this crowded field of cultural go-betweens. He is young and
potent, the heir to the old "Cantonese going home to die." His upbringing and self-awareness places him on a level with Crow, Buck,
and the rest. James is not only the next in line after the businessman, journalist, and missionary to stake a claim to this transpacific
circuit. In a fit of rage over their young daughter Louise's steadfastly
American defiance, the Liangs send the three remaining children
back to China in order to punish them, transferring guardianship
to James. He replaces his father—the jaded scholar, the lazy Confucian—as the head of the family. When James's siblings repeat the
Pacific crossing years later, they describe a "fellow on board [their
ship] from Hollywood." Peter, James's younger brother, continues
his breathless account: "He's coming out here to shoot some pictures. It's a story about a GI—sort of a Chinese Madame Butterfly
story, he said, only the GI doesn't go away. He takes his gal home. He
said that while they don't want stories about white men and Negroes
getting married they don't mind Chinese any more. Pretty good,
isn't it?"[64] In the wake of the businessman, journalist, and missionary's respective arrivals on Chinese shores, the filmmaker has come
as well, in the hopes of using China as an authentic backdrop for
Orientalist fantasy.

However, James and his siblings later reject this proto-model minority positioning. After a spell in China, during which he has become
an aggressive nationalist, the younger brother Peter scoffs at a white

serviceman hoping to bring his sister Louise back to the States. "I'll be happier with Louise than I would with any regular American girl," the serviceman explains. "Besides, the baby will be easier to explain. And people aren't as old-fashioned as they used to be. You can't marry a Negro, but most people don't mind a Chinese." "Don't mind a Chinese!" Peter bellows in reply. "But we mind Americans, let me tell you!"[65]

Peter's attitude suggests that he has drifted far from the all-American identity that once defined him. Perhaps his inability to find a comfortable middle ground is why he must be martyred—he is murdered by the Kuomintang's secret police. It is important that the Liang siblings prize a flexibility of perspective, and it is this commitment to neither American nor Chinese nationalism that allows James and his oldest sister, Mary, to flourish. James's idealism threatens to sink him as he, like John Dewey Chang before him, realizes "there was no magic homeland."[66] But he and Mary eventually realize a shared vision of collaboration between the rural Chinese and the self-exiled Chinese Americans, devoting themselves to rebuilding their ancestral village—to living like the rural Chinese, but offering them the benefits of Western medicine and education.

They face many of the same challenges that had vexed the "peasants" in Buck's earlier novels. But they draw upon a deeper reserve of experiences and perspectives, becoming, within the text, China's last line of defense—against Communism, postfeudal corruption, and factionalism. As with "His Own Country," it would take the full gradient of Chinese American experiences to discover a solution to China's social and political turmoil. There's something faintly ironic about the fact that Buck and John Day had been so instrumental in helping overturn the Chinese Exclusion Act, for these stories will their characters back to the ancestral land. It was a strange way to wield their influence, yet it just underscored the ultimate goal: a healthy, democratic China.

As the John Day Company readied *Kinfolk* for publication, the publishing house's staff began to wonder: who was Liang Wen Hua? Was he based on a real person? He certainly resembled Buck's rival, Kiang Kang-Hu. But didn't he also share similarities with the Chinese writer Lin Yutang, another John Day author?

Lin was a well-known Chinese writer and translator who had been educated throughout Asia, Europe, and the United States. He first met Buck and Walsh in the early 1930s and had, over the course of the decade, published a number of bestselling books and translations of Chinese classics in the United States. His style was folksy, witty and, most importantly, inoffensive, and he wrote about everything from Chinese philosophy to the Chinese disdain for cheese. He had moved to New York at the invitation of Buck and Walsh, writing and lecturing on all things Chinese—much like Liang. A contributor to magazines like *Reader's Digest, Colliers, Harper's, Asia,* and *the Atlantic,* Lin was perhaps the most prominent Chinese "expert" of his time, nearly rivaling Buck's influence.[67]

There is speculation that Buck borrowed elements of Lin's flighty personality for the character of Liang. In 1940, Lin had made a show of moving his family from America back to China out of solidarity with the nationalist war effort. They suffered through three harsh months and quickly returned to the United States. Buck's impression of Lin never recovered.[68] But if Lin recognized traces of himself in the character Liang, he kept it to himself. In a memo to his staff, Walsh denied the resemblance. In fact, Lin's wife, Liao Tsui-feng, had written Buck a letter telling her how much she had enjoyed *Kinfolk*. She guessed that Buck had based the character of Liang on Lin's "cynical" nephew while Liang's wife was clearly inspired by Buwei Wang Chao, wife of the prominent linguist Yuen Ren Chao. Mostly, though, Liao wanted to congratulate Buck on another perceptive work. "As a whole, your technique is so different in this book and I am sure the American public as well as the Chinese will thoroughly enjoy your book. You thoroughly understand the psychology of the Chinese in New York, as well as that of the Chinese in China."[69]

The irony is that neither Lin nor his wife actually understood "the psychology of the Chinese in New York." They were an itinerant family who traveled primarily in elite Western circles. Lin himself demonstrated very little knowledge of the struggles of those in Chinatown or the historical forces that had shaped their lives—he was probably even more clueless about the typical Chinese American experience than Liang Wen Hua. But in the mid 1940s, Walsh sensed that the reading public's interest in China was finally on the wane.

He encouraged Lin to write about the experiences of Chinese immigrants in America. Lin had been raised in rural China and educated at elite institutions abroad. At the time, he was living in Cannes and working for UNESCO. Walsh was dogged in his attempts to educate Lin, bombarding him with newspaper articles, historical tracts, and sociological studies to help him flesh out his characters and their daily struggles. As the literary historian Richard Jean So has noted, it was ironic that Walsh had enlisted Lin to write a book about Chinatown.[70] When Walsh and Buck had first encountered him years earlier, he had represented a kind of transpacific cosmopolitanism that was prized in China-watching circles. Now, he was being asked to use his authenticity and authority as a famous Chinese writer to detail the struggles of countrymen with whom he shared very little in common.

In 1948, Lin published *Chinatown Family*. Like Buck's stories, Lin's novel is set during the Chinese Exclusion Era, when immigration from China into the United States was nearly impossible. The story opens with two young teens, Tom and Eva Fong, arriving from the mainland to reunite with the rest of their family. Their father, Tom, Sr., had arrived decades earlier as a laborer, eventually sponsoring and financing the immigration of the rest of his family.

Tom, Sr. is the proud owner of a laundry business, and despite the fact that his life is described as a "struggle triumphant," emphasis is placed on the family's considerable successes. The children trade tales of the awful plight of Chinese laborers during California's Gold Rush yet they celebrate them as "stories of survival." Tom, Sr. considers the difficulty of maneuvering the reprehensible Exclusion Act to bring his family over but still finds the optimism to conclude that "the immigration officials were merely obstacles Heaven placed in the path of men determined to achieve success with patience and persistence."[71] When the younger Tom looks in his father's face, "there is no record to tell what he had gone through . . . [his face] concealed a whole load of emotions seldom expressed. It also expressed patience and endurance as if it was saying, 'We shall see who has the last laugh.'"[72]

There is no sense of conflict or tension throughout *Chinatown Family*, only a constant return to harmony and random strokes of good fortune. One of the sons marries the daughter of an Italian immigrant, and over time the families become inseparable. Chinese and American business methods are pragmatically fused together, insuring profit for all. When a freak accident claims the life of Tom, Sr. near the story's end, his guilt-ridden killer gives the family a handsome sum, and they conclude that everything worked out just fine.

Lin uses the characters—per Walsh's request—to stitch together a history of the Chinese in America, ostensibly in the hopes of alerting readers to the austere charms of these oft-ignored communities. The Fongs embody the touchstones of the Chinese immigrant experience, from the pernicious Chinese Exclusion Act to their family laundry. Consider the character of Uncle Tuck, the head of a local Chinatown guild. He had arrived on the West Coast as a laborer, during the dying days of the Gold Rush. He worked his way down the coast, eventually linking up with a band of laborers and forging eastward, across the country. In his fifties—having already lived the generic, itinerant life of a migrant laborer—Tuck reached New York City. A natural leader and skilled fighter, he became a cornerstone of this radically different, urban Chinese American community. At one point, his path even intersects with true history, as Lin suggests that Tuck's intellectual prowess had impressed none other than Sun Yat-sen, the Chinese political revolutionary. Heading a guild in New York's Chinatown, Tuck is a bridge between communities—middle class Chinese Americans uptown, grimy immigrants downtown, city officials, and the local police.

Buck and Lin's crisscrossing stories present Chinatown as a site of struggle and existential doubt but also transpacific possibility— a testing ground for new identities not beholden to nationalistic urges or shortsighted views on history and progress. The enclave of Chinatown itself becomes a model of fusing cultures, though the unions imagined by *Chinatown Family* are ultimately impossible ones. The strange tranquility of Lin's book suggests a hope that the reconciliation of East and West can be quiet, tidy, and passive. Despite placing his family within a matrix of racist institutions and having them lead a tedious, backbreaking day-to-day existence, Lin maintains an upbeat tone. Despite exclusion, labor restrictions, antimiscegenation—Tuck remains philosophical. In fact, this full gamut of experiences has only made him more thoughtful about the human condition. When young Tom asks him about the oft-circulated story of a crew of bandits who had nearly killed him in Wyoming, Tuck laughs: "There are cutthroats in every country. But cutthroats are not bad people. There are no bad people. Nobody is bad. All people are very much the same. Some are a little better, and some are a little worse. That is all."[73] Despite a life that testifies to the contrary, the United States, Tuck concludes, "is a great country."[74]

What can we make of Lin's Chinatown, where conflict is rare and patience is the only virtue? One possible answer lies within Lin's own cosmopolitan worldview, forged by an itinerant, stateless, and ultimately privileged existence. Throughout the 1930s he had moved freely, exempt from the bonds of poverty and decades of racism that might have stifled his characters' lives. This interest in the plight of Chinese Americans was but a momentary blip on the long arc of Lin's career. Lin had written *Chinatown Family* at his publisher's behest while living in Cannes. In the two decades that followed its publication, he would move back to New York, then to Singapore, Hong Kong, and Taiwan.

John Day's late-1940s flirtation with the Chinese American experience would come to seem like an aberration. The publisher had briefly marshaled its considerable resources to advance an ambitious political agenda around the privileged perspectives and superhuman dignity of Buck, Colman, and Lin's Chinatown youth. In essence, it was a last-ditch effort to revitalize middlebrow interest in China's fate by offering a new kind of character. The conversation was growing stale; the market for such books was shrinking. The period of interest that had roughly begun with *The Good Earth* effectively ended once the Cold War inflected that interest with a pronounced ideology. By the time the Communists assumed control in 1949, the democratic China and go-between Chinese Americans envisioned by these books would come to seem like bizarre fantasies. When Chinese Americans began publishing their own stories in the 1950s, they were carried by different themes and desires. Popular novels like Jade Snow Wong's *Fifth Chinese Daughter* and C. Y. Lee's *The Flower Drum Song*—adapted to great acclaim for stage and screen—celebrated family ties, themes of gritty perseverance, and the hard-won possibilities of assimilation. The Chinese American was a useful new archetype, though not in the way John Day had anticipated. While the Chinese American experience did little to prolong the American middlebrow interest in China's future, it was an experience that could be used to sell those abroad on America's future. The success of *Fifth Chinese Daughter*, for example, resulted in Wong's State Department-funded speaking tour of Asia in 1953. It was a different kind of flirtation with the Chinese American experience: this time the goal was the hearts and minds of Asians, not Americans.

China had been lost. The conversation that Buck and her circle had so thoroughly controlled was going on elsewhere. But there was still blame to go around.

7

Too Big to Fail

ONCE UPON A TIME, H. T. Tsiang had set out to write a novel "somewhat like *The Good Earth* but much better."

It was the mid-1930s, a period when it seemed like any American with a typewriter and some firsthand knowledge of Shanghai could publish a book about China, and Tsiang still believed that a career as a writer was well within his reach. But, as we witnessed in the previous chapters, he never tasted the success he felt he deserved. Not only had the major publishing houses rejected him, so had the proletarian art world's presumably friendlier niche of left-leaning artists and readers. Tsiang never understood his stalling career as an indictment of his talents; he read his misfortune as a problem of the market. His first novel, *China Red*, was self-published in 1931, the same year that Pearl Buck's *The Good Earth* awakened millions of Americans to the cause of China. While Buck quickly became the era's most influential voice on China, Tsiang wandered New York City, hawking copies of his self-published novels to anyone who would listen to his harried sales pitch. By the time he wrote *And China Has Hands*, he was driven by an intense, almost paranoid animosity toward Buck and all she represented. She became the symbol for this market that conspired to exclude him. Perhaps he could never overcome her power but he sought revenge wherever possible. As we saw in Chapter 5, Tsiang had taken his final shot at Buck in the closing pages of *And China Has Hands*. He revealed this novel and its luckless characters to be a joke of sorts, an attempt to imagine different, far less successful pathways for the author Buck and her prized creations:

> Poor Wong Wan-Lee, who had made no ten thousand fortunes, was a failure; but his cousin Wong Lung had made a million and had become the hero of The Good Earth—Horatio Alger!
> Poor Pearl C, who had become no star, was a failure; but her cousin Pearl B, had married her boss, a publisher.[1]

In Chapter 3, we considered the ways in which best-selling authors like Buck or Carl Crow became real-life characters spurring America's rediscovery of China. Not only did their books shape the interests of American readers, their own life stories did as well. Here, Tsiang was collapsing this distance, equating Wang Lung, *The Good Earth*'s sympathetic protagonist, with the fine fortunes of Buck, his celebrated creator. Buck and her fictions drove the American conversation on China. Meanwhile, Tsiang and his poor characters—the reluctant martyr Wong Wan-Lee, the naïve Pearl Chang—were but also-rans. His feeling of abjection grew so overwhelming that he inserted himself into this novel as an annoying "Chinese fellow who was trying to sell his own book," pestering the rest of the characters at every turn. It was a hint at larger frustrations. Tsiang had witnessed the rise of the "China hands," American experts whose experiences in China were devoured by middlebrow readers. As the title of his final novel suggested: China had hands, people like Buck, Crow, Edgar Snow, assorted journalists, travelers, diplomats, and businessmen. Tsiang, despite his American education and firsthand experience of the Chinese government, was never allowed to become one of these authorities.

As we shall soon see, Buck herself was not immune to feelings of insecurity regarding her status as a China expert. She, too, would set off into her fictional worlds to settle a score against the publisher and fellow China advocate Henry Luce, her most bitter rival. But for now, let us consider the underdog Tsiang's final years. What if we take seriously these moments in Tsiang's novels when he offered himself to us as a character? What desires were left unfulfilled in the unfinished manuscript titles he left behind—*A Floating "Chinaman"* or *Shanghai Newyork Moscow—An Odyssey of a Chinese Coolie*?

What happens when we arrange the various books, letters, and official documents that constituted his life and try to read it all as a single, coherent text? Maybe Tsiang himself was the "floating Chinaman," the "coolie" forever orbiting the scene. In the end, he left behind a far stranger and no less visionary life story. Tsiang was, it turned out, a character in someone else's drama: for years, he was one of thousands of leftist sympathizers under FBI surveillance.

H. T. Tsiang was not the Chinese American the public desired. In the last chapter, we surveyed the brief emergence of popular novels that approached the Chinese American not as an intellectual curiosity but as a political project. For a fleeting moment, established authors and editors imagined the Chinese American as a figure of privilege, a mediator between nations who deserved a place alongside the businessman, missionary, and journalist in bridging the transpacific divide. But not everyone could crisscross the Pacific as easily as Buck or her influential cohort. Tsiang found himself in a permanent sense of geographical dislocation, unable to chisel away at an American cultural marketplace more interested in Buck's peasants or the fictional detective Charlie Chan, and unwilling to return to an increasingly contentious China. He operated on the extreme periphery of New York's literary community, his promiscuous relationship to literary convention embodying a desire to invent a new language capable of representing the transpacific circulation of ideas that so moved him.

By 1940, Tsiang was on Ellis Island, awaiting a hearing on his case to stay in the United States, despite the fact that he had violated the terms of his student visa. As we saw in Chapter 5, he spent much of his detention writing letters to friends and comrades begging for legal assistance and expressing a paranoid fear that the United States government was monitoring his artistic output. Was this just another sign of his eccentric, attention-starved nature? Whenever he had written himself into his novels, he had tended to exaggerate his career's highs and lows. Would the government actually target someone whose works were experimental, self-published and profoundly unpopular?

Perhaps this is a way of thinking through a more philosophical question of scale: what can we learn from a figure who was so obscure? What might we glean from a character who sold very few books, who distributed those books in an ad hoc and occasionally hectoring manner, whose outsized sense of self compelled him to shout into the microphone or mug for the camera on those rare occasions he found himself near a spotlight? What can we draw from someone for whom the kindest thing might be to say that he was "misunderstood" in his time?

These were questions I kept trying to answer as I grew ever more enchanted with Tsiang's work. There were certainly aspects of his oeuvre that were forward thinking, even zanily self-aware in a way that anticipated avant-garde artistic and cultural movements that would not emerge for decades. But my argument here is not that we recognize Tsiang as some sort of lost visionary whose peculiar style predicted our present, a temptation that attends most discoveries of sui generis oddballs in the archives. I do not believe that Tsiang was unduly overlooked. His blast radius was tiny and sporadic; there is a reason he remained obscure. He longed to be part of a conversation about China and Chinese people, a conversation that was always taking place somewhere else—in sight but out of reach. Barred entry, he aspired instead to be a barnacle on the ship of Buck; to be a scourge; to mock, critique, and haunt this conversation to which he was not invited. I remain interested in the conditions that spurred his career—conditions that remain familiar to many marginalized thinkers and writers still today. The world he was trying to breach feels astonishingly contemporary, as does his utter illegibility to many who purported to know his kind.

In the end, Tsiang did not have to go back to China. By 1943 he had, like many proletarian artists, relocated to Hollywood,[2] where his production of *The Hanging on Union Square* played for over five years. Stars like Vincent Price, Gregory Peck, Orson Welles, Rita Hayworth, and Alfred Hitchcock came to see it, and Tsiang himself became a very minor Hollywood celebrity. Throughout the 1950s, he also performed *Wedding at a Nudist Colony*, a weekly, one-man show based on Shakespeare's *Hamlet* featuring Freudian analysis, anticapitalist rants, sound effects borrowed from Chinese theater, and a tin can in place of Yorick's skull.

He gradually migrated from playwriting to appearing in movies like *Behind the Rising Sun*, *The Keys of the Kingdom*, *Tokyo Rose*, and

The Babe Ruth Story as well as television shows like *I Spy, Bonanza,* and *My Three Sons.* Perhaps he appreciated the irony of acting in 1945's *China Sky*—adapted from a novel by Pearl Buck. He became a pioneering Asian American actor, though he was often cast in stereo-typical or subservient roles that traded on his yellow skin.

In the end, he was not the anonymous and forgotten man depicted in his novels. He had earned a following—a secret one consisting of undercover FBI agents, confidential informants, and friends ea-ger to attest to his ultimate harmlessness. Unbeknownst to him, FBI and INS agents in Los Angeles, San Francisco, and New York were compiling reports on Tsiang's background, known associates, asso-ciations, and movements.

Tsiang was not alone. During the Cold War, the FBI routinely spied on Americans with left-leaning sympathies. They were par-ticularly interested in enclaves like Chinatown, wary that these immigrant communities were hotbeds of Communist organizing. The example of New York's Chinese Hand Laundry Alliance, an organization with which Tsiang was loosely affiliated in the 1930s, is instructive. Starting in 1954, the FBI installed "technical surveil-lance" on the telephone of the Alliance's main office, hoping that the group's members would "converse freely in the Chinese lan-guage without fear of being detected." But they also attempted to engage members directly.[3] As one laundryman would later recall, "The FBI harassed us for more than twenty years. They could not find anything to indict us, but they kept harassing us. In those years, every week I received two calls from FBI agents. What did they say on the phone? Nothing. They just checked whether you were there. They wanted to cause fear among our members."[4] Most impor-tantly, the atmosphere of paranoia and patriotic duty could be used to the FBI's advantage. Members of the Chinatown establishment, more concerned with assimilation than the interests of the working class, often encouraged surveillance and FBI harassment of groups like the Alliance.[5]

What kind of life do Tsiang's files narrate? What range of possi-bilities do they allow for Tsiang? And more broadly: how might we detect Tsiang's refusal of the narratives of his life drafted by his secret government monitors? Bureaucratic documents aspire to make all subjects accountable and legible.[6] To paraphrase the political theorist James Scott: what did the state see?

Tsiang's file consists of about fifty pages culled from three reports. They were each filed in 1951. Two of the reports originated in Los Angeles and one in San Francisco, with assistance provided by FBI and INS agents in New York. By now, China had been "lost" to the Communists, and the promise of the Chinese American had begun to fade. The file recounts narratives sourced from an anonymous crowd, convened to debate Tsiang's potential threat as an underground agitator. Once the agents concluded that Tsiang's political activities were quite harmless, the files measured his fitness for citizenship.

Given the passionate irreverence that ruled Tsiang's everyday life, it is strange to regard his life in such concrete terms. The file attempts to discern self-representation from testimonial and observation, in the hopes of establishing some reliable sense of how he might be categorized: a threat to national security? Harmless? An alien? A potentially loyal citizen, albeit one with an unusual sense of humor?

Agents and informants attended meetings where Tsiang was present and interviewed fellow travelers, mentors, and friends. According to his file, Tsiang was under suspicion of being an "internal" or domestic security threat. On September 10, 1951, a Los Angeles field agent filed its most substantial report on him. It begins with a few brief paragraphs summarizing the competing versions of his identity: "Subject observed at Communist Party and Communist Party front meetings in Los Angeles. Regarded by local Chinese sources as harmless 'character and crackpot.' Subject described self as 'Red' to one source, indicating self to be pro-Communist."[7] The agent completes the synopsis of his findings by noting the many "strong endorsements" Tsiang had received for his books and poems. The bulk of this report consists of a narrative of his artistic endeavors since settling in Los Angeles, though supplementary reports shade in his life in New York as well.

Taken as a whole, the file is, in its own way, an admirable piece of scholarship. Tsiang himself never penned so straightforwardly comprehensive an account of his life and times. Over the course of a couple dozen pages, the agent reconstructs his movements in remarkable detail, sifting and searching for a clue as to his true motives. There are sad observations of minor debts, low-paying jobs as a busboy, poor health, poor attendance as a student, and poor grades. The file considers a chorus of opinions—informants, undercover field agents, old landlords, teachers, relatives, and coworkers. An informant "of known reliability" describes a meeting of the Hollywood Communist Club where Tsiang made a desperate appeal for members to buy tickets to a one-man play he was staging. Another informant told the agent that the League of American Writers had helped fund a stage adaptation of Tsiang's *The Hanging on Union Square* in 1944. The informant noted that the play had received considerable praise in the September 27, 1942, issue of the *Daily Worker*.[8] From the perspective of this curious agent, perhaps this network of support and praise was a sign of Tsiang's secret influence.

Tsiang was certainly busy in those days. He attended Communist splinter group meetings, receptions, parties, and bazaars throughout Southern California. Sometimes he was there to drum up tickets sales for his theater productions, other times he would sit quietly and listen. At "Fred's Birthday Ball," he and a "good looking" actress with reddish-brown hair performed a short play titled *Revolution at Canton*.[9] At a local meeting of the Jewish People's Fraternal Order, Tsiang chatted up an undercover agent. He tried to convince him to come see his plays. "The admission fee was $1.00 plus tax." He then handed the agent a sheet of paper reprinting reviews from local newspapers.[10]

Tsiang's file does not depict him as some luckless loner, adrift and unheard. It places him within an eclectic network of friends, supporters, artists, fellow travelers, and secret informants. Sometimes he was even the life of the party. But opinion on Tsiang's fitness for citizenship was divided. "REDACTED stated that whereas TSIANG is considered by many Chinese and others to be pro-Communist, he has never been seen trying to influence others. REDACTED does not consider TSIANG to be a bad or subversively inclined individual and stated that he might even consider recommending TSIANG for continued residence in the United States, at least insofar as his potential dangerousness might be concerned."[11] In contrast, another informant said "he would never grant United States citizenship to TSIANG if the decision were up to him."[12]

These reports on Tsiang do not slot comfortably into any lineage of writing with aesthetic or symbolic aspiration—these are files that compile data. They help narrate, through the choices made by now-anonymous agents about how to deploy the testimony of now-anonymous informants, a set of political possibilities. Among the other life details one gleans from these files, those that recur begin to take on the feeling of fact. Tsiang had difficulties paying his rent, for example. He was a "harmless 'character and crackpot'" or an "eccentric" "screwball"[13] but never a serious, steely Communist, despite his own claims to the contrary. An informant "stated that the subject strikes him as all talk, and he could not visualize TSIANG as a saboteur despite the fact he appeared to be definitely 'left-wing.'"[14] The playwright Clifford Odets remarked to the investigators that Tsiang was "one of the finest, sweetest and most Christian-like men he has ever met,"[15] while a different informant considered him "a harmless character who due to his eccentricity would never be given any important work by the Communists or the Soviets."[16]

The investigators recount and occasionally excerpt Tsiang's literary accomplishments with the same discriminating air as critics and publishers. Passages are reprinted and closely read for any trace of serious Communist sympathizing, as though these FBI agents are book reviewers combing the text for traces of authorial intention. Tsiang would have appreciated that someone read his works closely enough to detect its leftist leanings. In his work on French literary culture, the historian Robert Darnton writes about Joseph d'Hémery, the French police inspector tasked with monitoring the book trade between 1748 and 1753. A careful reader of the writers he was policing, d'Hémery inadvertently composed one of our first sociologies of literature. Surveying d'Hémery's trove of surveillance files, Darnton carefully notes the limitations of reading "police work as witch-hunting." There were no underground plots to uncover, nor were these authors chosen because they were suspected of subversion. Instead, it might be more accurate to say that d'Hémery worked on behalf of a bureaucracy interested in collecting data on its subjects and their daily pursuits. "It really represents something less familiar and more interesting: information gathering in the age of absolutism."[17] In Darnton's view, these police files cannot be taken "as hard nuggets of irreducible reality" we use to reconstruct the past.[18] They represent moments when d'Hémery himself became a writer, composing a secret, wide-lens narrative about France's burgeoning literary culture.

This is not to discount the trauma of surveillance. But despite the starkly different context—the Cold War certainly was an era of "witch-hunting"—I am drawn to Darnton's call to read police surveillance as a kind of authorship. What conventions and expectations guide these accounts? What do they reveal about their secret authors? In her work on the Soviet secret police, the literary critic Cristina Vatulescu has attempted to identify "the poetics of the personal files, its narrative devices, its rhetorical figures, as well as the shifting contexts of its production and reception."[19] She astutely notes the necessity to shape these dissident lives into "biographies," if only to better understand and control the circumstances that had produced an oppositional underground.[20]

What, then, did these agents make of Tsiang's life and art? Large portions of the reports are redacted, a graphic reminder of history's gap-filled remoteness. Ornate signatures identify the agents who filed these reports, many of whom were quite renowned within the bureau: Edward Scheidt was one of J. Edgar Hoover's original "G-Men" in the 1930s before becoming director of the FBI's New York field office. R. J. Abbaticchio, Jr. worked in Houston and along the West Coast before retiring to work with the Nevada Gaming Commission. C. H. Carson and R. B. Hood were special agents with considerable experience monitoring Hollywood. Their confidential informants rest in peace behind black streaks, though the details and settings of their accounts suggest that many might have been fellow leftists or Asian immigrants.

Years are condensed to mere sentences. But the file lingers on a few anecdotes depicting Tsiang's eccentricities. While the reports are devoid of humor, certain moments feel serendipitously Tsiang-like in their retelling. In 1950, Tsiang was nominated to the Board of Directors of the Southern California Council of American-Soviet Friendship. "However, his nomination was countered with a comment from another unidentified person that although TSIANG was a good man for the job, he had recently been drinking too much to be considered thoroughly reliable. REDACTED advised that TSIANG was not elected to the Board of Directors."[21] Another time, Tsiang was at the counter of a Chinatown shop when "a white man" remarked that Tsiang "was certainly 'pink.'" The accusation irked Tsiang who, "in a tone of braggadocio responded, 'Pink!—Hell, I'm as Red as that.' At this point, TSIANG indicated with his finger some red colored object lying on the counter."[22] It is hard to imagine that this anecdote was reproduced as an indication of Tsiang's true leanings. After all, just a few pages over, the informant suggests that his leftist sympathies were not matched by any fearsome work ethic: "It is REDACTED's opinion that TSIANG is absolutely opposed to work and would not resort to work, particularly physical labor, unless he were actually starving."[23]

It is strange to recognize moments when these agents have made editorial choices. Midway through one lengthy report on Tsiang's whereabouts, the agent mentions "Ask The Wind! Ask The Dust! (An Ode to Thought Control)," a mimeographed poem Tsiang had begun distributing to friends and followers. The agent begins with a dutiful summary of Tsiang's work: "This is a poem in which a hungry poet is being attacked by a hungry wolf followed by a little running dog. The poet is pictured as being consumed by the wolf and later resurrects himself by bursting from the wolf's stomach, thus destroying the wolf."[24] The agent never tries interpreting the poem's symbolism or its titular reference to "thought control." But for reasons unexplained, the agent did feel it necessary to reproduce the poem's final verses in full. In the end, the poet finds strength in the knowledge that his art will outlast them all: "They will last longer than any hungry wolf / Or any little running dog of the money king!"[25]

This file will outlive him, too.

This has been a story about the vesting of authority: how it is acquired, how it gets transcribed onto paper, how it travels.

There are two version of this story at play. In the first, Buck uses her authority to cast light on the plight of the Chinese Americans and their Chinatowns. She and her husband, John Day Company publisher Richard Walsh, encourage others to do the same. There is a generative tension in reading these files about Tsiang against these literary representations of Chinese Americans by Buck and her cohort: they offer competing narratives of the Chinese American possibility. In scrambling our expectations around the categories fact and fiction, we realize how mutually constitutive the two are—how, in the case of Tsiang, these texts converge in the same discursive field. On one hand, creative works aspire toward a condition of truth, a sense that a fictional Chinese American might animate discussion of real life politics; on the other hand, surveillance documents that aspire toward the collection of truth end up beholden to narrative convention, the need to resolve loose threads and to imagine a real-life person's life experiences as raw materials for a sensible story. The constitution of a Chinese American subject is a practice that is both notional and embodied. While these various representations of Chinese Americans were drafted for different reading audiences, they stage a fascinating debate about both the possibilities and limitations of this identity, as well as what it meant to be a good, immigrant citizen in postwar America.

The second version of this story comes to us in Tsiang's files, an unofficial biography collaboratively penned by a far-flung cast of government agents and confidential informants. In the context of a failed literary career, these joyless agents author the most committed criticism available of Tsiang's body of work. An immigration official named Marks Rosen concluded that Tsiang definitely posed no danger to the United States, though opinion remained divided as to whether he was a Communist. Perhaps the answer could be found in subtext: "I have been unable to establish whether he belongs to any Communistic organizations or whether he is actively engaged in any Communistic activities. In this connection it will be noted that his book 'China Red' printed in 1929, although not written in the first person, seems to be an account of the alien's transition from an anti-Red to a Communist . . ."[26] An FBI agent follows Rosen's lead, and the report continues by reprinting page 159 of *And China Has Hands*, one of the instances when Tsiang himself appeared in his novel to harangue passers-by into buying his books. Tsiang's playful irony had not fooled the FBI; they recognized the secret, underground politics buried deep within his novels.

It is possible that these FBI and INS agents were Tsiang's most faithful readers, sensitive to his eccentric performance, parsing his poems and novels for hidden meanings. Once his art was decoded and defanged, they set out trying to reduce his wondrous, contradictory life into staid lines on an official document: measurable indicators of age and height, years spent in various cities, a list of newspapers that had published his poetry. But he still squirmed free of their attempts to categorize him. Tsiang's voice begins to emerge from within the reports. To a publisher who had helped with one of his books, Tsiang seemed "just a little crazy"—an apt description.[27] An official with the American Civil Liberties Union who had worked on Tsiang's deportation case concluded that he was somewhat "nutty," a word Tsiang would have appreciated.[28] We might read Tsiang's occasional, quoted interjections, as moments when he is clamoring for a chance to speak as well. Under "Education," for example, the agent reports that Tsiang "studied for ten years and received no degree." The agent continues: "The subject's comment with respect to this situation was"—and the FBI agent quotes Tsiang—"'You don't have to be a Ph.D. to be a writer or a poet.'" His self-representation could not be assimilated into the entry fields of the report, and his denial of the authority conferred by a PhD loops back to his own DIY artistic career, littered with rejection letters from publishers who viewed him an illegitimate forecaster of China's future.

On the rare occasion that Tsiang did run afoul of the law, it was, as the reports note, for public drunkenness. These arrest records demonstrate Tsiang's awareness that the Chinese American identity was mediated through popular representations: under "title," there are various phonetic spellings of his name. One of the aliases listed by officers during his arrests: "Charlie Chan," the hero of Earl Derr Biggers's pulp fiction and the most famous "Chinaman" of his time.[29]

I would like to imagine that Tsiang chose this name. He played the racist stereotype for laughs, spoofing the ways in which one Chinese was often made to stand in for all. As Chi-chen Wang and Harold Isaacs observed, to the average American, China meant Charlie Chan and *The Good Earth*. Just as Liang Wen Hua, the niggling academic from Buck's *Kinfolk*, would scoff at the influence novels about peasants had had on the American imagination, here, Tsiang expresses a similar dismay at how Charlie Chan, the fictional Chinese detective, has rendered all others inconsequential. He often referred to himself in relation to Chan in his letters to Rockwell Kent. But unlike Buck's refusal, grounded upon the belief that Liang shaded in the diversity of the Chinese American community, Tsiang's appropriation of Chan's name is not a claim to a more capacious identity. Rather it suggests an ironic subversion of the techniques of government—it refuses the possibility of compliance and good citizenship.

Or maybe "Charlie Chan" was the alias Los Angeles' police officers gave any drunken Chinese man—a kind of racist, alien version of "John Doe." Maybe this was how limited their imaginations could be. The entry fields in the FBI field reports, after all, echo the exhausted permutations of Chinese, American, and Chinese American identity that drove the works of Buck and her fellow John Day liberals. Together, this broader field of representations from without help lend context to Tsiang's own cultural productions and his subversive irreverence. These concerns are related: we might say that the relative freedom he experienced as a writer, beholden to no genre or convention, reflected the degree of freedom he sought as a subject formed by the transpacific. He felt emboldened to refuse the patriotic Chinese American identities made famous by Buck and Lin Yutang. Although Buck's novels aspire to fictional exploration and the FBI reports hope to do little more than convey data, both pursue a similar question: that is, the degree to which one's experiences as both Chinese and American might be exploited politically in the coming years, for good or bad.

What would Tsiang have thought of these reports? If given the chance, perhaps his response would have been similar to that of the painter Arnold Mesches, who reproduced pages of his 1950s surveillance files as part of a collage series called "*The FBI Files*."[30] Or maybe he would have woven sly allusions to surveillance into his works—think Richard Wright singing "The FB Eye Blues"—and returned the gaze of the FBI "ghostreader."[31]

Tsiang probably would have been surprised to know that his file depicted him in such nonthreatening terms—as someone who was "all talk." At this point, he had ceased to be the author of his own story. A reminder of Tsiang's ultimate powerlessness comes during a section devoted to his activities in New York. The local field agent had interviewed a range of Tsiang's friends and associates, including

Richard Walsh, head of the John Day Company. Walsh told the agent that Rockwell Kent had written him a letter "requesting that the firm give favorable consideration to the subject's writings." Walsh explained that he had rejected Tsiang's manuscripts "for lack of literary merit."[32] We glimpsed Kent's letter in Chapter 1. He had tried to appeal to his friend Walsh's sympathies. Tsiang, he explained, had completed a couple books but they were "still-born works which, brought out under his imprint and marketed in restaurants and on street corners, can be said to have not been really published."[33] In the immediate context of Tsiang's struggle to establish himself as a writer, Kent's letter felt dismissive and condescending, a chilling illustration of his position far beyond the margins of the publishing world: To have not been really published.

But Tsiang might have taken comfort in knowing that his work survived anyway. His life's work was studied and then archived in the filing cabinets of the FBI—a more secure resting place, perhaps, than any library. I came across Tsiang's file while browsing the archives of the late historian Josephine Fowler. I did not know it would be there. As I leafed through the pages and realized what I was reading, I felt a strange sense of pride. I could not believe that such a thing existed. I felt that Tsiang had, in a very bizarre way, made it: he had left something behind. The file had a heft and density. It had, in the words of the anthropologist Ilana Feldman, an aura of "facticity and potency."[34]

The files were meant to discipline him, to make him legible to a bureaucracy that needed to parse friend from foe. Even here, he refuses his place. What did the coming decades hold for the Chinese Americans, Elizabeth Colman asked her audience of elite China watchers, somewhat melodramatically, in 1946? Tsiang, in his resistance of Colman and Buck's perfectly hybrid citizen, embodies one answer. There is something valuable, if not humbling, about considering the failed futurisms of the past. But as with any inquiry into the past, there are limitations to what we can discover. One particularly lengthy assessment of Tsiang's character states that he did not seem like a "bad or subversively inclined individual." This informant "might even consider recommending Tsiang for continued residence in the United States, at least insofar as his potential dangerousness might be concerned." The informant revealed that he had once joked with Tsiang about this contradictory aspect of his politics and personality. Tsiang replied with a laugh, before offering a response, which was redacted.[35]

Once upon a time, Pearl Buck was not the immovable force that Tsiang imagined her to be. As FBI agents were writing their own version of his odyssey, Buck feared that she was losing her stature as America's premier authority on all things Chinese.

In the 1930s and 1940s, Buck's control over this field of conversation seemed unshakeable. Theodore Harris, her friend and biographer, recalled one press conference when a reporter essentially asked why she did not have a direct line to the White House:

> Pearl Buck undoubtedly knows more about China and the Chinese people, more about Asia and Asian people, cultures and governments than any other American and possibly more than any other person alive. Why is it that we do not ask her opinion of or her advice on our current Asian policies?[36]

But as China became more of a geopolitical priority, her esteem waned. Buck's faith in the Chinese people—her idealization of grassroots solutions to the problems of modernity—began to seem a quaint and outdated perspective. By World War II, there were simply more and more qualified experts to consult for advice on Asian policies.

Owen Lattimore, the influential political advisor and scholar of China and Central Asia, mused on the state of the China expert in a 1945 book entitled *Solution in Asia*. The problem requiring a solution was the postwar structure of East Asia. Up until recently, he explained, Americans had been receiving their knowledge on Asia from a small and not particularly qualified community of writers and thinkers, few of whom understood these nations in any substantive way. After all, many of them did not even speak the language:

> Even the routine work of reading and excerpting local newspapers was most commonly done by "native" clerks. It was altogether exceptional to find a newspaperman who could conduct an interview in an Asiatic language, or read a local newspaper, or

who made it a habit to travel widely in the interior of Japan or West to the East. When they interpreted the East to the West it was natural for them to stress those aspects which indicated the need of more money for missionary work. Many of the most influential books on the politics and even the history of Asia were written by men who could not read source materials in the language of the people whose affairs they authoritatively discussed.[37]

Lattimore acknowledged the important role that traders, missionaries, and diplomats played in brokering these new forms of transpacific exchange. In Chapter 3, we encountered some of the go-betweens who assisted both sides: compradors, clerks, traveling salesmen, translators, students. But as the two nations entered a period of more formalized exchange—a period of higher global stakes—Lattimore lamented the appallingly low bar for "expertise" within the diplomatic realm.

> It was a common experience to hear a lecture or read an article, by an "expert," describing China as a chaos of militarists, opium, squeeze, concubines, Communists and malevolent encroachment on foreign interests. Perhaps a week later there would be offered a lecture or article describing the Chinese as a democratic people, guided by a devoted band of wise political leaders who were preparing, among other things, an unlimited field for American enterprise and profit. How far did he feel, at the time, that he had reliable criteria for judging the relative expertness of experts who contradicted each other?[38]

As we witnessed in Chapter 3, the rise of the China expert meant that this massive, foreign land of "four hundred million" became whatever Americans saw fit to imagine it as. There is a temptation to try and guess which experts Lattimore blames for American misperceptions. It should be noted that he was generally supportive of Buck's writings, having positively reviewed Buck's 1933 translation of the Chinese epic *All Men Are Brothers*.[39] But Lattimore's lament echoes those of the various Chinese figures we have thus far encountered: Kiang Kang-Hu, the Chinese scholar and politician who wondered why Americans were so entranced by the backwards China of *The Good Earth*; Chi-chen Wang, the Columbia University professor who was vexed by the American conflation of modern China with Chinatown and Charlie Chan; and Tsiang, motivated by his scorn for Buck and the broader publishing industry. Even Buck herself expressed concern over the expert class that spoke on behalf of China.

The end of World War II would be a decisive moment and Lattimore believed that it was up to the public to hold their experts accountable for their ideas. By the mid 1940s, Buck's influence had begun to recede. She had opposed Chiang Kai-Shek, who would remain a powerful—and, for Americans, highly visible—figure shaping China's postwar landscape. She had drawn on wartime sympathies to help overturn the Chinese Exclusion Act; she had opposed Japanese internment. But her influence was increasingly limited to the domestic sphere. Soon, the Cold War would lay waste to the previous era's half-sketched idealisms.

In 1951, in the autumn of her fame, Buck published a book titled *God's Men*.[40] It is an exceedingly bitter book about the diverging paths of two men, Clem Miller and William Lane. They first meet as small boys in turn-of-the-century China, then again in the United States once each has discovered his true calling. Miller would dedicate himself to charity, eventually perishing under the awesome weight of his grand ambition to end world hunger. In contrast, Lane is more interested in controlling the world than saving it. He is probably the most villainous character of Buck's considerable oeuvre. With a hollow heart—Buck insists on reminding readers of Lane's profound inability to feel anything—and megalomaniacal spirit, Lane founds a brilliantly simple and astonishingly profitable newsmagazine that preys on the malleability of the American middlebrow. From his perch atop the masthead, Lane carefully shapes his American readers' view of the world, particularly their sentiments toward his birthplace of China. He is imperious and condescending; he is a failed writer out of touch with the common man, damned with the occasional bout of erectile dysfunction.

God's Men is a thinly veiled attack on the life and ideas of *Time-Life* publishing magnate Henry Luce.[41] Luce is undoubtedly Lane—subtlety was not one of Buck's strengths. Like Luce, Lane's father—named Harry, Luce's real-life nickname—is a kind-hearted American missionary posted in China. Lane's sister is named Henrietta—an obvious variation if not feminization of the name Henry. Like Luce, Lane attends the Chefoo School in China. Luce enrolled at Yale while the fictional Lane went to Harvard. Both Luce and Lane depend on upstanding right-hand men (Miller draws on elements of *Time* cofounder Britt Haddon and editor Theodore White); both divorce their first wives; and both throw the full support of their magazines behind Chiang Kai-shek and the nationalist Kuomintang.

Why did Buck devote an entire novel to literary character assassination? Buck and Luce had not always been at odds. As the children of missionaries ("mish-kids") they had each spent their formative years in China, bearing witness to rebellion and revolution. Each expressed momentary skepticism toward the missionary enterprise, though its spirit would suffuse their transpacific visions later in life. The experience of growing up in China might have shaped their notions of identity as well. Buck and Luce were made aware of just how unusual their childhoods had been as soon they arrived in the United States for schooling. When Buck moved to Virginia to attend Randolph-Macon Women's College, she was known on campus as "the freak who could speak Chinese." She felt little innate attachment to American culture and identified instead with the modest, striving classes, whether they hailed from Anhui or upstate New York. She continued to work through this sense of alienation well into her career, uncertain whether she felt more American or Chinese. Luce suffered a much harsher introduction to the politics of national identity. As a child, he attended the Chefoo School in Yantai, its hallways ruled by British classmates priggishly chauvinistic against Americans like him. Upon moving to Connecticut for boarding school, however, he was recast as Chinese. His fellow students at the Hotchkiss School promptly gave Luce the nickname "Chink" and frequently made light of his Chinese hometown.[42] Decades later, his Chinese roots still amused his rivals. In 1948, the influential conservative pundit Westbrook Pegler penned a bizarre column in quasi-Chinese pidgin casting doubt on the anti-Communist credentials of "Chinaboy Henry Luce"—also known as "Fuey Pi-yu," a funky Chinese name invented by Pegler—and his "velly plitty" wife.[43]

There were certainly moments when it seemed that Buck and Luce might end up on the same side of history. They had briefly met when the latter visited Shanghai in 1931, keeping in touch through the 1930s and early 1940s and collaborating on a number of aid and assistance programs for China. He founded and raised money for United China Appeal, an umbrella group for various Chinese relief organizations, going so far as to mail every single *Time* subscriber a letter asking for donations. He convinced wealthy, powerful captains of industry and culture to publicly support these causes—many of them were motivated less by events in China than the potential repercussions of snubbing Luce and his stable of magazines.[44] Luce had publicly supported Buck's efforts to repeal the Chinese Exclusion Act. They were both anti-Communist. But in the mid-1940s, Luce began to distance himself from the leftist "Pearl Buck crowd."[45] They fundamentally disagreed on how best to configure the long-term interests of these two nations. Luce had placed his faith in industry and conservative governance, supporting Chiang Kai-shek and Soong May-ling. From 1927 to 1955—owing, one assumes, to Luce's input—Chiang or Soong appeared on the cover of *Time* eleven times. Buck detested political elitism, especially the overly Westernized ways of Chiang and Soong. Instead, she hoped for a common future built on cooperation, patience, and a bottom-up political moderation.

Buck retained faith and earnest fascination in China's toiling masses. "I spoke Chinese first, and more easily. If America was for dreaming about, the world in which I lived was Asia," she would later write. "I did not consider myself a white person in those days."[46] Like Luce, she opposed anarchy and Communism. But, as someone who felt more Chinese than American, she also sought to understand the conditions that compelled the dispossessed toward such extreme ideas. In contrast, Luce held little interest in the daily experiences of the average Chinese or, for that matter, American. Luce's understanding of China was confined to his family compound and he knew very little of the language.[47] After leaving for a Connecticut boarding school in 1914, he would not return to China until brief visits in 1932 and 1941.[48] Instead, he cherished abstraction, big ideas, clearly defined structures and principles, versions of America and China that were purely conceptual.

As their careers evolved—and as the situation in China during the interwar period became increasingly tenuous and factionalized—they sought to use their influence in different ways. Where Buck's politics were difficult to pin down, Luce was proudly "biased in favor of God, the Republican party, and free enterprise."[49] Where Buck enjoyed considerable public acclaim, Luce worked behind the scenes, becoming one of the most influential and innovative publishers of the twentieth century. His portfolio of magazines, touching on everything from current affairs to sports to the emergent language of corporatism, changed the way Americans engaged with ideas. While he lacked Buck's public renown, Luce had direct access to the corridors of power, to say nothing of his army of writers, photographers, and editors. In the first half of the twentieth century, Luce was the only private citizen who could rival Buck's influence when it came to positioning the Chinese within the American imagination.

In the last chapter, Tsiang, an outsider to any and all aboveground conversations about China, frolicked in the possibilities of revenge. Nobody had paid him much mind—it was his last resort. When he made the characters of *And China Has Hands* the mocking, sarcastic "cousins" of Buck and her austere *Good Earth* farmer, it was, at root, an expression of his utter invisibility. By attacking not just Buck but her publisher husband as well, Tsiang was dramatizing the extent to which the establishment had overlooked him.

It would have been unimaginable to Tsiang that Buck herself could possibly feel so powerless. Perhaps he would have delighted at the absurd irony of it all. Celebrated for her modesty and class, *God's Men* captured Buck in a moment of nasty desperation. The only reason for writing *God's Men*, it would appear, was to express her profound disillusionment with Luce and his heavy hand in steering China's fate.

Buck—the Nobel-winning best seller—exacts her revenge on Luce by casting Lane as a clumsy, inefficient, and insecure writer. While in college, he retreats to his room one night to write "something about a man's soul finding its own country, but he could not satisfy his fastidious taste in words. His poetry was not good enough and he tore the sheets into bits and threw them into the wastepaper basket."[50] He realizes that his great ambitions cannot compensate

for his reclusive core and total lack of charisma.[51] He vies to become chief editor of the Harvard *Crimson*, only to lose the post to
none other than Franklin Roosevelt: "William never forgave Franklin Roosevelt. He had already begun to believe that the people anywhere in the world were clods and fools and now he was convinced
of their folly. The Boers who fought England were clods and fools.
The Chinese he remembered upon the streets of Peking were clods
and fools."[52]

Lane's days are free of joy or humor; he is unable to vibe with the
"common man," and he is anxious about his identity as an American
because of the constant bullying he suffers at the hands of British
classmates—Luce experienced the same childhood injuries.[53] He begins to regard everyone around him with consternation and fear."[54]
While her literary character assassination of Luce echoed sentiments
shared by many that the publisher was a master manipulator, these
are projections rooted in petty jealousy.[55] Who among us would pass
up the chance to bedevil a powerful enemy with a humiliating epi-
sode of erectile dysfunction?

Lane pours this negative energy into his work, and soon his magazine boasts a circulation in the millions.[56] Though he is ashamed of
his father's missionary career, Lane's work is inflected with a providential verve. He understands himself as one of history's "unexplained
great men," the child of seemingly ordinary parents who ascends to
a God-like stature as "a leader unexplained."[57] Even when his dying
father reminds Lane to listen to his conscience, he completely mis-
interprets the advice.[58] Heading a publishing empire eerily similar
to Luce's, Lane aspires to become the "king" of the common man:
"I think the people can be guided to better things."[59] As circulation
numbers grow, so too does his hubris, and in a climactic scene reminiscent of a real-life exchange between Luce and his once-trusted
associate editor Theodore White, Lane exclaims, "I don't care what
Chinese people are saying. I never care what any people say. I am
interested in telling them what to say."[60]

Where Lane's frigidity extended to his own sporadic organ, his
childhood friend Clem Miller is offered as a soulful and attentive
alternative.[61] He pursues a radically different path from Lane's,
though their lives are intimately intertwined. Miller marries Lane's

sister, the awkwardly named Henrietta, and he remains optimistic and compassionate toward his common man. The Buck biographer Peter Conn has noted the similarities between Miller and Clifford Clinton, a California restaurateur who founded the charity Meals for Millions. But Miller also shares much in common with Buck herself. The city unnerves him—just as it did Buck.[62] Where Lane's arrival in America only deepens his sense of alienation from his parents' land, Miller sees "a country fit for dreams."[63] Lane allies himself with Chiang Kai-shek and Miller invests his faith in Sun Yat-sen, who will uplift the Chinese people by giving them the power of self-determination.[64] Buck uses Miller to deny the missionary paternalism that had compelled generations of Americans abroad:

> Clem had no interest in saving souls, for he had a high and unshakeable faith in the souls of men as he saw them, good enough as God had made them, except when the evils of earth beset them. And these evils, he was convinced, rose first of all from hunger, for from hunger came illness and poverty and all the misery that forced men into desperation and then into senseless quarrels. Their souls were degraded and lost because of the clamoring hunger of their bodies. As simply as his father had left his home and followed God's call across the sea, so simply now did Clem believe that he could cure the sorrows of men and women and their children.[65]

While Lane seeks to control and manipulate those around him, Miller accidentally builds an empire of affordable, community-minded grocery stores.[66] Guilt-riddled by his own growing wealth, the kind-hearted Miller commits himself to charity. Miller's goal to end world hunger might seem as idealistic as Buck's own work advocating on behalf of the common masses. But, as a skeptical review in *Time*—Luce's magazine—coyly suggested, Miller's altruistic business sense could have been sourced from Buck's own life. The previous year, she had suggested that the United States replace the Voice of America with "a chain of dime stores all over Asia."[67]

The *Time* review grouses that *God's Men* is less a novel than it is "an exercise in puppetry" pitting the infallible, Horatio Alger-esque

Miller against the "ruthless" Lane and his "Buck-chosen set of inferiority complexes." The chasm between Lane and Miller stands
in for two distinct versions of America. Near the end of *God's Men*,
the two friends compare their ambitions. Lane—"shocked to the
soul"—dismisses the socialist air of Miller's schemes: "You mean the
government ought to feed the people? That's the welfare state!" As
Miller protests that the nation is only as strong as its people, Lane
measures America according to its greatest men. He has pulled himself up from his bootstraps, he claims, and this, finally, is his "faith as
an American."[68]

We might pause here and consider the real-life version of this American "faith." Buck was, after all, working with the raw materials of
Henry Luce's actual life. Much like the FBI agents hoping to make
sense of Tsiang's fragmentary life, Buck dug through Luce's biography for clues that might explain his arrogance. She was rewriting the
text of his life with maximum bias.

What was Buck getting at by recasting Luce's patriotism in such
callow terms? Luce's missionary parents had embarked for China in
1897. They held fairly conventional views about American might and
Chinese inferiority. Over time, the elder Luce came to admire the virtues and achievements that comprised Chinese history. Instead of civilizing them, he felt he was a "missionary in reverse" learning from the
proud, diligent people he had come to uplift.[69] While this idealization
of China shaped the younger Luce's thinking, Henry's horizons are
also defined by a distant, imaginary America. His firsthand familiarity with the realities of China prevented him from sharing the very
abstract faith that Western visitors had in the nation.

Luce had learned how to become an American while a student at
the Hotchkiss School in Connecticut.[70] Assimilation meant master-
ing new codes, from the rules of football and whims of American
slang to hierarchies of class and taste. But coming of age alongside his
comfortably American classmates gave language to the vague sense
of disconnection that brewed within him. When upperclassmen noticed that Luce had listed his hometown as "Wei Hsien, China," they
decided to give him the nickname "Chink." As the Hotchkiss literary
magazine joked, he "must have sneaked in thru Mexico or Canada."[71]

While both Luce and the fictional character Lane prized the China of their youth, they both resist attempts to cast the ancient civilization as a salve against the West. Buck depicted Lane's hesitancy as the lingering scorn of a youth filled with humiliation and embarrassment. But Luce offered a more nuanced account of his childhood, remarking that it was only the idealized images of China that had made it across the Pacific. The view from the ground, as Buck, too, frequently reminded her American readers, was very different: "I loved China, but I was immunized against illusions about her. What the rich tourists and the great intellectuals like John Dewey and Bertrand Russell never understood was that Chinese civilization had fallen into terrible decay. They saw only the outward forms of a graceful old culture. But the dynamism was gone."[72]

Much like Buck, Luce saw his transpacific upbringing as an asset. It gave him the background to dampen down the exuberant images of China depicted by the so-called experts and "great intellectuals." It also gave him a kind of romantic distance from the idea of America. Throughout his life, Luce would often remark that his worldview had been shaped by the fact that he could never lay claim to an American hometown—a quintessential marker, he believed, of authentic identity. Instead of knowing "the American-in-particular," he romanticized "the American-in-general," embracing the nation as a coherent teleology, a set of ideas, a promise.[73] Later in life, he acknowledged the extent to which his formative, childhood distance from America's material realities had deepened his faith in what the nation could become. "I probably gained a too romantic, too idealistic view of America. This was not simply because America looked better at a distance," he explained, it was because he had grown up surrounded by selfless, compassionate missionaries. He knew a range of Chinese people, "good, bad, very bad and indifferent," and he was probably more sympathetic toward them than most "mish-kids." But his sense of the world was defined by the Americans of his childhood, who were exclusively "good Christian people."[74]

With this exaggerated sense of American character—and without a feeling of Main Street rootedness—Luce had difficulty connecting with the common man—an aspect of his personality that Buck exaggerated in *God's Men*. Yet this did not prevent Luce from creating a publishing empire that captured the imagination of America's emergent middle class. *Time, Life, Sports Illustrated, Fortune, Architectural Forum*, and *House and Home:* his magazines celebrated every facet of American life. In the February 7, 1941, issue of *Life* magazine, Luce published his most famous piece of writing, an editorial titled "The American Century." The ideas animating Luce's essay had been marinating for quite some time. He had borrowed the phrase "American Century" from H. G. Wells, while the notions of duty and obligation had been inspired by conversation with people like Walter Lippman and Archibald MacLeish. At its most basic level, Luce's piece called for the United States to relinquish its isolationist stance and dive headlong into World War II. The spreading of democracy around the world, Luce argued, was an American responsibility. "The American Century" put forth a "logic of internationalism" that essentially compelled the United States to share its "abundant life" with the rest of the world. Most importantly, Luce's vision of progress was one that was global in scope—and it anticipated the American rise. From ancient Rome to Genghis Khan through the "Chinese emperors," Lenin, and Hitler, the great leaps in world history had been sustained by collaboration, the crossing of borders. "But what internationalism have we Americans to offer?"[75]

The bombing at Pearl Harbor months later would make Luce's plea irrelevant; but the enthusiasm for promoting American ideas abroad would proliferate considerably during the Cold War. "The American Century" became shorthand for America's postwar arrogance, and traces of that come through in Luce's prose, his sense of urgency and panic. "Friends and allies of America? Who are they, and for what? This is for us to tell them."[76] After the war, the nation's responsibility would turn outward, not simply as a political or economic force but as a beacon for hope. "To lead the world would never have been an easy task. To revive the hope of that lost opportunity makes the task now infinitely harder than it would have been before."[77] A month after publishing the essay, Luce was on the road drumming up interest in United China Appeal (later renamed United China Relief), making dozens of speeches on behalf of the poor Chinese. Clearly, China was still on his mind, despite its absence from "The American Century."

This is not to suggest that Luce's career was guided by his Chinese childhood, as Buck claimed hers was. But perhaps those formative experiences compelled him to see the world differently than his peers. His upbringing undoubtedly shaped his desire to project American ideas abroad, particularly his childhood exposure to the supposed best that America had to offer, the "good Christian people" who had devoted their lives to enlightening the Chinese. For Luce, America was only ever an abstraction.

Buck recognized the providential roots of "the American Century." She invented her own version of Luce's essay in *God's Men*. Lane gives the following speech at a banquet celebrating his magazine's readership reaching one million:

> It is the hour of American destiny.
> —We have been sowing and now we are about to reap. I see the harvest in terms of the whole world.
> —The world will listen to our voices, speaking truth.
> —We are young but we have learned in our youth to control the forces of water and air—the forces which are locked into ore and coal.
> —Old countries are dying and passing away. England is weak with age, an ancient empire, her rulers grown tired. France is sunk in dreams and Italy slumbers. But we of America, we are awake. The name America will be heard among every people. It is our time, our hour. It is we who will write the history of the centuries to come . . . [78]

Lane's speech exaggerates the ideas and language of Luce's "American Century," from the term "American destiny" to his vigorous appraisal of the nation's exceptional nature. In Buck's retelling, Lane calls for nothing short of imperial domination. "I supposed your preacher father is somewhere in you, after all," his wife remarked. "I wasn't preaching," Lane replies harshly. "I was telling the truth."[79]

We have encountered a range of characters so far, many of who drew on their own experiences to imagine a transpacific future. For the American missionaries and traders who first sailed the Pacific, this was a *tabula rasa*, a new frontier for our goods, ideas, and way of life. Buck's skepticism with the missionary enterprise and faith in the common folk compelled her to rail against all forms of elitism, whether it was Chinese intellectuals or disconnected American policy-makers. She imagined a shared future built on civility, equality, and a grassroots democratic culture. For Tsiang, the transpacific would be an open, free, riotously hybrid space where discrete nationalities and prescribed identities would dissolve. The transpacific was a space of possibility: it was a new arena for class struggle. For Carl Crow and the first waves of modern businessmen, the transpacific took the shape of a market—one that still required some degree of mutual cooperation and understanding. For Luce, this was a space to be filled with American ideas and American might.

Luce felt an obligation to use his magazines to publish works that brought China into clearer, closer view. He worked closely with various think tanks and advocacy groups, dreaming of establishing an "intellectual Manhattan Project for Asia."[80] He often described feeling a "moral obligation" to provide thoughtful treatment of China to American readers.[81] But such passions immunized Luce from maintaining a balanced sense of Chinese political realities. Luce remained faithful to Chiang's regime even as the Nationalist army was, in the famous words of a high-ranking American official, "rotten with corruption."[82] Under Luce's leadership, *Time* continued to publish flattering, pro-Chiang dispatches, often against the wishes of his own China correspondents. In 1943, after a great deal of deliberation, Luce finally agreed to publish an essay by Buck that was critical of Chiang. Despite Luce and Buck's personal differences, a greater need had compelled them. Buck's essay, "A Warning about China," appeared in *Life* magazine, echoing Luce's hope that Americans not turn their backs on China.

Finally, then: Luce was the one who could rival Buck's influence as well as her authority. There was nothing she could do. Her corrosive bias notwithstanding, the version of Luce that Buck created for *God's Men* helps to make their rivalry legible. They were both obsessed with China, for they each saw China as their birthright. She wrote what she could within the confines of Luce's journalistic empire; she did what she could as an advocate and organizer. Ultimately, neither of their visions won out. By 1949, China had been lost to the Communists—an outcome neither of them had desired. Nothing could be done about it. So Buck, like Tsiang, returned to a world of her own creation and made up a character named William Lane. It was a world she could control.

After bombarding readers of *Time* and *Life* with cover stories about the heroes of Chinese nationalism from the 1930s through World War II, Luce shifted the focus of his magazines away from China in the late 1940s. Despite what he believed to be his best efforts, the world had allowed China to fall into the hands of the Communists. It was not until the 1960s, as he approached the end of his life, that Luce's mind would wander back toward the land of his youth.

In a 1965 speech to the Commonwealth Club of San Francisco entitled "Even More Important than Communism," Luce laid out the foundation for what his confidante John Jessup described as a "transpacific dialogue."[83]

The speech opens with Rudyard Kipling's famous opening from "The Ballad of East and West"—the same lines that Tsiang had lampooned years earlier in *China Red*. But Luce greeted Kipling's words with optimism. "I would say that East and West have just barely begun to meet. Whether a real meeting of the minds will occur remains very much to be seen."[84] Luce hoped to spend his last years promoting such a meeting.

For Luce, the onus was on the United States to make the first move and engage China, an echo of the spirit that underscored "The American Century." But this encounter would not be one-sided; rather it would be an overture toward the establishment of "one worldwide civilization."[85] The West had an enormous amount to gain from a serious, respectful engagement with the "Oriental" world:

Indeed, it is perhaps only in a serious confrontation with the East that the West can rediscover, even recreate, a knowledge of itself. There is one other thing. In trying to explain itself to the East, the men of the West will not only rediscover the meaning of the West; they will also discover with more precision what, in the year 1965, is most lacking in the West—whatever that deficiency may be. Thus they—and we—will end up learning from the East. The future of mankind depends on the response of the East to the West. And that depends on whether the West knows what it has to say.[86]

Much like Buck before him, Luce held Asia up as a mirror for Western values. In this new configuration, the relationship between the United States and Asia—or, as he states here, the Occidental and the Oriental—worked both ways: the Orient desired access to Occidental technology, while the Occidental world needed an Oriental standard of measurement to figure out "what . . . [was] most lacking." By looking eastward, perhaps Americans could "recreate . . . a knowledge of itself."[87]

The last speech of Luce's life was an address to students at the University of California at Santa Barbara on February 1, 1967. It was titled "Toward Compatible Systems"[88] and it retraced much of the same territory as his Commonwealth Club speech. But it ended with a disarming vision of the future that Buck (or her *God's Men* surrogate, the indefatigable Clem Miller) could have never imagined.

This was no longer the "American Century." It was time for the East and the West to merge into one: "[T]he biggest truth is that all mankind is moving into a future world, whose shape and manner of life we can hardly imagine . . . An astonishing future lies predictably ahead. It is into that future that we all go together—or, at any rate, our children, children of the West and children of the East."[89]

Luce passed away three weeks later.

By 1967, H. T. Tsiang had retired from show business. The previous year, he had made his final credited appearance as an actor, playing a character named Ching Fa on the television series *Gunsmoke*. He had done quite well for himself in Hollywood, going from dinner theater and playwriting to acting on the big screen. He even rubbed shoulders with some of America's most beloved stars.

In 1960 Tsiang appeared alongside Frank Sinatra, Sammy Davis, Jr., and the rest of the Rat Pack in *Ocean's Eleven*. He was credited with the role of "houseboy." He spends one entire scene shuffling about on his knees. Tsiang never lost his knack for aggressive chumminess.

That year, he took out a small ad in a Hollywood paper to wish the film's director, Lewis Milestone, a happy birthday. He identified himself as "the crazy house boy" and asked Milestone to pass his regards to Frank Sinatra—"I'm still chewing on his last paycheck."

He died in 1971. He is buried in Evergreen Cemetery in Los Angeles. His tombstone misidentifies his birth year as 1906 rather than 1899.

Two years later, Buck died. Having faded from influence in the last decades of her life, she spent the 1960s and 1970s pursuing more personal causes: adoption, humanitarian aid, and the fate of the world's impoverished children.

Ultimately, none of these figures, all of who were idealists in their own way, lived to see any new accord between the tumultuous old land of their youths and the haughty, bulging one of their adulthoods. One wonders what stories Buck would have told had she lived to write her final book, a completion of the family saga begun with *The Good Earth*. All that survives is a possible title: *The Red Earth*.[90]

Conclusion

The Floaters

"Why can't I write about China?"

A set-piece that plays out on college campuses nationwide: a writing workshop, a diverse array of students, a knotty provocation lobbed at someone who dares write about people with whom they appear to share little in common. In this case, it is a scene from Don Lee's *The Collective*, a 2012 novel about a trio of idealistic, young Asian American friends in the 1990s trying to find their way as artists. This small moment will vex them for years to come. A white student named Kathryn Newey has submitted a short story set in China during the Cultural Revolution. Her classmates praise her work, each one adding a new layer of admiration to the initial consensus that this is a wonderful piece of writing. But a Korean American student named Joshua Yoon protests: "I guess I'll have to be the lone dissenter here."[1] He explains that he found the story craven, melodramatic, and "completely offensive." He argues that Newey—described by another character as a "dowdy girl from Duluth"[2]—has no "right writing a story about China."[3] She is baffled and indignant: "I'm Caucasian, so I can't write about Chinese people? What about Pearl S. Buck? She won the Pulitzer for *The Good Earth*. She got the Nobel Prize."[4]

Newey's self-defense leaves Yoon cold, particularly her mention of Buck. Isn't that interesting? he wonders. "They'll give the Pulitzer to a white woman for a novel about Asians, but no Asian American novelist has ever won a Pulitzer."⁵ In *The Collective*, it is Yoon who holds the most fixed ideas about literature and identity. He has probably inherited his disregard for Buck. His comments fall in line with a long tradition of Asian American artists suspicious of Buck for both her representation of the Chinese as well as her privileged position as the child of white missionaries. It is a criticism built into the very origins of Asian American literature itself: she is one of the enemies identified in the introduction to 1974's *Aiiieeeee!*, the first anthology of Asian American literature.⁶ But there is an interesting wrinkle to Yoon's latter-day embrace of this party line. The story that Yoon, a Korean American adoptee raised in Harvard Square, had submitted to their workshop was about war in Southeast Asia. While it was beautifully written, it nonetheless described a history and place foreign to him. At best, it was a relationship born of proximity. As an Asian American writing about Asia, though, nobody in the workshop thought to question his "right" to do so.

Within the setting of the writing workshop—a setting that stands in for the rough draft stage of history—the specter of Buck ushers in a complicated set of questions. How are we to identify people like Buck or even Luce—white Americans raised in China? Consider Buck's lifelong preference for Asia to America:

> Do you know, whenever I go to Asia, I fall back into the old patterns of my life there. One never recovers from Asia! It makes no difference where in Asia I go—Korea, Japan, India, it doesn't matter—suddenly I'm at home again. I love the people and they know it. They, in turn, accept me as theirs. It's not that I don't love my country—I do. But perhaps I'm never as comfortable with any Westerner as I am with an Asian.⁷

It is not hard to imagine how Yoon might react to such a statement. Our contemporary approach to identity rarely allows for such broad, flexible affiliations. We have difficulty taking seriously claims rooted in empathy rather than experience. As Buck continues: "By birth and ancestry, I am an American, and by choice and belief I am a Christian. But by the years of my life, by sympathy and feeling, I am Chinese."⁸

We might stretch Joshua Yoon's protest to its logical ends: does Buck have a "right" to write about the Chinese? Does that "right" extend to Chinatowns and Chinese Americans? Does he?

The book I have written has focused on the acquisition and maintenance of authority. It has been the story of how writers and travelers lacking outstanding credentials became regarded as experts; of go-betweens, translators, and immigrants helping Americans imagine a future based on transpacific harmony; of publishers and markets and what it means to sit just outside of the prevailing wisdom. In other words, this has been a story about the structural conditions that produced the images and ideas about China that circulated American culture in the interwar years. But it was individuals who made this structure legible as they maneuvered and adapted to its possibilities. Scaled down to the level of the interpersonal, these questions of authority were recast in somewhat moralistic terms of authenticity and birthright: of who possessed the right to speak on behalf of China. These individuals engaged in serious and consequential debate on the future of China and the United States. Lurking beneath the surface were interpersonal tensions: jealousy and envy, animosity and projection, fantasies of revenge disguised as calls for sturdy debate.

Perhaps it was inevitable that such a tight, crowded field of conversation would become so self-aware. Despite America's longstanding fascination with China, the popular demand for knowledge about China did not emerge until the phenomenal success of *The Good Earth*. The broad focus of my book has been on the aftermath of that moment, how a circle of Chinese and Americans interested in the two nations' shared fate responded to the surge of interest in all things Chinese that followed Buck's ascension. This new demand for knowledge about China created opportunities for Americans like Carl Crow and Alice Tisdale Hobart, who converted their personal experiences into best-selling tales from a new trade frontier. This market was less hospitable to Chinese writers like Kiang Kang Hu and H. T. Tsiang, who assailed Buck for her reliance on the archetype of the hard-working Chinese peasant. As the translator Chi-Chen Wang discovered, even those uninterested in attacking Buck's representation of China had to at least reckon with her. Even the all-powerful Buck was not above the fray, as we saw with *God's Men*, her novel-length evisceration of the publisher and fellow China-obsessive Henry Luce. It was a strange gesture that echoed Tsiang's most desperate attacks on her: if the means to control the discursive field are beyond you, why not make your rivals into a character that you *can* control?

As peculiar as it might have been for Buck to claim that she was Chinese by "feeling," there was clearly something unusual to her perspective. Perhaps we should consider what it would mean to take Buck's sentiment seriously. How might Buck's perspective help bring larger flows of people, things, and ideas into focus? Buck may have made a career out of writing about China, but it would be incorrect to label her a careerist, for *The Good Earth* created this field of conversation almost by accident. This has been a book about the boundaries that circumscribed that field of conversation—the marketplace of ideas about China. But it has also been about unintended consequences. Although the figures comprising this book were primarily concerned with China, their fascination with events elsewhere held material consequences for those in the United States. Popular authors like Buck, Lin Yutang, Carl Crow, or Alice Tisdale Hobart did not set out to affect the representation of Chinese in America or to say anything meaningful about Chinese American immigrant culture; for them, Chinatown was merely the local manifestation of a bigger picture. It is a version of what Arif Dirlik, writing about our present, describes as the "metaphorical rim" upon which Asian America is located:

> Asian America is no longer just a location in the United States, but is at the same time a location on a metaphorical rim constituted by diasporas and motions of individuals. To understand Asian Americans it is no longer sufficient to comprehend their roots in U.S. history or, for that matter, in countries of origin, but a multiplicity of historical trajectories that converge in the locations we call Asian America.[9]

I have been drawn to these "trajectories," particularly the efforts made by competing rivals to steer them. By situating all of these different authors and books along this "metaphorical rim," a transpacific circulation of ideas emerges: the construction of Chinese character for American readers, the tangential interest in Chinese Americans and Chinatowns, the campaign to end the Chinese Exclusion Act, the exclusion of outlying Chinese voices from the fray. The resonances between the 1930s and the present, then, come into clearer focus. The question becomes: how do a series of conversations about and literary power struggles over China in the 1930s help us think about the present?

The effect of *The Good Earth* continues through today. Let us return for a moment to *The Collective*. That Lee still invokes Buck in 2012 suggests that the questions vexing writers and readers decades ago remain relevant today. Buck still symbolizes something powerful to Americans and Chinese alike. My book has considered her immediate effect in America, and it was inspired by the general renewal of interest in her life and work over the past two decades. For American readers, there have been absorbing new biographies by Peter Conn and Hilary Spurling, an endorsement from Oprah Winfrey's influential book club, new editions of her obscure novels. Her legacy among the Chinese is somewhat more complicated. There are now academic conferences in China devoted to Buck's influence. Her house in Nanjing has been restored. Against the backdrop of China's ascension, Buck has come to be regarded as the rare, visionary Westerner sensitive to China and its culture. She is part of the language again. A few years ago, I picked up a zine by the photographer Li Kejun titled *The Good Earth*.[10] He takes portraits of Chinese farmers and then manipulates them until their glee seems exaggerated and almost garish. When I asked his publisher why Li had chosen this title, he shrugged. It was just a familiar name.

In 2010, Anchee Min published *Pearl of China*, a novel about Buck's life told from the perspective of a fictional Chinese friend. As a child raised during the Cultural Revolution, Min was taught to denounce Buck as a "cultural imperialist." She moved to the United States at the age of 27, teaching herself English and eventually writing a string of successful memoirs and historical novels set in China. During the book tour for her best-selling 1994 memoir *Red Azalea*, Min met an "elderly white lady" who asked if she knew Buck's work. "Before I could reply, she said—very emotionally and to my surprise—that Buck had taught her to love the Chinese people. She placed a paperback in my hands and said it was a gift. It was the *Good Earth*."[11] Min read it on the flight home, sobbing the whole way through. "I had never encountered any author, including the most respected Chinese authors, who wrote about our peasants with such admiration, affection and humanity."[12]

In a way, popular authors like Min occupy a similar, intermediary role as Buck did in the 1930s, offering American readers sympathetic, accessible, and relatable tales of old China. It is a similarity not lost on Min herself. *Pearl of China* is an attempt to recuperate Buck's reputation as someone who truly understood the Chinese. The novel recounts Buck's life from the perspective of her childhood neighbor, Willow, a character Min created as a composite of Buck's various, real-life Chinese friends. As one would expect, Willow and her family are initially uncertain about the arrival of the missionaries. Although he works closely as an apprentice to the Bucks, Willow's father initially understands his religiosity as more of a pragmatic performance than true faith. Willow herself is mesmerized by Buck's position between two cultures, as when Buck explains, "My parents use a fork and a knife; I use chopsticks."[13]

Just as Willow's father eventually sees the light, she herself begins to internalize Buck's way of seeing the world. When Willow explains with resignation that her husband has begun to abuse her, Buck is horrified. She is the one who convinces the heretofore dutybound Willow not to accept such a fate: "This is slavery!"[14] Buck helps Willow understand the reality of her surroundings, most notably the myopia of China's intellectual class and their preference of "fantasy over reality." As Buck explains, "It's easier to close one's eyes on disease and death."[15] In *Pearl of China*, this is the context that produces *The Good Earth*. Buck's desire to tell American readers about her spiritual homeland of China feels urgent, defiant. "I believe in my Chinese stories. No other Western author can come close to what I offer—what life is really like in the Orient. For God's sake, I'm living it. The Chinese world cries out for exploration. It's like America once was—fertile and full of promise."[16] Buck workshops early drafts of *The Good Earth*, seeking out feedback from Chinese readers about its tone and authenticity, and everyone she encounters instantly loves it. (In real life, *The Good Earth* went through at least eight pirated Chinese translations in the 1930s and 1940s; one of these translations went into twelve successive editions.)[17]

After the success of *The Good Earth*, Buck spends much of the novel's remainder overseas in the United States. *Pearl of China*, then, becomes a novel of Willow's travails as someone left behind, steadfast in her allegiance to Buck's enlightened worldview, even during the Cultural Revolution. Perhaps the strangest moment comes when Min imagines Buck's symbolic importance to high-ranking party officials, including Mao Zedong himself. At one point, Mao asks an advisor if she is "a friend or an enemy" and plots to coopt her influence.[18] "Pearl Buck is read in every country on the world map. Her books have been translated into over a hundred languages! If Edgar Snow is a tank, Pearl Buck is a nuclear bomb."[19] Mao eventually brands Buck an agent of Western imperialism and Willow is summoned before the party leaders. When she refuses to publicly denounce her friend, she is sent to a prison labor camp near Tibet.[20] She becomes known as the "evil twin sister of Pearl Buck."[21] As Willow wastes away in prison, she wonders "whether Pearl would be amused or horrified at the fact that Mao had considered converting her into a proletarian"—a question about legacy and reception that might as well stand in for Min's own novel.[22]

I have often wondered whether Buck, Tsiang, Crow, and the rest would be "amused or horrified" by *A Floating Chinaman*. Throughout this book, I have been interested in the dynamic of writers writing about other writers. It seems a way to understand the creation and refinement of ideas, as well as the spirit of competition that underlies all critical endeavors. The stakes were at once intellectual, personal, and professional. This is not to say that the construction of knowledge is always beholden to rivalries and whims. But the acquisition of authority is always a contest; there are always other claimants to the status of expert. The shape of this particular contest just happened to be very clear. All of these different figures vied to offer the most authoritative version of America and China's transpacific future. In the case of Tsiang writing about Buck or Buck writing about Luce, the underlying drivers of envy or ideological animosity always lurked on the edge of the page.

What motivated Min? *Pearl of China* feels like a reclamation project, an attempt to restore Buck's reputation as someone who could mediate between China and the United States. Buck's politics were too ambiguous for the Cold War and her influence waned. She longed to return to China but her visa requests were turned down. *Pearl of China*, then, is also an attempt to make amends for China's treatment of Buck throughout the Cold War—to imagine what might have happened had China acknowledged and embraced her influence. Buck had been denied the chance to return to China in 1972 as part of Richard Nixon's delegation. As a Chinese diplomatic official explained to her: "In view of the fact that for a long time you have in your works taken an attitude of distortion, smear and vilification toward the people of new China and its leaders, I am authorized to inform you that we cannot accept your request for a visit to China."[23]

In *Pearl of China*, Willow ends up meeting Nixon during his visit to Buck's hometown and the two commiserate about how her beloved China now treats her.[24] In the 1980s, as relations between the nations warm and China begins recognizing the trauma of the Cultural Revolution, Willow, who has survived a century's worth of tumult, finally gains recognition as a "national treasure"—a moment that foreshadows Buck's eventual redemption.[25] *Pearl of China* is, finally, not just an attempt to rescue Buck's reputation—to make amends for the past. It is also Min's attempt to assert Buck's usefulness for understanding the present.

It can certainly feel as though history is repeating itself. "You know the remarkable thing about China," a Swedish friend remarked to Henry Luce at a party in the early 1940s, "is that everyone who comes here becomes enchanted with the tremendous possibilities for achieving whatever it is they want to achieve."[26] Luce had grown up in China at the turn of the century—a far more tumultuous time. A few decades later, China represented a land of opportunity. Of course, not everyone found whatever it was they were looking for in China. Edgar Snow arrived in his early twenties via the same Missouri-Shanghai pipeline that had brought Crow there earlier. "I had come to the East looking for the 'glamor of the Orient,' searching for adventure."[27] Instead, Snow encountered thousands of famine-stricken men, women, and children dying before his eyes.

Yet he stayed in China, eventually writing the classic 1937 account of Mao's rise, *Red Star over China*.

Still, Americans in the 1930s would have been forgiven for assuming that all it took to succeed in China was to simply go there. A version of this transpacific wonder returned in the 1990s and 2000s. We can attribute the renewal of interest in Buck, Crow, and Hobart in part to the renewed fascination with China that has attended its economic liberalization. New go-betweens have emerged: expatriates-turned-authors, journalists, business executives, academics. As China has grown into its stature as one of America's fiercest rivals, a steady stream of stories, stoked with equal parts fear and bemusement, have emerged as shorthand explainers for the nation's changing culture. These stories merely have to carry the possibility of being true, as the bar for expertise is still set dismayingly low. The *China Daily Show*, a satirical website presumably run by Western expats living in China, posted a wickedly sarcastic typology of modern-day China experts. The character types were familiar to anyone who has traveled in China: diplomatic workers, smarmy consultants, graduate students, and journalists. "After spending a certain amount of time in China— a month, maybe more—a deeper and more nuanced understanding of this complex country of 1.4 billion is practically guaranteed."[28]

The American fascination with China has been driven primarily by money. China's economy has grown at an astonishing rate over the past thirty years. A new generation of journalists and business executives echo the breathless optimism offered by Carl Crow and Standard Oil decades ago. Americans throughout the 2000s were regaled with tales of all that was possible in China, as the lure of distant markets only exacerbated the extent to which America's own economy was falling into disarray. Today, the transpacific is made legible through prospective trade agreements like the Trans-Pacific Partnership and chatter about Pacific Rim trading partners.[29] Over the past decade, there has been a steady stream of books about China: business etiquette manuals, tales of impending economic or military rivalry, rags-to-riches memoirs about a P. R. flak turned TV star and an itinerant journalist who became a rock star.[30] In 2007, James McGregor, an American journalist and business executive, published an update of Carl Crow's *Four Hundred Million Customers*. His title: *One*

Billion Customers. These echoes across time reinforce our sense that China is a puzzle waiting be solved. The past returns to embolden those setting across the Pacific today.

At last: what about H. T. Tsiang, the perpetual outlier? His work claimed but a tiny blast radius. But if others have returned to prominence for their seeming relevance to the present, then why not ask what Tsiang might teach us? The renewed interest in people like Buck and Crow comes from their comparative success. Why not imagine a trajectory in which Tsiang was not ignored and rebuked? What if we were to write a fable of Tsiang's struggle, just as Min did in *Pearl of China?*

In the late 1990s, officials in Tsiang's native Nantong began compiling a list of anyone who had ever left the town and made a name for him or herself. In America, Tsiang was just another struggling writer, barely remembered if at all. Back home, however, Tsiang's exploits had long been celebrated as brave and heroic. He was a local boy made good, working in the Chinese government, venturing to America and publishing in both Chinese and English. Although he never returned, he remained well known in Nantong, thanks in part to the efforts of his proud sister and her children. New editions of his Chinese essays and stories were published. His American output, however, remained a mystery until the early 2000s, when academics from Nantong University discovered all the correspondences he had left behind—the letters, short poems, and scraps of stories that he had sent to Kent. One of them traveled to the United States and returned with copies of all these wondrous new documents. A team of scholars translated these works and published them in 2008.[31] In their eyes, these joke-filled letters between Tsiang, Kent, and others suggested a deep bond, perhaps even the possibility of a deep friendship between China and America. There was nothing desperate or strange about any of it.

So Tsiang survives—in FBI files, in the present-day imagination of his countrymen. But I prefer to dwell in the possibilities of his past. *A Floating Chinaman* has been an attempt to reconstruct and reassess the conditions of Tsiang's oeuvre—to scrutinize the motivations of someone who stood against trajectories that today seem inevitable. My book has been animated by a speculative desire to imagine a world in which his ideas were not relegated to the margins.

I borrowed the title of this book from one of Tsiang's unfinished novels, mentioned once in a letter to Theodore Dreiser. Later, Tsiang would advertise a novel in progress called *Shanghai Newyork Moscow—An Odyssey of a Chinese Coolie*, which was presumably the same, never-to-be-completed work. The scale of this "odyssey" is absolutely staggering. It is difficult to imagine a novel capturing this entire picture of global complexity—the ceaseless flow of ideas and things, the universal lure of the proletarian movement as it takes root from nation to nation. Spurned by publishers and readers alike, why not set out to chronicle a world in motion? Nobody was going to take him seriously anyway. As I discussed in Chapter 5, the most likely explanation is that Tsiang whittled this proposal down to a more manageable size and wrote *And China Has Hands* instead. But I would like to imagine that Tsiang's *A Floating Chinaman* was simply too ambitious to bring into focus. Of course we will never know. There is a unique mystery to unfinished projects; the temptation for the future generation is to try and complete them.

This reading of Tsiang's life is admittedly a generous if not deeply romantic one. After all: how seriously can one take the ideas of a man known throughout 1950s Los Angeles for a one-man adaptation of *Hamlet* set at a nudist colony?

My interest is not just in the reasons for his seeming obscurity but how he responded to the realization that he would never be invited to the party—how it propelled him toward his daring artistic extremes. His situation was sui generis; it would be a stretch to claim that he anticipated any models of identity. He arrived during the Chinese Exclusion Act and his career essentially ended decades before he could be absorbed into the category of the Asian American.

I was drawn to Tsiang's title for its evocative strangeness, its undercurrent of defiance. He had already denounced the "Chinaman"—in his first novel, *China Red*, he had made light of this epithet, wondering how a term so descriptive could contain such hate. But what does it mean to float? Does it suggest that one merely drifts and meanders, carried by the weight of the wind? Or does it contain a different set of possibilities? To float might mean to fly free of commitments—to control one's own destiny.

I became fascinated with this word. In present-day China, the "floating population" (*liudong renkou*) refers to the millions of migrant laborers who have traveled far from home in search of work. Because social benefits are provided based on a home registration system, these workers, who have helped spur the country's rapid modernization, often find themselves unable to access basic public services. As some Chinese commentators put it, they are like undocumented immigrants within their own country.

In 1911, the politician and labor theorist Austin Lewis wrote of the "vast mass of floating proletarians."[32] These were unskilled and often uneducated workers, members of the "overflowing supply of undifferentiated labor" that served at the whim of a structure beyond their control.[33] For Lewis, their free-floating movements were what robbed them of a political voice:

> The roads are full of them at some seasons. They are not tramps in the general acceptation; in fact, they are not tramps at all, except so far as they are frequently obliged to travel on foot from place to place in search of work. They are objects of persecution and graft to the police and the authorities of the small towns. They are subjected to many indignities, in some places they are domed [*sic*] to the rock-pile and the jail, not because of what they have done, but because of what they are.[34]

As a result of their itinerant, "floating" status, they could never fulfill the residential qualifications to vote. "Their apparent isolation from ordinary life, their nomad habits, their fluidity would seem to prohibit their taking any important part in that sequence of events called the revolution."[35] But Lewis saw reasons for hope. In recent years, the "floating proletariat" had begun organizing themselves outside of the political process. They had succeeded in driving up farm wages and maturing toward "self-realization."[36] To float, then, was to be at the whim of capital. But it was also about scheming for ways to harness that fluid, wandering status and effect material change. In Tsiang's version of *A Floating Chinaman*, it was this beleaguered Chinese worker, beholden to the caprices of the "almighty dollar," who planted the seeds of revolution from continent to continent. This was the utopian possibility: a consciousness floating from city to city; laborers recognizing that "they are not tramps at all" but a silenced majority; a reserve army of labor; a free-ranging insurrection.

The roads are full of them.

The floating proletariat was surplus labor—a concept familiar to Tsiang. When the Chinese workers who had been drawn stateside to work the mining towns and railroads were no longer needed, the only solution was to regulate their flow through the Chinese Exclusion Act.

I am mesmerized by this metaphor of floating—it unfixes our inherited ideas about identity; it scrambles our sense of the inevitable.

Tsiang probably imagined the "floating Chinaman" as a character bedeviled by capital, drifting with the wind, following work across the continents. What does it mean to recognize one's own status as surplus to requirements? To be conscious that you are no longer desired or necessary? As a writer, Tsiang was part of the "undifferentiated" mass far beneath the recognition of Buck and her cohort. Once he realized that he would never penetrate this world, he was liberated to float just beyond the safety of its orbit. Tsiang would not have allowed *A Floating Chinaman*—his version—to be a story of victimization: after all, he embodied a version of this "floating" Chinese laborer, looking to rouse all who crossed his path. Despite the sense of abjection that coursed through his writing and regardless of his air of self-importance, all of his books somehow ended on a note of revolutionary optimism. I would like to imagine that the "Chinaman" Tsiang created, much like him, was a character that recognized the power of being unfixed and unnamable. Someone who floated free of the categories and possibilities meant to discipline them.

To float is to rise above.

NOTES

ACKNOWLEDGMENTS

INDEX

Notes

Introduction

1. Ed Park, "Chinese Whispers," *The Village Voice* (New York), January 16, 2001, web.
2. Edward Vining, *An Inglorious Columbus* (New York: D. Appleton and Company, 1885), 11.
3. Ibid., 224, 448–450, 520.
4. Ibid., 231.
5. Ibid., 262–326.
6. Ibid., 19.
7. Charles Godfrey Leland, *Fusang, or the Discovery of America by Chinese Buddhist Priests in the Fifth Century* (London: Trübner and Company, 1875).
8. Elizabeth Robins Pennell, *Charles Godfrey Leland: A Biography* (New York: Houghton Mifflin, 1906), 120. Italics in original.
9. Marlon K. Hom, *Songs of Gold Mountain: Cantonese Rhymes from San Francisco Chinatown* (Berkeley: University of California Press, 1987), 4.
10. Henriette Mertz, *Pale Ink* (Chicago: Ralph Fletcher Seymour, 1953), 20.
11. Harold Isaacs, *Scratches on Our Minds: American Images of China and India* (New York: John Day, 1958), 11.
12. Ibid., 28, 12.
13. Ibid., 47.
14. Ibid., 50.
15. Ibid., 79–80.
16. Ibid., 87.
17. Ibid., 80.
18. Ibid., 155.
19. H.T. Tsiang, *Poems of the Chinese Revolution* (New York: Liberal Press, 1929).

241

20. H. T. Tsiang, *China Red* (New York: Liberal Press, 1931), back matter.

21. Secretary (on behalf of Theodore Dreiser) to H. T. Tsiang, 15 December 1930, folder 6226, Theodore Dreiser Papers, Kislak Center for Special Collections, Rare Book and Manuscripts, University of Pennsylvania Libraries, Philadelphia.

22. H. T. Tsiang to Theodore Dreiser, 31 December 1930, folder 6226, Theodore Dreiser Papers.

23. This is most likely a reference to Henry James's *The American Scene*, a collection of his travel writings published in 1907. *The American Scene* is notable for its somewhat unkind attitude toward early twentieth century American immigrants.

24. H. T. Tsiang, *The Hanging on Union Square* (New York: H.T. Tsiang, 1935).

25. H. T. Tsiang, *And China Has Hands* (New York: Robert Speller, 1937).

26. H. T. Tsiang, *China Marches On* (New York: H.T. Tsiang,1938).

27. H. T. Tsiang to Rockwell Kent, 7 January 1941, Rockwell Kent Papers, Smithsonian Archives of American Art, Washington, D.C.

28. See: Isaacs, *Scratches on Our Minds*; Michel Oksenberg and Robert Oxnam, eds., *Dragon and Eagle—United States-China Relations: Past and Future*, (New York: Basic Books, 1978); and R. David Arkush and Leo Lee, eds., *Land Without Ghosts: Chinese Impressions of America from the Mid-Nineteenth Century to the Present* (Berkeley: University of California Press, 1993).

29. Janet Hoskins and Viet Nguyen, eds., *Introduction to Transpacific Studies: Framing an Emerging Field* (Honolulu: University of Hawaii Press, 2014), 2.

30. Yunte Huang, *Transpacific Imaginations: History, Literature, Counterpoetics* (Cambridge, MA: Harvard University Press, 2008), 4–5.

31. For recent works that illustrate the importance of reexamining late-nineteenth and early-twentieth century American cultural history as important sites of early identity formation, see: Colleen Lye, *America's Asia: Racial Form and American Literature, 1893-1945* (Princeton, NJ: Princeton University Press, 2009); Yunte Huang, *Transpacific Displacement: Ethnography, Translation, and Intertextual Travel in Twentieth-Century American Literature* (Berkeley, CA: University of California Press, 2002); John Kuo Wei Tchen, *New York Before Chinatown: Orientalism and the Shaping of American Culture* (Baltimore, MD: Johns Hopkins University Press, 2001); Keith Lawrence and Floyd Cheung, eds., *Recovered Legacies: Authority and Identity in Early Asian American Literature* (Philadelphia, PA: Temple University Press, 2005); Josephine Lee, Imogene Lim, and Yuko Matsukawa, eds., *Recollecting Early Asian America: Essays in Cultural History* (Philadelphia, PA: Temple University Press, 2002).

32. John K. Jessup, *The Ideas of Henry Luce* (New York: Atheneum, 1969), 196–197.

33. Tsiang to Kent, 15 April 1941, Rockwell Kent Papers.

1

Theoretical China

1. Rockwell Kent to Bennett Cerf, 23 August 1941, Rockwell Kent Papers, Smithsonian Archives of American Art, Washington, D.C.
2. Richard Walsh to Kent, 20 September 1941, Kent Papers.
3. Benson Lee Grayson, *The American Image of China* (New York: Ungar, 1979), 2.
4. John Fairbank has diagnosed this early twentieth-century ambivalence as a result of the perennial confusion over the United States' relationship with China. Despite a deep-seated fascination with China dating back to the colonial period, Fairbanks argues that the United States simply had difficulty figuring out a coherent way of understanding its Pacific neighbor. Also see: Paul Varg, *The Making of a Myth: The United States and China, 1897–1912* (East Lansing: Michigan State University Press, 1968).
5. Seth Low, "The Position of the United States among the Nations," *Annals of the American Academy of Political and Social Science* 26 (July 1905): 1–16.
6. Ibid., 2.
7. Ibid.
8. Akira Iriye expands on this view, observing that this enduring fascination with the markets of China and Japan was the result of a persistent tension between expectation and action: "The disparity between image and reality, expectation and achievement, is striking. Perhaps it was for this very reason that Americans always exaggerated the promise of an Asian market. The longer it failed to materialize, the greater the need would be to overcome frustrations and paint a picture of what might have been and what might yet be." Quoted in Hongshan Li and Zhaohui Hong, eds., *Image, Perception, and the Making of U.S.-China Relations* (Lanham, MD: University Press of America, 1998), 30.
9. Patricia Neils, ed. *United States Attitudes and Policies toward China: The Impact of American Missionaries* (New York: East Gate Books, 1990), 9.
10. Paul Varg, *Missionaries, Chinese, and Diplomats* (Princeton, NJ: Princeton University Press, 1959), 3.
11. Jerry Israel, *Progressivism and the Open Door: America and China, 1905–1921* (Pittsburgh, PA: University of Pittsburgh Press, 1971), 9.
12. Ibid., 126.
13. Frederick Jackson Turner, *The Frontier in American History* (New York: Henry Holt Company, 1935), 296–297.
14. C. Y. Tang, "The Cycle of Civilization," *Chinese Students' Monthly*, January 1918, 111. Also see: "Tang Wins the State Contest," *The Beloit College Round Table*, February 17, 1917, 1.
15. Charles Beard, "Introduction," in Charles Beard, ed., *Whither Mankind* (New York: Longmans, Green, 1928), 5, 8.

16. Hu Shih, "Civilizations of East and West," in Beard, *Whither Mankind*, 31.

17. According to historian Paul Varg, missionary volunteers "were seldom religious aesthetes, although the spiritual drive was central in their lives. They reflected the normal excitement over an unusual career in an unusual corner of the world, free from the more prosaic patterns of the ministry or a position in business at home." Varg, *Missionaries*, vii–viii.

18. Pearl S. Buck, *My Several Worlds: A Personal Record* (New York: John Day, 1954), 10.

19. Pearl S. Buck, "Is There a Case for Foreign Missions?" *Harper's*, January 1, 1933, 144.

20. Theodore Harris, *Pearl S. Buck: A Biography* (New York: John Day Books, 1969), 59.

21. Buck, *My Several Worlds*, 10.

22. Nora Stirling, *Pearl Buck: A Woman in Conflict* (Piscataway, NJ: New Century Books, 1983), 31.

23. Hilary Spurling, *Pearl Buck in China* (New York: Simon and Schuster, 2010), 70.

24. Buck, *My Several Worlds*, 125.

25. Peter Conn, *Pearl Buck: A Cultural Biography* (Cambridge: Cambridge University Press, 1996), 49.

26. Stirling, *Pearl Buck*, 29.

27. Ibid., 86.

28. Conn, *Pearl Buck*, 56.

29. Buck, *My Several Worlds*, 139.

30. Pearl Buck, *East Wind, West Wind* (New York: John Day, 1930).

31. Though the events are undated, one can deduce from plot details that the book begins around the year 1910.

32. Peter Conn notes an early iteration of the farmer-protagonist in Buck's 1926 short story "Lao Wang, the Farmer." Conn, *Pearl Buck*, 89.

33. John Tebbel, *A History of Book Publishing in the United States*, Vol. 3, *The Golden Age between Two Wars, 1920–1940* (New York: R. R. Bowker, 1978), 163–165.

34. Stirling, *Pearl Buck*, 101–102.

35. S. J. Woolf, "Pearl Buck Talks of Her Life in China," *New York Times*, August 14, 1932, SM7.

36. Henry Seidel Canby, "The Good Earth," *Book of the Club Month News*, February 1931, 1.

37. See: Conn, *Pearl Buck*, 131–132; Colleen Lye, *America's Asia: Racial Form and American Literature, 1893–1945* (Princeton, NJ: Princeton University Press, 2005), 204–206.

38. Canby, "The Good Earth," 1.

39. Conn, *Pearl Buck*, 131; Blake Allmendinger, "Little House on the Rice Paddy," *American Literary History* 10 (Summer, 1998), 362.

40. Buck, *The Good Earth*, 88.

41. Ibid., 75.

42. Ibid., 87.
43. Ibid., 56.
44. Ibid., 87.
45. Ibid., 219.
46. Ibid., 212.
47. Ibid., 29–30.
48. P. S. Hutchinson, "Breeder of Life," *Christian Century*, May 20, 1931, 683.
49. Stirling, *Pearl Buck*, 105–106.
50. Woolf, "Pearl Buck Talks."
51. Liu Haiming, "Reception in China Reconsidered," in Elizabeth J. Lipscomb, Frances E. Webb, and Peter Conn, eds., *The Several Worlds of Pearl S. Buck* (Westport, CT: Greenwood Press, 1994), 58–59.
52. Ibid., 58.
53. Ibid.
54. Theodore Harris, *Pearl S. Buck: A Biography* (New York: John Day Company, 1969), 140.
55. "In Praise of the 'Good Earth,'" *Chinese Digest*, March 1937, 2.
56. Kiang Kang-Hu, *On Chinese Studies* (1934; repr. Westport, CT: Hyperion Press, 1977), 275.
57. Ibid., 266.
58. Ibid., 269.
59. Ibid., 268.
60. Ibid., 266.
61. Ibid., 267.
62. Ibid., 264.
63. Ibid., 267.
64. Ibid., 270–271.
65. Ibid., 274.
66. Ibid., 272–273.
67. Liu, *The Several Worlds of Pearl S. Buck*, 61.
68. Spurling, *Pearl Buck in China*, 216–217. Liu Haiping and Peter Conn guess that Lu's harsh assessment might have been based on a poor translation. Conn, *Pearl Buck*, 374.
69. Spurling, *Pearl Buck in China*, 200.
70. Stirling, *Pearl Buck*, 109.
71. It should be noted that Buck was likely referring to the Evan King translation of Lao She's novel that was published in the United States in 1945. King's version deviates quite radically from the original, as he invented characters, rearranged events, and created a new ending. For the White letter, see Spurling, *Pearl Buck in China*, 185.
72. Spurling provided this quote from Snow, which originally appears in Stirling's 1970s interview notes: "I was surprised to find how the young Chinese intellectuals hated it. They were violent about it ... also the missionaries disliked it. In fact, almost nobody living in China liked it at all, for different reasons . . . They wanted to make a good impression on

the foreigners, and also they wanted to avoid facing facts themselves and to avoid doing anything to remedy the situation." Spurling, *Pearl Buck in China*, 200.

73. Michael Hunt, "Pearl Buck—Popular Expert on China, 1931–1949," *Modern China* 3, no. 1 (January 1977): 40.

74. Woolf, "Pearl Buck."

75. Kiang, *On Chinese Studies*, 367.

76. Ibid., 373–374.

77. Buck, *The Good Earth*, 113.

78. Ibid., 107–108.

79. Ibid., 107.

80. Ibid., 95.

81. Ibid., 107.

82. Ibid.

83. Ibid., 123.

84. Ibid., 124.

85. Ibid.

86. Ibid., 125.

87. Ibid., 126.

88. Ibid., 111.

89. Wendy Larson and Richard Kraus, "China's Writers, the Nobel Prize, and the International Politics of Literature," *The Australian Journal of Chinese Affairs* 21 (January 1989): 148.

90. Larson and Kraus, "China's Writers," 148.

91. Ibid.

92. See Hunt, "Pearl Buck."

93. Stirling, *Pearl Buck*, 202–203.

94. Thomas Hischak, *American Literature on Stage and Screen* (Jefferson, NC: McFarland, 2012), 83.

95. Conn, *Pearl Buck*, 186.

96. Hunt, "Pearl Buck," 34.

97. Harold Isaacs, *Scratches on Our Minds: American Images of China and India* (New York: John Day, 1958), 155.

98. Chi Chen Wang, introduction to *Ah Q and Others: Selected Stories of Lusin* (New York: Columbia University Press, 1941), vii.

99. Frank Chin, Jeffrey Paul Chan, Lawson Fusao Inada, and Shawn Wong, eds., *Aiiieeeee! An Anthology of Asian American Writers* (1974; repr. New York: Mentor, 1991), xxii.

100. Peter Conn, "The Rehabilitation of Pearl Buck," *The Asia Society* (blog), August 7, 2012, http://asiasociety.org/blog/asia/rehabilitation-pearl-buck.

101. The literary historian Chris Vials has also written about the long shadow cast by Buck during this time, particularly as it pertained to the alternative approaches to "realism" pursued by Tsiang and other Asian immigrant writers. Chris Vials, *Realism for the Masses: Aesthetics, Popular Front Pluralism, and U.S. Culture, 1935-1947* (Jackson, MS: University Press of Mississippi).

102. Kent to Walsh, 15 September 1941, Kent Papers.

103. H. T. Tsiang, *And China Has Hands* (New York: Robert Speller, 1937), 154.

2

Naïve Melody

1. Tsiang's tombstone gives his date of birth as 1906; a *New Yorker* article published in 1935 claims he is 32. Rion Bercovici, "Novelist," Talk of the Town, *The New Yorker*, July 6, 1935, 10.
2. Floyd Cheung, "H.T. Tsiang: Literary Innovator and Activist," *Asian American Literature: Discourses and Pedagogies* 2 (2011), 58.
3. Floyd Cheung, introduction, H. T. Tsiang, *And China Has Hands* (1937; repr. New York: Ironweed Press, 2003), 7–15.
4. Scott Seligman, *The First Chinese American: The Remarkable Life of Wong Chin Foo* (HJOng Kong: Hong Kong University Press, 2013).
5. Chih-ming Wang, *Transpacific Articulations* (Honolulu: University of Hawaii Press, 2013), 42.
6. Jessica Ching-Sze Wang, *John Dewey in China: To Teach and to Learn* (Albany: SUNY Press, 2007), 33.
7. Bercovici, "Novelist," 10.
8. Cheung, "H. T. Tsiang," 64.
9. Tsiang specifically thanks Thorndike and Dewey in the acknowledgments for his first collection, *Poems of the Chinese Revolution*.
10. H. T. Tsiang, *Poems of the Chinese Revolution* (New York: H.T. Tsiang, 1929), 4.
11. Ibid., 2.
12. Ibid.
13. Ibid.
14. Ibid., 3.
15. Ibid., 13–14.
16. Ibid., 13.
17. Ibid., 9.
18. The poem predates Lao She's *Rickshaw Boy*, a by-the-bootstraps best seller published in America during World War II.
19. Tsiang, *Poems*, 5.
20. Tsiang, *Poems*, 6.
21. Ibid., 7.
22. Ibid.
23. Ibid., 8.
24. Ibid.
25. Ibid., 12.
26. Ibid.
27. Judith Tick, *Ruth Crawford Seeger: A Composer's Search for American Music* (New York: Oxford University Press, 1997), 192.
28. Tick, *Ruth Crawford Seeger*, 191.
29. Joseph Straus, *The Music of Ruth Crawford Seeger* (Cambridge, UK: Cambridge University Press, 1995), 8–9.

30. Tick, *Ruth Crawford Seeger,* 192.
31. For more on the uneasy relationship between Asian immigrant writers and the proletarian arts movement, see Chris Vials, *Realism for the Masses: Aesthetics, Popular Front Pluralism, and U.S. Culture, 1935-1947* (Jackson, MS: University Press of Mississippi), 110–148.
32. Cheung, "H.T. Tsiang," 67.
33. H. T. Tsiang, *China Red* (New York: Liberal Press, 1931), front matter.
34. Secretary (on behalf of Theodore Dreiser) to H. T. Tsiang, 15 December 1930, folder 6226, Theodore Dreiser Papers, Kislak Center for Special Collections, Rare Book and Manuscripts, University of Pennsylvania Libraries, Philadelphia.
35. Tsiang, *China Red,* back matter.
36. Ibid., 9.
37. Ibid., 11.
38. Ibid., 39.
39. Ibid., 12.
40. Ibid.
41. Ibid., 13.
42. Ibid.
43. Ibid., 26.
44. Ibid., 19.
45. Ibid., 24.
46. Ibid., 25.
47. Ibid., 26–27.
48. Ibid., 112.
49. Ibid., 145–146.
50. Ibid., 155.
51. Ibid., 105–106.
52. Ibid., 107.
53. Ibid.
54. Ibid.
55. Ibid.
56. Ibid.
57. Ibid., 95.
58. Ibid., 117.
59. Ibid., 120.
60. Bercovici, "Novelist," 10.
61. Tsiang, *China Red,* 18.
62. Ibid., 65.
63. Ibid., 51.
64. Ibid., 139.
65. Ibid., 141.
66. Ibid., 156.
67. Ibid., 95.
68. Ibid., 21–22.

69. Rockwell Kent to Richard Walsh, 15 September 1941, Rockwell Kent Papers, Smithsonian Archives of American Art, Washington, D.C.

70. Tsiang, *China Red*, 54.

3

Four Hundred Million Customers

1. Paul French, *Carl Crow: A Tough Old China Hand* (Hong Kong: Hong Kong University Press, 2006), 15.

2. Paul Varg, *The Making of a Myth: The United States and China, 1897–1912* (East Lansing: Michigan State University Press, 1968), 15.

3. John A. Thomas, "Selling and Civilization," *Asia*, December 1923, 949.

4. For a general overview on the different schools of thought, see Michael Hunt, "Americans in the China Market: Economic Opportunities and Economic Nationalism, 1890s–1931," *Business History Review* 51, no. 3 (Autumn 1977).

5. Varg, *The Making of a Myth*, 38.

6. Malcolm Cowley, "A Farewell to the 1930's," *The New Republic*, November 8, 1939, 42.

7. Cowley, "A Farewell," 42.

8. French, *Carl Crow*, 19.

9. Jerry Israel, "Carl Crow, Edgar Snow, and Shifting American Journalistic Perceptions of China," in Jonathan Goldstein, Jerry Israel and Hilary Conroy, eds., *America Views China: American Images of China Then and Now* (Bethlehem, PA: Lehigh University Press, 1991), 150.

10. Carl Crow, *Four Hundred Million Customers: The Experiences—Some Happy, Some Sad of an American in China* (1937; repr. Norwalk, CT: Eastbridge Books, 2003), 3.

11. Ibid., 125.

12. Ibid.

13. Ibid., 26.

14. Ibid., 27.

15. Pearl Buck, *The Good Earth* (1931; repr. New York: Washington Square Press, 1999), 11.

16. Michael Godley, "The End of the Queue: Hair as Symbol in Chinese Culture," *East Asian History* 8 (1994): 54.

17. Ibid., 70.

18. French, *Carl Crow*, 43.

19. Ibid., 43.

20. Crow, *Four Hundred Million Customers*, 14.

21. Ibid., 16.

22. Ibid.

23. Ibid., 24.

24. Ibid., 219.

25. French, *Carl Crow*, 251.

26. Ibid., 94.
27. Crow, *Four Hundred Million Customers*, 2.
28. Ibid., 1.
29. Ibid., 2.
30. Ibid., 318.
31. Ibid.
32. Ibid.
33. Yen-Ping Hao, *The Comprador in Nineteenth Century China: Bridge between East and West* (Cambridge, MA: Harvard University Press, 1970), 155.
34. Ibid., 11.
35. Ibid., 180.
36. Ibid., 184.
37. Ibid., 209–210.
38. Ibid., 55.
39. Ibid., 61.
40. Noel Pugach, "Standard Oil and Petroleum Development in Early Republican China," *Business History Review* 45, no. 4 (Winter 1971): 454.
41. Walter LaFeber, *The New Empire: An Interpretation of American Expansion, 1860–1898* (Ithaca, NY: Cornell University Press, 1963), 23.
42. Carl Crow, *Foreign Devils in the Flowery Kingdom* (1940; repr. Hong Kong: Earnshaw Books, 2007), 41.
43. Mary Brown Bullock, *The Oil Prince's Legacy: Rockefeller Philanthropy in China* (Washington, DC: Woodrow Wilson Center Press, 2011), 12.
44. Varg, *The Making of a Myth*, 41.
45. Sherman Cochrane, *Encountering Chinese Networks: Western, Japanese, and Chinese Corporations in China, 1880–1937* (Berkeley: University of California Press, 2000), 19.
46. Ibid., 31.
47. Ibid., 38.
48. Ibid.
49. Crow, *Foreign Devils*, 42–43.
50. Ibid., 43.
51. Pugach, "Standard Oil," 452.
52. Crow, *Foreign Devils*, 43.
53. Ibid.
54. Pugach, "Standard Oil," 452. Also mentioned in David Rockefeller, *Memoirs* (New York: Random House, 2002), 243.
55. Cochrane, *Encountering Chinese Networks*, 32.
56. Ibid., 33.
57. Alice Tisdale Hobart, *Yang and Yin: A Novel of an American Doctor in China* (Indianapolis, IN: Bobbs-Merrill, 1936), 104.
58. H. T. Tsiang, *Poems of the Chinese Revolution* (New York: Liberal Press, 1929), 13.
59. Hans Schoots, *Living Dangerously: A Biography of Joris Ivens* (Amsterdam: Amsterdam University Press, 2000), 137.

60. Cochrane, *Encountering Chinese Networks*, 31.

61. "Light in the Orient," *Standard Oil Bulletin*, November 1913, 16.

62. James Thomas Gilliam, "The Standard Oil in China (1863–1930)" (PhD dissertation, Ohio State University, 1987), 94.

63. Crow, *Foreign Devils*, 44.

64. Nora Stirling, *Pearl Buck: A Woman in Conflict* (Piscataway, NJ: New Century Publishers, 1983), 50.

65. Pearl S. Buck, *My Several Worlds: A Personal Record* (New York: John Day, 1954), 139.

66. Hilary Spurling, *Pearl Buck in China* (New York: Simon and Schuster, 2010), 126. According to Spurling, details of Hobart's initial encounter with Buck appear in Hobart's review of *The Good Earth* for the July 20, 1931 issue of the *Saturday Review*. I was curious to learn more about their meeting but I was unable to find this source. The *Saturday Review* was not published on that date. Furthermore, Florence Ayscough, not Hobart, reviewed *The Good Earth* for the paper.

67. Lady Dorothea Hosie, "Bringing Light to China," *Saturday Review of Literature*, October 21, 1933, 201. Also, the back inside flap of the *Oil for the Lamps of China* dust jacket features an advertisement for *The Good Earth*.

68. Alice Tisdale Hobart, *Yin and Yang* (Indianapolis, IN: Bobbs-Merrill, 1936), 7.

69. *Pidgin Cargo* was republished in 1934 using Hobart's preferred title, *River Supreme*.

70. The Yangtze as a site of conquest, contemplation and renewal is also the subject of John Hersey's *A Single Pebble*. John Hersey, *A Single Pebble* (New York: Knopf, 1956).

71. Hobart, *River Supreme*, 7.

72. Ibid., 24.

73. Ibid.

74. Ibid., 27.

75. Ibid., 276.

76. Ibid., 53.

77. Ibid., 207.

78. Ibid., 159.

79. Ibid., 190.

80. Ibid.

81. Alice Tisdale Hobart, *Oil for the Lamps of China* (New York: Grosset and Dunlap, 1933), preface.

82. Ibid., 12.

83. Ibid.

84. Hao, *The Comprador in Nineteenth Century China*, 13–14.

85. Hobart, *Oil*, 15.

86. Ibid., 13.

87. Ibid., 16.

88. Ibid.

89. Ibid., 14.
90. Ibid., 16.
91. Ibid., 36.
92. "Chances in China," *New York Times*, February 15, 1914, section 8, page 9. Also: "Obituary: W. E. Bemis," *Fuel Oil Journal*, January 1916, 98.
93. "Chances," 9.
94. Hobart, *Oil*, 63.
95. Ibid., 29.
96. Ibid., 26.
97. Ibid., 58.
98. Ibid., 75.
99. Ibid., 172.
100. Ibid., 175–176.
101. Ibid., 306.
102. Ibid., 370.
103. Ibid., 276.
104. Ibid., 381.
105. Hosie, "Bringing Light to China," 201.
106. Margaret Wallace, "When East and West Meet in China," *New York Times*, October 8, 1933, BR6.
107. Hobart, *Oil*, 117.
108. Ibid., 207.
109. Ibid., 185.
110. Ibid., 325.
111. Ibid., 336.
112. Ibid., 354.
113. Ibid., 350.
114. Ibid., 355.
115. Hobart, *Yang and Yin*, 128.
116. Ibid., 290.
117. Alice Tisdale Hobart, "Business Men in China," *Saturday Review*, October 16, 1937, 16.
118. Hobart, *Oil*, 370.
119. Ibid., 402.
120. Ibid., 403.

4

Pink Flag

1. Rion Bercovici, "Novelist," Talk of the Town, *The New Yorker*, July 6, 1935, 10.
2. Hilary Spurling, *Pearl Buck in China* (New York: Simon and Schuster, 2010), 193–194.
3. H.T. Tsiang, *Poems of the Chinese Revolution* (New York: Liberal Press, 1929), 4.

4. Michael Folsom, "Introduction: The Pariah of American Letters" in Michael Folsom, ed., *Mike Gold: A Literary Anthology* (New York: International Publishers, 1972), 7.

5. Michael Gold, "Towards Proletarian Art," in Michael Folsom, ed. *Mike Gold: A Literary Anthology* (1921; repr. New York: International Publishers, 1972), 62.

6. See Mark Morrisson, *The Public Face of Modernism* (Madison: University of Wisconsin Press, 1991) and Michael Denning, *The Cultural Front: The Laboring of American Culture in the Twentieth Century* (New York: Verso Press, 1998).

7. Michael Gold, "A Proletarian Novel?" *New Republic*, June 4, 1930, 74.

8. Michael Denning and others argue that the movement peaked in 1934, the year of the general strikes, when stalwarts of the literary mainstream began to take notice of these underground journals, experimental magazines, and working class-themed stories.

9. Dening, *The Cultural Front*, 223.

10. Joseph Freeman, "Introduction" in Granville Hicks, ed., *Proletarian Literature in the United States: An Anthology* (New York: International Publishers, 1935), 12.

11. Ibid., 18.

12. Ibid., 19.

13. Malcolm Cowley, "What the Revolutionary Movement Can Do for a Writer," in Henry Hart, ed., *American Writers' Congress* (International Publishers: New York, 1935), 62.

14. Ibid., 64.

15. Malcolm Cowley, "A Farewell to the 1930's," *The New Republic*, November 8, 1939, 42.

16. Cowley, "What the Revolutionary Movement," 60–1.

17. Ibid. 64.

18. H. T. Tsiang, *The Hanging on Union Square* (New York: Liberal Press, 1935), 3.

19. Ibid., 9.

20. Ibid., 7.

21. G. Thomas Tanselle, *Book Jackets: Their History, Forms, and Use* (Charlotteville: The Biographical Society of Virginia, 2011).

22. John Tebbel, *A History of Book Publishing in the United States, Vol. 3, The Golden Age between Two Wars, 1920-1940* (New York: R. R. Bowker, 1978), 321.

23. Tebbel, *A History of Book Publishing*, 326.

24. The history of negative book blurbs is a fairly short one. In 1741, the satirist Henry Fielding published *Shamela*, a parody of Samuel Richardson's *Pamela* that went so far as to lampoon all the gushing praise reproduced in Richardson's original. Alan Levinovitz, "I Greet You in the Middle of a Great Career: A Brief History of Blurbs," *TheMillions.com*, February 1, 2012, http://www.themillions.com/2012/02/i-greet-you-in-the-middle-of-a-great-career-a-brief-history-of-blurbs.html.

25. Tsiang, *Hanging*, 12.
26. Ibid., 13.
27. Ibid., 16.
28. Ibid., 11.
29. Tsiang, *Hanging*, 17.
30. Ibid., 20.
31. Ibid., 30.
32. Ibid., 24–25.
33. Ibid., 59.
34. Ibid., 64.
35. Ibid., 66.
36. Ibid., 185.
37. Ibid., 207.
38. Ibid., 42.
39. Ibid., 71.
40. Ibid., 73.
41. Ibid., 78.
42. Ibid.
43. Ibid., 47.
44. Ibid., 30.
45. Ibid., 155
46. Ibid., 189–190.
47. Ibid., 190.
48. Ibid., 191.
49. Ibid., 190.
50. Ibid., 191.
51. Ibid., 86.
52. Ibid., 112.
53. Ibid., 177.
54. Ibid., 178.
55. Ibid., 160.
56. Ibid., 176.
57. Ibid., 180.
58. Ibid., 181.
59. Ibid.
60. Ibid., 201.
61. Ibid., 205.
62. Ibid., 207.
63. Ibid., 59.
64. Ibid., 207.
65. Ibid., 208.
66. Ibid.
67. Denning, *The Cultural* Front, 244.
68. Tsiang, *Hanging*., back matter.
69. Ibid., 108.
70. Ibid., back matter.

5

Down and Out in New York City

1. R. David Arkush and Leo Lee, eds. *Land Without Ghosts: Chinese Impressions of America from the Mid-Nineteenth Century to the Present* (Berkeley: University of California Press, 1993), 171.

2. Ibid., 179.

3. Ibid., 181.

4. Jon Lee, *Chinese Tales Told in California* (San Francisco: Work Projects Administration, 1940), 1.

5. Ibid., 5.

6. H. T. Tsiang, *And China Has Hands* (New York: Robert Speller, 1937), 18.

7. Michael Denning, *The Cultural Front: The Laboring of American Culture in the Twentieth Century* (London: Verso Books, 1997), 231.

8. Ibid., 241–242.

9. Elaine Kim, *Asian American Literature* (Philadelphia: Temple University Press, 1982), 109.

10. H. T. Tsiang to Theodore Dreiser, 31 December 1930, folder 6226, Theodore Dreiser Papers, Kislak Center for Special Collections, Rare Book and Manuscripts, University of Pennsylvania Libraries, Philadelphia.

11. Max Kohler, "Un-American Character of Race Legislation," *Annals of the American Academy of Political and Social Science* 34 (September 1909): 284.

12. Ibid., 284.

13. See Guanhua Wang, *In Search of Justice: The 1905–1906 Chinese Anti-American Boycott* (Cambridge, MA: Harvard University Press, 2002).

14. Harriet L. Moore, "Global Strategy for Global War," *Far Eastern Survey* 12 (1943): 108.

15. H. T. Tsiang, *Poems of the Chinese Revolution* (New York: H.T. Tsiang, 1929), 7.

16. Ibid., 7.

17. John Kuo Wei Tchen, "Introduction" in Paul Siu, *The Chinese Laundryman: A Study of Social Isolation* (New York: NYU Press, 1987), xxiii.

18. Renqiu Yu, *To Save China, To Save Ourselves: The Chinese Hand Laundry Alliance of New York* (Philadelphia: Temple University Press, 1992), 82.

19. Ibid., 62–63.

20. See Paul Siu, *The Chinese Laundryman: A Study of Social Isolation* (New York: NYU Press, 1987).

21. Tsiang, *And China*, 10.

22. Ibid., 10.

23. Ibid., 21.

24. Ibid., 23.

25. Ibid., 25.

26. Ibid, 141.

27. Ibid., 109.

28. Ibid., 47.

29. Ibid., 49.
30. Ibid., 76.
31. Ibid., 77.
32. Ibid., 55.
33. Ibid., 57.
34. A nearly identical remark about Chinese national cuisine is made in *China Red*.
35. Ibid., 27.
36. Ibid., 28.
37. Ibid., 128.
38. Ibid., 127.
39. Ibid., 29.
40. Ibid.
41. Ibid.
42. Ibid.
43. Ibid., 35.
44. Tsiang, *The Hanging*, 189–190.
45. Tsiang, *And China*, 30.
46. Ibid., 31.
47. Ibid., 32.
48. Ibid.
49. Ibid., 33.
50. Ibid., 159.
51. Ibid., 102.
52. Ibid., 103.
53. Ibid., 104.
54. Ibid.
55. Ibid., 62.
56. Ibid., 57.
57. Ibid., 85.
58. Ibid., 86–87.
59. Ibid., 86.
60. Ibid., 88.
61. Ibid., 156.
62. Ibid., 158.
63. See Julia Lee, "The Capitalist and Imperialist Critique in H. T. Tsiang's *And China Has Hands*," in *Recovered Legacies*, eds. Floyd Cheung and Keith Lawrence (Philadelphia: Temple University Press, 2005).
64. Tsiang, *And China*, 163.
65. Ibid., 163.
66. Ibid., 161–162.
67. Ibid., 159.
68. Ibid., 154.
69. Sina Nafaji, David Serlin and Scott A. Sandage, "The Invention of Failure: An Interview with Scott A. Sandage," *Cabinet* 7 (Summer 2002): http://www.cabinetmagazine.org/issues/7/inventionoffailure.php.

70. Rion Bercovici, "Novelist," Talk of the Town, *The New Yorker*, July 6, 1935, 10.
71. Judith Halberstam, *The Queer Art of Failure* (Durham, NC: Duke University Press, 2011), 9.
72. Ibid., 88.
73. Ibid., 4.
74. Joel Fisher, "Judgment and Purpose" in Lisa Le Feuvre, ed. *Failure: Documents of Contemporary Art* (Cambridge, MA: MIT Press, 2010), 118.
75. Ibid., 121.
76. H. T. Tsiang, *China Marches On* (New York: Published by Author, 1938), 4.
77. Ibid., 4.
78. Ibid., 5.
79. Ibid., 9.
80. Ibid., 13.
81. Ibid., 32.
82. Rockwell Kent to H. T. Tsiang, 14 January 1941, Rockwell Kent Papers, Smithsonian Archives of American Art, Washington, D.C.
83. Kent to Tsiang, 15 September 1941.
84. Tsiang to Kent, 17 January 1941.
85. H. T. Tsiang, "Top-Side," 1940.
86. Tsiang to Kent, 7 January 1941.
87. Eleanor Roosevelt to H. T. Tsiang, 26 November 1938.
88. For more on the performative aspects of Tsiang's Ellis Island writings, see Aaron Lecklider, "H.T. Tsiang's Proletarian Burlesque: Performance and Perversion in *The Hanging on Union Square*, *MELUS: Multi-Ethnic Literature of the U.S.* vol. 36 (Winter 2011), 87–113.
89. Tsiang to Kent, 15 April 1941.
90. Tsiang to Kent, 18 January 1941.
91. Tsiang to Kent, 2 February 1941.
92. H. T. Tsiang to Bruce Bliven, 12 May 1941.
93. Tsiang to Kent, 2 February 1941.
94. H. T. Tsiang to Shirley Johnstone, 14 April 1941.
95. Kent to Tsiang, 25 May 1941.
96. H. T. Tsiang to Stephen Early, 30 May 1941.
97. H. T. Tsiang to Vito Marcantonio, 18 April 1941.
98. Lewis Gannett to Eleanor Roosevelt, 12 December 1940.
99. Waldo Frank, "The Case of H. T. Tsiang," *The New Republic*, April 28, 1941, 605.
100. Tsiang to Kent, 18 April 1941.
101. Tsiang to Kent, 12 March 1941.
102. Tsiang to Kent, 21 April 1941.
103. Tsiang to Hu Shih, 5 June 1941.
104. Tsiang to Kent, 5 June 1941.
105. Rockwell Kent to Bennett Cerf, 23 August 1941, Rockwell Kent Papers, Smithsonian Archives of American Art, Washington, DC.
106. Richard Walsh to Rockwell Kent, 20 September 1941.

107. Walsh to Kent, 20 September 1941.
108. Tsiang to Kent, 21 September 1941.
109. H. T. Tsiang to Richard Walsh, 22 September 1941.
110. Ibid.
111. Tsiang to Kent, 25 September 1941.
112. Tsiang to Walsh, 29 September 1941.
113. Tsiang to Walsh, 30 September 1941.
114. Tsiang to Walsh, 9 October 1941.
115. Walsh to Kent, 20 October 1941.
116. Tsiang to Kent, 11 December 1941.
117. Tsiang, *And China*, 103.

6

Pacific Crossings

1. Chi Chen Wang, introduction to *Ah Q and Others: Selected Stories of Lusin* (New York: Columbia University Press, 1941), vii.
2. Hilary Spurling, *Pearl Buck in China* (New York: Simon and Schuster, 2010), 216–217. Peter Conn guesses that it might have been based on a poor translation. See Peter Conn, *Pearl Buck: A Cultural Biography* (Cambridge, MA: Cambridge University Press, 1996), 374.
3. Charlotte Brooks, *Alien Neighbors, Foreign Friends* (Chicago: University of Chicago Press, 2009): 80–81.
4. Ibid., 91.
5. Gloria Heyung Chun, *Of Orphans and Warriors: Inventing Chinese American Culture and Identity* (Piscataway, NJ: Rutgers University Press, 1999), 36.
6. Ibid., 33–34.
7. Wang, *Ah Q*, xvii.
8. Ibid. vii, ix
9. Ibid., ix.
10. Columbia University Press Archive, Columbia University Rare Books and Manuscripts Library, Box 237, Folder 1, letter dated February 15, 1940.
11. James Hevia, "Leaving a Brand on China: Missionary Discourse in the Wake of the Boxer Movement," *Modern China* vol. 18 (July 1992), 304–332.
12. "Specialist houses like John Day Co., noted for its long list of books on Asia, many of them inspired by the publisher's wife, Pearl Buck, had a plethora of titles to advertise." See John Tebbel, *A History of Book Publishing in the United States*, Vol. 4, *The Great Change, 1940–1980* (New York: R. R. Bowker, 1981), 16.
13. Conn, *Pearl Buck: A Cultural Biography*, 159–160.
14. George Thomas Kurlan, *The Directory of American Book Publishing, From Founding Fathers to Today's Conglomerates* (New York: Simon and Schuster, 1975), 155.
15. Elizabeth Colman, *Chinatown, USA* (New York: John Day Company, 1946), 9.
16. Conn, *Pearl Buck: A Cultural Biography*, 245.

17. Colman, *Chinatown*, 9–10.
18. Ellen Wu, *The Color of Success: Asian Americans and the Origins of the Model Minority* (Princeton, NJ: Princeton University Press, 2014), 46.
19. Ibid., 48.
20. Pearl Buck, *The Chinese Children Next Door* (New York: John Day Company, 1942).
21. Conn, *Pearl Buck: A Cultural Biography*, 273–274.
22. Wu, *The Color of Success*, 51.
23. Colman, *Chinatown, USA*, 15.
24. Ibid., 12.
25. Ibid., 30.
26. Ibid., 23.
27. Ibid., 14.
28. "Downtown Merchants," *Chinese Digest*, November 15, 1935, 7.
29. "In Praise of the 'Good Earth,'" *Chinese Digest*, March 1937, 2, 11.
30. Ibid., 8.
31. Ibid., 16.
32. Chun, *Of Orphans and Warriors*, 21.
33. Ibid., 27.
34. Ibid., 28.
35. Robert Dunn, "Does My Future Lie in China or America?" *Chinese Digest*, May 15, 1936, 3.
36. Ibid., 13.
37. Chun, *Of Orphans and Warriors*, 21.
38. Kaye Hong, "Does My Future Lie in China or America?" *Chinese Digest*, May 22, 1936, 3.
39. Ibid.
40. George Grace, "Firecrackers," *Chinese Digest*, June 19, 1936, 14.
41. Pearl Buck, *A House Divided* (1935; repr. New York: John Day Company, 1965), 154.
42. Ibid., 155.
43. For more on Buck, Soong, and their effect American perceptions of China, see: Karen Leong, *The China Mystique: Pearl S. Buck, Anna Ma Wong, Mayling Soong and the Transformation of American Orientalism* (Berkeley: University of California Press, 2005).
44. Pearl Buck, *The Woman Who Has Changed and Other Stories* (1942; repr. New York: John Day Company, 1979), 75.
45. Ibid., 92.
46. Pearl Buck, *Today and Forever: Stories of China* (New York: John Day Company, 1941), 92.
47. Ibid., 106.
48. Ibid., 111.
49. Ibid., 115.
50. Ibid., 124.
51. John Dewey, *The Middle Works, 1899–1924* (Carbondale, IL: Southern Illinois University Press, 1983), 217.

52. Pearl Buck, *Kinfolk* (New York: John Day Company, 1949), 1.

53. Ibid., 2.

54. Ibid., 3.

55. Ibid., 4.

56. Ibid., 5.

57. Buck, *The Chinese Novel* (New York: John Day, 1939): 12.

58. Buck, *Kinfolk,,* 29.

59. Ibid., 208–209.

60. Ibid., 11.

61. Gloria Heyung Chun, "Go West … to China": Chinese American Identity in the 1930s," in K. Scott Wong and Sucheng Chan, eds., *Claiming America: Constructing Chinese American Identities during the Exclusion Era* (Philadelphia: Temple University Press, 1998), 165–190.

62. Buck, *Kinfolk*, 43–44.

63. Ibid., 47.

64. Ibid., 135.

65. Ibid.

66. Ibid., Buck, *Kinfolk,,* 358.

67. Chun, *Of Orphans and Warriors*, 52.

68. Nora Stirling, *Pearl Buck: A Woman in Conflict* (Piscataway, NJ: New Century, 1983): 206–207.

69. Richard Walsh to Quentin Boss, June 2, 1949, box 261, folder 5, Archives of John Day Company, Princeton University.

70. Richard Jean So, "Collaboration and Translation: Lin Yutang and the Archive of Asian American Literature," *Modern Fiction Studies* 56, no. 1 (Spring 2010), 40–62.

71. Lin Yutang, *Chinatown Family* (1948; repr. Philadelphia: Temple University Press, 2007), 6.

72. Ibid., 10.

73. Ibid., 71–72.

74. Ibid., 71.

7

Too Big to Fail

1. H. T. Tsiang, *And China Has Hands* (New York: Robert Speller, 1937), 154.

2. Michael Denning, *The Cultural Front: The Laboring of American Culture in the Twentieth Century* (New York: Verso Press, 1998), 257.

3. Renqiu Yu, *To Save China, To Save Ourselves: The Chinese Hand Laundry Alliance of New York* (Philadelphia: Temple University Press, 1995), 191.

4. Ibid., 186.

5. Ibid., 165.

6. Lisa Gitelman, *Paper Knowledge: Toward a Media History of Documents* (Durham, NC: Duke University Press, 2014), 2.

7. FBI, 100–32590 (Los Angeles), 1.

8. Ibid., 21.

9. Ibid., 23.

10. Ibid., 23–24.

11. Ibid., 27.

12. Ibid., 2.

13. Ibid., 26.

14. Ibid., 28.

15. Ibid., 13.

16. Ibid., 27.

17. Robert Darnton, *The Great Cat Massacre and Other Episodes in French Cultural History* (New York: Vintage Books, 1985), 158–159.

18. Ibid., 157.

19. Cristina Vatulescu, *Police Aesthetics: Literature, Film, and the Secret Police in Soviet Times* (Palo Alto, CA: Stanford University Press, 2010), 14.

20. Ibid., 32.

21. FBI, 100–32590 (Los Angeles), 26.

22. Ibid., 28.

23. Ibid.

24. Ibid., 24.

25. Ibid.

26. Ibid., 15.

27. Ibid., 12.

28. Ibid., 13.

29. Ibid., 30.

30. Arnold Mesches, *The FBI Files* (Brooklyn: Hanging Loose Press, 2004).

31. William J. Maxwell, *FB Eyes: How J. Edgar Hoover's Ghostreaders Framed African American Literature* (Princeton, NJ: Princeton University Press, 2015).

32. FBI, 100–32590 (Los Angeles), 12.

33. Rockwell Kent to Richard Walsh, 15 September 1941, Rockwell Kent Papers, Smithsonian Archives of American Art, Washington, D.C.

34. Ilana Feldman, *Governing Gaza: Bureaucracy, Authority, and the Work of Rule, 1917–1967* (Durham, NC: Duke University Press, 2008), 35.

35. FBI, 100–32590 (Los Angeles), 27.

36. Theodore Harris, *Pearl S. Buck: A Biography* (New York: John Day Company, 1969), 269.

37. Owen Lattimore, *Solution in Asia* (Boston: Little, Brown and Company, 1945), 6–7.

38. Ibid., 7.

39. Hilary Spurling, *Pearl Buck in China: Journey to the Good Earth* (New York: Simon and Schuster, 2010), 146.

40. Pearl Buck, *God's Men* (New York: John Day, 1951).

41. Peter Conn, *Pearl S. Buck: A Cultural Biography* (Cambridge: Cambridge University Press, 1996), 325–332. Stuart Creighton Miller, *The Unwelcome Immigrant: The American Image of the Chinese, 1785–1882* (Berkeley: University of California Press, 1969): 14–15.

42. Alan Brinkley, *The Publisher: Henry Luce and His American Century* (New York: Knopf, 2010), 34. Still, these experiences did little to dissuade Luce from publishing racist portrayals of other Asians. During World War II, Buck wrote him a letter reminding him that using "yellow" pejoratively when discussing the Japanese could offend the Chinese as well (Brinkley, *The* Publisher, 316).

43. Wentworth Pegler, "Luced Remarks About Fuey," *Milwaukee Sentinel*, August 27, 1948, sec. 1.

44. Robert Herzstein, *Henry R. Luce: A Political Portrait of the Man Who Created the American Century* (New York: Scribner, 1994), 188–189.

45. Patricia Neils, *China Images in the Life and Times of Henry Luce* (Savage, Maryland: Rowman and Littlefield, 1990), 182.

46. Spurling, *Pearl Buck*, 2.

47. Brinkley, *The Publisher*, 15.

48. Ibid., 273.

49. Ibid., 7.

50. Buck, *God's Men*, 82.

51. Ibid., 118.

52. Ibid., 117.

53. Buck, 10–11.

54. Ibid., 117.

55. See David Cort, *The Sin of Henry R. Luce: An Anatomy of Journalism* (Secaucus, NJ: Lyle Stuart, Inc. 1974) and James L. Baughman, *Henry R. Luce and the Rise of the American News Media* (Boston: Twayne, 1987).

56. Ibid., 201.

57. Ibid., 115.

58. Ibid., 218.

59. Ibid., 155.

60. Ibid., 337.

61. Ibid., 355.

62. Ibid., 291.

63. Ibid., 84.

64. Ibid., 195.

65. Ibid., 151.

66. Ibid., 218.

67. "The Real Dope," *Time*, April 23, 1951.

68. Buck, *God's Men*, 299.

69. Neils, *China Images*, 23.

70. Brinkley, *The Publisher*, 34.

71. Ibid.

72. Ibid., 28.

73. Jessup, *Ideas*, 381.

74. John Kobler, *Luce: His Time, Life and Fortune* (New York: MacDonald, 1968), 3–4.

75. Jessup, *Ideas*, 117.

76. Ibid., 112.

77. Ibid., 115.
78. Buck, *God's Men*, 208.
79. Ibid., 209.
80. Jessup, *Ideas*, 212.
81. Neils, *China Images*, 132.
82. Herzstein, *Henry R. Luce*, 293.
83. Jessup, *Ideas*, 206.
84. Ibid., 207.
85. Ibid., 208.
86. Ibid., 213.
87. Ibid.
88. Ibid., 215.
89. Ibid.
90. Hunt, "Pearl Buck—Popular Expert on China, 1931–1949," *Modern China* 3, no. 1 (January 1977), 59.

Conclusion

1. Don Lee, *The Collective*, 88.
2. Ibid.
3. Ibid., 89.
4. Ibid.
5. Ibid., 90.
6. Colleen Lye, *America's Asia* (Princeton, NJ: Princeton University Press, 2009), 204–205.
7. Theodore Harris, *Pearl S. Buck: A Biography* (New York: John Day Company, 1969), 117.
8. Nora Stirling, *Pearl Buck: A Woman in Conflict* (Piscataway, NJ: New Century Publishers, 1983), 27.
9. Arif Dirlik, "Asians on the Rim: Transnational Capital and Local Community in the Making of Contemporary Asian America," *AmerAsia Journal* 22, no. 3 (1996): 13.
10. Li Kejun, *The Good Earth* (Vancouver: 88 Books, 2012).
11. Anchee Min, *Pearl of China* (New York: Bloomsbury, 2010), 277.
12. Ibid., 278.
13. Ibid., 31.
14. Ibid., 77.
15. Ibid., 95.
16. Ibid., 116.
17. Hilary Spurling, *Pearl Buck in China* (New York: Simon and Schuster, 2010), 229.
18. Min, *Pearl of China*, 205.
19. Ibid., 206.
20. Ibid., 210.
21. Ibid., 222.
22. Ibid., 233.

23. Liu Haiping, "Reception in China Reconsidered" in Elizabeth J. Lip-scomb, Frances E. Webb, and Peter Conn, eds., *The Several Worlds of Pearl S. Buck* (Westport, CT: Greenwood Press, 1994), 57.

24. Min, *Pearl of China*, 253.

25. Ibid., 260.

26. John K. Jessup, *The Ideas of Henry Luce* (New York: Atheneum, 1969), 196–197.

27. Edgar Snow, *Red Star over China* (1938; repr. New York: Grove Press, 1968), 214–215.

28. "Which China Expert Are You?" *ChinaDailyShow.com*, September 25, 2014, http://chinadailyshow.com/which-china-expert-are-you/.

29. See David Palumbo-Liu, *Asian/American: Historical Crossings of a Racial Frontier* (Stanford, CA: Stanford University Press, 1999); Rob Wilson, *Re-Imagining the American Pacific* (Durham, NC: Duke University Press, 2000); Janet Hoskins and Viet Nguyen, eds., *Introduction to Transpacific Studies: Framing an Emerging Field* (Honolulu: University of Hawaii Press, 2014).

30. Rachel DeWoskin, *Foreign Babes in Beijing* (New York: Norton, 2006) and Alan Paul, *Big in China: My Unlikely Adventures Raising a Family, Playing the Blues and Becoming a Star in Bejing* (New York: Harper, 2011).

31. Yu Li Zi, ed. *Jiangxizengdangan* (Jinan, China: Qi Lu Press, 2008).

32. Austin Lewis, *The Militant Proletariat* (Chicago: Charles H. Kerr and Company, 1911), 32.

33. Ibid., 33.

34. Ibid.

35. Ibid., 33–34.

36. Ibid., 34.

Acknowledgments

DURING MY SECOND YEAR of graduate school, my friend Salamishah lived down the street from me, and we used to walk to campus together, chatting about our work and daydreaming about what the future held. She was very wise—she had started the program a year before me—and one of her observations in particular stayed with me. I'm sure she wasn't the first person to declare that a scholar's first book is always, in some remote way, autobiographical. But, as I was then in desperate search of a dissertation topic, she was the first person to say this to me when the idea held some vague relevance to my life.

In the years since, I have grown deeply invested in the figures comprising this book. I wasn't always researching and writing, but I was constantly thinking about them. There are some aspects of this story that appeal to my suspicions about power and influence, and there are some aspects that appeal to my sense of humor. I have been sustained over this time by my (at times worrying) obsession with the mischievous, leftfield Chinese writer H. T. Tsiang, chasing his tale from self-published epics to personal letters to an FBI file. I felt a strange sense of attachment to him, a connection to his story's wayward arc, a sympathy for how he thought he had been misunderstood. As I put this book to rest, my fascination with Tsiang's maverick path leaves me humbled and deeply appreciative for the friends and colleagues who have supported, protected, and inspired me along the way.

I am indebted to Werner Sollors for his vision, generosity, and patience with me, particularly as I initially resisted his suggestion to dig through the work of Pearl Buck. Yunte Huang inspired and challenged me, completely reorienting my assumptions and beliefs. Luke Menand gave me the confidence to write however I wanted to write. It was in a course taught by Akira Iriye and Rebecca McLennan where I began thinking about the global contexts within which identities are forged. Elements of this project took shape in courses taught by Eileen Chow, Gwendolyn DuBois Shaw, Evelyn Brooks Higginbotham, and John Stauffer, as well as conversations with Kwame Anthony Appiah, Elvis Mitchell, and Doris Sommer. Thanks to Stephanie Macarais-Alusow, Christine McFadden, and Arthur Patton-Hock for making my life much easier at critically stressful junctures. My deepest affection for the talented and inspiring thinkers I befriended in graduate school: Salamishah Tillet, Dagmawi Woubshet, Suleiman Osman, Matt Briones, and Judy Kertesz; Chinnie Ding, Cameron Leader-Picone, Namwali Serpell, and Julia Lee; George Blaustein and Yael Schacher; Brian Hochman, Jack Hamilton, Maggie Gram, and Tim McGrath. I remain eternally grateful to Lindsay Waters, who took an interest in this project very early on and practically willed it into existence. And we both thank Amanda Peery, who carefully shepherded my manuscript into publishable shape. Thanks, as well, to several Harvard University Press alums: Phoebe Kosman, Hannah Wong, and Shanshan Wang.

I conducted much of my research while a visiting scholar at the Center for the Study of Ethnicity and Race at Columbia University. Thanks to Gary Okihiro for bringing me into the Center's vital community. Emma Gregoline, Peter Hahn, Sam Sweet of *All Night Menu*, and Jenny Romero of the Margaret Herrick Library appeared at fortuitous moments to provide crucial research assistance. The story this book tells would have been woefully thin had it not been for the help and expertise of Nancy Shawcross of the Rare Book and Manuscript Library at the University of Pennsylvania, Nicolette Dobrowolski of the Special Collections Research Center at Syracuse University, Kate Rivers of the Library of Congress, and Barbara Burg of Widener Library at Harvard University.

This book evolved thanks to colleagues who poked, prodded, asked tough questions, made suggestions, or, in an entirely indirect way, simply modeled something important for me: Werner, Yunte, Luke, Eileen, Floyd Cheung, Paul Farber, Shelley Fisher Fishkin, Joshua Harmon, Joseph Jeon, Evan Kindley, Amitava Kumar, Josh Kun, Kiese Laymon, Sunyoung Lee, Greil Marcus, Rani Neutill, Sukhdev Sandhu, Nikhil Pal Singh, Min Hyoung Song, Jack Tchen, Oliver Wang, and Eric Weisbard. On the rare occasion I presented this research at conferences, I always came away reenergized: my thanks to the participants in the "Transpacific Encounters" session at the 2013 meeting of American Comparative Literature Association and the H. T. Tsiang *Hanging on Union Square* event at NYU's A/P/A Institute. Conversations with Werner, Luke, Larry Buell, Glenda Carpio, and Denise Khor were a highlight of a productive 2009–2010 spent back at Harvard. I'm grateful to Harvard University's Committee on Ethnic Studies and the English Department for their generous research support.

I've been fortunate to find a supportive network of colleagues at Vassar, particularly in the English Department and the American Studies program. My thanks to Carlos Alamo, Peter Antelyes, David Bradley, Lisa Brawley, Heesok Chang, Eve Dunbar, Wendy Graham, Bill Hoynes, Michael Joyce, Jonathon Kahn, Amitava Kumar, Kiese Laymon, Leonard Nevarez, Sarah Pearlman, Hiram Perez, Erendira Rueda, Matt Schultz, and Tyrone Simpson. Thanks, as well, to Brian Chickery for reviving my school laptop on more than one occasion. Lastly, I acknowledge the Office of the Dean of the Faculty and the Louise Boyd Dale Memorial Fund of Vassar College for their generous support of this project. Completion of this book would have been impossible without the support of the New America Foundation.

It was the late Michael Rogin who first gave me the confidence to pursue life as a writer or an academic or maybe both. I hope he understood the deep impression he left on my life. I began my side career as a journalist shortly before graduate school, which probably explains why this book was such a long time coming. I owe everything to the editors and fellow writers who appeared in my life at just the right time: Oliver Wang and Jeff Chang; Chris Bohn, Ed Park, and Sasha Frere-Jones; Reihan Salam and David Wallace-Wells.

To the friends and editors who bought me a drink, played me a song, made me laugh, taught me how to read and write, and, most importantly, talked to me about anything and everything *except* for how this book was coming along: Michael Agger, Zach Baron, Harish Bhat, Jon Caramanica, Dan Chamberlin, Anthony Chang, Kris Chen, Youmna Chlala, Brian Coleman, Michael Endelman, Sean Fennessey, Nick Follett, Franklin at the Corner Bistro, Sasha Frere-Jones, Nathaniel Friedman, Sarah Goldstein, Brittany Gudas, David Haglund, Will Hermes, Sarah Honda, Andy Hsiao, Sonjia Hyon, James Hughes, Kiwa Iyobe, John and John at Jack's Rhythms, Jay Caspian Kang, E. Tammy Kim, James Kim, June Kim, Kirby Kim, Nick Klein, Sean Kundu, Eugene Kuo, Makkotron, Brett Mallard, Jefferson Mao, Paraag Marathe, Benjamin Meadows-Ingram, Kyle Nelson, Piotr Orlov, Michael Parayannilam, Betty M. Park, Joseph Patel, Peter Relic, Gaby Ross, Chris Ryan, Greg Scally, Leonard Shek, Amy Tai, Herb Tam, Derek Walmsley, David Wang, Jessica Wang, and Stephanie Wang. Thanks to Willa, even though she is a dog and therefore cannot read.

I feel incredibly lucky to have found community—a word I take very seriously—at a few points in my professional life. In particular, a shout-out to the late, great Soundings and the Asian American Writers Workshop. My love to anyone and everyone associated with either. This book will always remind me of the places where I spent the most time avoiding it: 1369, Central Kitchen, Cheapo Records, Harvard Bookstore, In Your Ear, Other Music, Stereo Jack's, and WMBR in Cambridge; Absolute Bagels, Big City Records, the Hungarian Pastry Shop, St. Mark's Books, and WXOU in Manhattan; 34th St. in Astoria; Weekend Records and Kos Kaffe in Brooklyn; Jack's Rhythms in New Paltz; WVKR in Poughkeepsie.

I would never have finished this without the careful insights and good vibes of Ken Chen, Pete L'Official, Richard Jean So, and Oliver Wang. Ken, Pete, and Rich are the teammates I've always wanted: brilliant and playful, encouraging but rigorous, generous, always open to trading unpopular, draft-stage ideas. It's rare to find people who make you feel so young and old at the same time. The same goes for Oliver Wang—as close to a mentor as I have had in my professional life and the model for what it means to be a good dude. To

Ken Ishida: I picked up a pen hoping I might one day write myself back into those days when you were still around. Stay true.

My parents showed me the world and then let me explore it on my own terms. They let me dream, and I will spend the rest of my life trying to live up to their example.

And, finally: Carol, who knows when to listen and when to tell me to stop talking. Your love gives my life meaning, your laughter is the only music I will ever need.

Index